THE STORY OF EVERYTHING

AS TOLD IN THE URANTIA BOOK

AN OVERVIEW BY

MICHELLE KLIMESH

Square Circles Publishing

THE STORY OF EVERYTHING
As told in *The Urantia Book*
An overview by Michelle Klimesh

Cover artwork and design: Patricia Fearey

SQUARE CIRCLES PUBLISHING
www.squarecirclespublishing.com

ISBN: 978-0-9982556-1-3
Library of Congress Control Number: 2002096218

INTRODUCTION

In August of 1994, Wayne and Ute Ferrier started an online study group for students of *The Urantia Book*. Their idea was to read from the beginning of the book and discuss each paper via email. I joined in their study.

Within a few months, the founding members of the online study group dropped away, but I continued to post weekly impressions of each paper. Occasionally other readers—Kevin Brown, Juan Juan, Bud Kagan, and Jim and Cheryl McCallon—contributed offerings while I was out of town.

One night I read the first sixty essays in order. I was stunned to discover that I was writing a condensation of *The Urantia Book*.

From time to time other readers of *The Urantia Book* asked if I was planning to publish the series as a book. Parents wrote to tell me that their teenagers were reading my posts because they were easier to understand than the full text. One friend said that she was forwarding the digests on to her parents, who wanted to know what *The Urantia Book* was about but didn't want to read the whole thing.

One reader who suggested that I turn the digests into a book was Saskia Raevouri of Square Circles Publishing. Starting in 1999, over the next few years Saskia read each condensed paper with me, suggested revisions, and eventually helped me to turn my words into a book. Without Saskia, *The Story of Everything* would not exist.

I love *The Urantia Book*. It gives me hope that there is sense in the universe, that there is order in apparent chaos, that good will triumph over evil, and that I can and will survive the seeming insanity of the strange planet of my birth. It soothes my weariness to open the pages of *The Urantia Book*. No mere digest will ever take its place.

Writing *The Story of Everything* deepened my view of life in the same way that seeing the first photograph of Earth from space gave me a new vision of our planet. I hope your experience in reading this revised edition will be equally valuable.

Michelle Klimesh
April 2017

CONTENTS

Part ii—The Local Universe

Part iii—The History of Urantia

Part iv—The Life and Teachings of Jesus

PART I

THE CENTRAL
AND
SUPERUNIVERSES

PART I
THE CENTRAL AND SUPERUNIVERSES

1—THE UNIVERSAL FATHER

The Universal Father is the first source and center of all things. He creates, controls, and upholds all there is. All enlightened beings worship God the Father and have one supreme ambition—to become like him.

Messengers from Paradise carry God's divine command throughout the universes: "Be you perfect, even as I am perfect." Humans cannot be perfect in the infinite sense, but can become complete in divinity of will, personality motivation, and God-consciousness.

The Father is known by many names, but reveals himself only by nature. God is primal reality and the source of all truth. He is universal spirit, eternal truth, infinite reality, and a loving father. Affectionate dedication to doing his will is the only gift of true value that humans have to offer God.

God is an eternal, infinite, true, good, and beautiful personality beyond the imagination of the human mind. He delights in his children. The manifestations of the Universal Father in the local universes are his Creator Sons. It is eternally true: "He who has seen the Son, has seen the Father."

God-knowing mortals have within themselves three experiential phenomena that constitute positive proof of God's existence: God-consciousness, God-seeking, and the desire to do God's will.

God is an eternal power, a majestic presence, and a glorious ideal. He is a perfect personality, a person who can know and be known, love and be loved. Personality is not just an attribute of God, it is the revelation of God to the universes. Human personality is the shadow cast by the divine personality. Mortals view personality from the finite toward the infinite, but God's perspective moves from the infinite to the finite.

The human body is literally the temple of God; a divine fragment of the Father dwells within each mortal mind. The benefits received from this presence of the divine Father are limited only by the mortal's capacity to receive and discern spiritual reality. God participates in the struggle of every imperfect soul in the universe who seeks to ascend. It is true that in all our afflictions he is afflicted, for in him we live and move and have our being.

Humans attain divine union through progressive spiritual communion with God and wholehearted, intelligent conformity to his will. Mind yielded to spirit becomes increasingly spiritual and ultimately will achieve oneness with the divine.

2—THE NATURE OF GOD

Our understanding of God is handicapped because our minds are limited. Humans can best understand the nature of God as it has been revealed through the life and teachings of Jesus.

God the Father unfailingly meets the ever-changing demand for himself all over the universe. He knows everything. Universe Sovereigns may engage in adventure; the Constellation Fathers may experiment; the system heads may practice; but the Universal Father sees the end from the beginning. To God, all time is present, there is no past or future. He is infinite in all of his attributes.

God is perfect. In the universes, perfection is relative, but on Paradise, perfection is undiluted. He is perfect in beauty and goodness; there is nothing lacking in his divine character. His justice is tempered with mercy. God is inherently kind, compassionate and merciful. It is never necessary to persuade him to love us; our need is wholly sufficient to insure the flow of his grace.

Everything good comes from God. Love is the dominant characteristic of his personality. The highest reason to love God is that he guides us, step by step, life by life, until we stand in his very presence. God literally sends his spirit to live and toil with us as we pursue the eternal universe career.

God is good; he is our eternal refuge. He heals the brokenhearted and binds up the wounds of the soul. It has been said that God loves sinners but hates sin. It is true that God loves sinners, but he has no attitude toward sin because sin is not a spiritual reality. Iniquity is inherently suicidal. The inevitable consequence of deliberate rebellion against God is loss of existence.

Divine truth is universal, but our understanding of truth is finite and therefore only relative. Evolving persons can be certain only as far as their own personal experience extends. That which is true in one part of the universe may be only partially true elsewhere. The search for truth requires a search for the creative design that pre-exists all universe phenomena.

Truth is both beautiful and good. Beauty is true and good. Goodness is true and beautiful. Health, sanity, and happiness are integrations of truth, beauty, and goodness in the human experience.

3—THE ATTRIBUTES OF GOD

God is omnipresent; he alone can be in numberless places simultaneously. He rules in the local universes through his Creator Sons who are discernible to lower orders of beings and can compensate for God's invisibility. God is greater than all of his combined creations. Although he exists throughout the universes, the universes can never encompass his infinity. God pervades the physical universes of the past, present, and future. He is the primordial foundation of material creation.

Individually, humans are indwelt by Father fragments, and the effective presence of God within each person is conditioned by the degree of cooperation provided. Fluctuations of God's presence are not due to whims of the Father but are directly determined by the mortal's choice to receive him. God has freely bestowed himself without limit or favor.

God is energy. He is the cause of all physical phenomena; he controls all power. The power of God does not function blindly, but it is nearly impossible to explain the nature of his laws. From the limitations of our mortal perspective, many actions of the Creator may seem arbitrary and cruel, but God's actions are always purposeful, intelligent, kind, and wise.

God knows all things. He is the only personality who knows the number of all the stars and planets. His consciousness is universal, his circuit encompasses all personalities. God is never subject to surprise. The potential force, wisdom, and love of God are not reduced by his self-bestowal on subordinate creatures and creations. If creation should continue eternally, the power of God's control from the Isle of Paradise would be adequate for such an eternally increasing creation; God would still possess the same potential as if his power had never poured forth into the universe. Likewise, sending Father fragments to indwell the mortals of numerous worlds in no way lessens the wisdom and perfection of truth of the all-powerful Father.

The nearest approach to God is through love. Finite mind cannot know the infinity of the Father, but it can feel the Father's love.

The uncertainties of life do not contradict the universal sovereignty of God. Creature life is beset with certain inevitabilities. To develop courage, we must grapple with hardships. To develop altruism, we must experience social inequality. Hope results from being faced with insecurity, and faith arises when we live in such a way that we know less than we can believe. The love of truth is created only in an environment where falsehood is possible. Idealism comes as we struggle for a better world. Loyalty cannot emerge unless we live with the possibility of betrayal, and unselfishness results only if we have a self-life to forsake. To appreciate pleasure we must live in a world where pain and suffering are possible. The only evolutionary world without error would be a world without free intelligence. Man must be fallible if he is to be free.

The sovereignty of God is unlimited. The universe was not inevitable. It was not an accident, neither is it self-existent; it is subject to the will of the Father. God the Father loves us, God the Son serves us, and God the Spirit inspires us in the adventure of finding the Father.

4—GOD'S RELATION TO THE UNIVERSE

Divine providence is not the childish material ministry that some mortals imagine it to be. Providence is possible due to related activities of spiritual beings who continuously work for the honor of God and for the spiritual advancement of his children. Providence is consistent with the perfect nature of God.

The watchword of the universe is progress.

God uses unlimited forces and personalities to fulfill his purposes and sustain his creatures. God creates, upholds, preserves, and renews all material and spiritual things. Without God, there would be no such thing as reality. The Father unceasingly pours energy, light, and life into his creations.

Much that appears haphazard to the human mind seems orderly and constructive to higher minds, but even high spiritual beings come across apparently fortuitous interassociations of forces, energies, intellects, and spirits. The medley of physical, mental, moral, and spiritual phenomena in the universes undoubtedly accrue to the glory of God.

Nature is the perfection of Paradise divided by the evil and incompletion of the unfinished universes. Evolution modifies nature, diminishing the error of relative reality while augmenting the content of Paradise perfection. It is wrong to worship nature. Although nature is pervaded by God in a limited sense, it is also a manifestation of the imperfect results of the universe experiment of cosmic evolution. Apparent defects in the natural world do not indicate corresponding defects in the character of God.

God is incapable of wrath or anger. These emotions are hardly worthy of human beings, much less of God. God is the only changeless being in existence; he is self-existent and independent. God is all-wise and all-powerful. He has no limits other that those which he imposes on himself.

God's absoluteness pervades all levels of universe reality. He is eternally motivated by love. In science, God is the First Cause; in religion, God is the Universal Father; in philosophy, God is the one being who exists by himself.

Human religious thought confuses associated Deity personalities with the Universal Father himself. This failure to recognize the difference between God the Father and the local universe creators and administrators is a source of great confusion on earth. Mortals also suffer from primitive concepts of God. The idea of appeasing an angry God, of winning the favor of Deity through sacrifice and penance represents a repulsive philosophy unworthy of an enlightened age of science and truth. It is an affront to God to teach that innocent blood must be shed to win his favor or divert his wrath. The human race is destined to know the beauty of character of the Universal Father, that which was so magnificently portrayed by Jesus when he sojourned on earth.

5—GOD'S RELATION TO THE INDIVIDUAL

A fragment of God lives within the intellect of every normal-minded, morally conscious human being. This fragment, the Thought Adjuster, guides mortals unerringly through the spiritual journey that leads into the presence of God the Father in Paradise.

God yearns for the association of every created being who can love him. Through the indwelling Adjusters, we can seek intimate personal communion with God's divine spirit as we advance inward through the ages toward Paradise. We cannot fail to attain the destiny God has established for us if we yield to the leading of his spiritual guidance.

The indwelling Thought Adjuster allows us to more fully discern the presence of other spiritual influences. Realization of contact with the Adjuster is primarily limited to the realms of the soul: lack of intellectual consciousness concerning the indwelling fragment does not disprove its existence. Proof of the divine Adjuster's work lies wholly in the fruits of the spirit that appear in the life of the believer.

Worship springs from a creature's spontaneous reaction to the recognition of the Father's nature and personality. Prayer contains an element of self-interest, but worship exists for its own sake. Mortals worship God, pray to and commune with the Son, and work out the details of earthly life with the offspring of the Infinite Spirit.

Nonreligious activities seek to bend the universe to the service of self; religious individuals seek to devote their activities to the service of the universe. Philosophy and art create bridges between nonreligious and religious activities by luring people into contemplating spiritual realities. Religious experience is essentially spiritual and cannot be fully understood by a material mind; the realities of religion are beyond mortal capacity of intellectual comprehension. Religious experience unifies human consciousness, promotes philosophic substantiation of ideal moral values, and leads to the spiritual satisfaction of worship—the experience of divine companionship.

God-consciousness includes the mind, the soul, and the spirit through the realization of the idea of God, the ideal of God, and the spirit reality of God. The experience of God-consciousness remains the same throughout history, even though the theological definition of God changes with each advancing epoch.

A human mind that possesses the capacity to distinguish right from wrong and to worship God, in union with a divine Adjuster, is all that is required to initiate the existence of an immortal soul. Eternal survival is wholly dependent on the choice of the mortal being. Survival is assured when the mind, soul, and Adjuster together believe in God and desire to be like him.

Personality, bestowed by God the Father, is one of the incomprehensible mysteries of the universe. Capacity for divine personality is inherent in the Adjuster, and capacity for human personality is potential in the cosmic-mind endowment of the human being. Mortal personality is observable as a functional reality only after the mortal mind is touched by the Adjuster.

The material personality and the prepersonal Adjuster together can create an immortal soul; mortal man alone either wills or inhibits the creation of this surviving self. No other being or agency in the universe can interfere with the sovereignty of mortal free will regarding eternal survival, and no creature can be coerced into the eternal adventure against his will.

The Universal Father is personally conscious of all personalities at all levels of self-conscious existence. As gravity is circuited in the Isle of Paradise, as mind is circuited in the Conjoint Actor, and as spirit is circuited in the Eternal Son, so is personality circuited and centered in the Universal Father.

6—The Eternal Son

The Eternal Son is the original Son of God, the Second Person of Deity, and the Second Great Source and Center. The Son is the spiritual center of the universe government and the personal manifestation of God the Father in the universe. The Son cocreates with the Father and shares the sonship experience with all other created beings; he loves us as both father and brother. Mercy is the essence of the Eternal Son's spiritual character. He reveals the love of God to the universes.

All spiritual beings are responsive to the drawing power of the Eternal Son. He is omnipotent in the spiritual realm. Although the Son does not personally function in the physical domains, his omnipresence constitutes the spiritual unity and cohesion of all creation. The spirit of the Eternal Son is with us and around us, but not within us as is the Thought Adjuster. The indwelling Father fragment adjusts the human mind to divine attitudes, and such a mind becomes increasingly responsive to the spiritual drawing power of the Son.

Personality is the exclusive gift of the Universal Father. The Son gives origin to a vast spirit host, but he creates personality only in conjunction with the Father or the Conjoint Creator. The Son's personality is divine and absolute; it cannot be fragmented. The spirit fragment of the Father dwells within us, the spirit of the Son surrounds us, and the two forever work as one for our spiritual advancement.

The Eternal Son is spirit and has mind, but not a spirit or mind which mortal mind can comprehend. The kind of mind that allies with spirit is not comparable to either material mind or mind that coordinates matter and spirit. The Son's mind is unlike any other in the universe except the Father's.

The Eternal Son is wholly spiritual. Since mortals are nearly entirely material, human understanding of the Son must await attainment of increased spiritual insight. The Son is a merciful minister, a divine spirit, and a spiritual power and personality. The Son is the sum of the First Source and Center, divested of all which is nonpersonal, extra-divine, nonspiritual, and purely potential.

As God is the Universal Father, the Son is the Universal Mother. The Father and Son are separate individuals, but in the administration of the universes they are so interrelated that it is not always possible to distinguish between them. God is the initiating thought and the Son is the expression, the Word. The Father is the bestower of human personality; the Son is the pattern of mortal personality attainment; the Spirit is the source of the mortal mind.

The Son is approachable through his Paradise Sons and through the patient ministry of the creatures of the Infinite Spirit. Throughout the local universe experience, a Creator Son will compensate for the inability of mortals to appreciate the significance of the Eternal Son in Paradise. As we progress toward Paradise, we will enjoy an ever-enlarging comprehension of the Eternal Son.

7—Relation of the Eternal Son to the Universe

The Eternal Son upholds the vast creation of spirit realities and spiritual beings. He is the sovereign of the spiritual universe because he controls the spiritual gravity circuit. Spiritual gravity functions independently of time and space; it is unreduced by time delays or space diminution. Sin and rebellion may interfere with the operation of a local universe, but nothing can suspend the spiritual gravity of the Eternal Son. The spirit-gravity circuit creates cohesion within the universe as a whole, as well as between individuals and groups.

The spiritual-gravity circuit is the secret of the Paradise ascension of surviving mortals. As time passes, ascenders become progressively less subject to material gravity and more responsive to spirit gravity. The spirit-gravity circuit literally pulls the mortal soul Paradiseward. This circuit is also the basic channel for the transmission of prayers from the human mind to the consciousness of Deity.

On Paradise, the Eternal Son's presence is spiritually absolute. He is not personally present in the superuniverses; his administration there is not discernible by created beings. In the local universes, the Eternal Son is present through the persons of the Paradise Creator Sons.

The ascension plan for material beings is a joint creation of the Father and the Son. The universal plan for the creation, evolution, ascension, and perfection of will creatures embraces three correlated undertakings. The Universal Father bestows Thought Adjusters on material will creatures and endows them with personality. The Eternal Son bestows his Creator Sons upon the evolutionary universes to manifest the love of the Father and the mercy of the Son to all creatures. The Infinite Spirit operates a tremendous enterprise of mercy ministry to all mortals. The Father, Son, and Spirit cooperate in the work of creation, control, evolution, revelation, administration, and if necessary, restoration and rehabilitation of the ascending creatures of the universes.

The Eternal Son cannot directly contact human beings, but he does draw near them by gradually down stepping himself. The Eternal Son and the Creator Sons can bestow themselves on lower order of created beings to share the experiences of intelligent will creatures of the universes. Incarnation is the technique by which the Son escapes from the fetters of absolute personality.

The Eternal Son's mercy and service characterize all orders of descending Sons of God. When the Father and the Son jointly project a new personal thought, this idea is instantly personalized as a new Paradise Creator Son. In spirit and nature, each Paradise Son is a perfect portrait of the Original Son. All Sons of God who originate in the Paradise Deities are in continuous communication with the Eternal Son. The Eternal Son has perfect knowledge concerning the activities of all orders of Paradise Sons, just as he has knowledge regarding everything of spiritual value existing in the hearts of all creatures in time and eternity.

The Eternal Son is a complete, exclusive, universal, and final revelation of the spirit and personality of God. He and the Father are one. In divine personality they are coordinate, in spiritual nature they are equal, and in divinity they are identical.

8—THE INFINITE SPIRIT

The time-bound mind of man must have a starting point for visualizing universe history. While a portrayal of sequential origin of Deity is helpful to the mortal mind as an explanation of the relationship of Deities, such a condescension does not preclude the fact that all three have existed eternally without beginning or end.

The members of the Trinity are distinct individuals in eternal association. If we imagine that God the Father is Thought and God the Son is Word, then God the Spirit is Action. In the instant that the Father and Son together conceived of infinite action, the Infinite Spirit sprang fully formed into being.

The existence of the Infinite Spirit set the stage of space for the drama of creation. In the instant of his creation, one billion perfect spheres materialized. The central universe of Havona was then embraced by physical and spiritual gravities, and the soil of life prepared for consciousness of mind manifest in the intelligence circuits of the God of Action. Upon these seeds of potential, creature personality appeared, and the presences of the Paradise Deities filled organized space and began to draw all things Paradiseward.

It is proper to name the Third Person of Deity the Infinite Spirit, but material creatures may also conceive of him as the Conjoint Creator, the Infinite Reality, the Universal Organizer, and the Personality Coordinator. He discloses the Father's infinity and the Son's mercy; he executes the purposes of the Father-Son. Ever and always, the Infinite Spirit is a mercy minister. As the Sons reveal the love of God, the Spirit reveals his mercy.

The Father delegates everything possible to the Son; likewise, the Son bestows all possible authority to the Spirit. Every post-Havona universe in existence was planned and created by partnership of the Son and the Spirit. The Spirit pledges all of his resources to the Father and the Son; he has dedicated all that he has to the plan of drawing will creatures to Paradise. The Infinite Spirit is devoted to fostering the ascension of material creatures, especially through the persons of the Creative Daughters, the local universe Mother Spirits.

The essence of the Spirit's divine character is everlasting ministry to mind. God is love, the Son is mercy, and the Spirit is the ministry of divine love and endless mercy to all creation. The Spirit is love applied to the individual minds of all the children of every universe. The Infinite Spirit is omnipresent. He is a universe presence, an eternal action, a cosmic power, a holy influence, a universal mind, and a true and divine personality. He is the Spirit whom all ascenders must attain before they approach the Father through the Son. In the administration of the universe the Father, Son, and Spirit are forever one, perfectly associated in the service of creation.

9—RELATION OF THE INFINITE SPIRIT TO THE UNIVERSE

The Third Source and Center is responsive to both spiritual and material reality. He is the universal coordinator, the correlator of all reality. The Infinite Spirit functions whenever energy and spirit associate; no reality can escape eventual relationship with him. Agents of the Infinite Spirit ceaselessly manipulate forces and energies throughout the universes.

The Infinite Spirit pervades all space. He is omnipresent without qualification, but is omnipotent only in the domain of mind. The Infinite Spirit possesses the unique power of antigravity, which he transmits to certain of his higher creatures. He also has powers that neutralize energy and transcend force by slowing energy to the point of materialization. The Conjoint Actor manipulates the forces and energies of Paradise, thus bringing into existence the universal and absolute mind.

The Conjoint Creator is not the source of energy, rather, he is the manipulator of energy. He has created power-control creatures—physical controllers, power directors, and power centers—who regulate and stabilize physical energies. These material energies are dependent on the absoluteness of the Eternal Isle. Paradise is the pattern of infinity, and the God of Action activates that pattern.

Energy is receptive and responsive to mind. Mind can be superimposed on energy, but does not need to be added to pure spirit because spirit is innately conscious. The insight of spirit transcends the consciousness of mind. Cosmic force responds to mind as cosmic mind responds to spirit. Mind establishes relationships between energy and spirit that suggest a mutual kinship in eternity.

The Third Source and Center bestows mind and is infinite in mind. If the universe should grow endlessly, his mind potential would remain adequate to endow limitless numbers of creatures with suitable minds. Through his associates, the Third Source ministers to all minds on all spheres. He is personally conscious of every intellect in all of creation.

The Conjoint Creator is the ancestor of the cosmic mind; he completely controls the universal mind circuit. The human mind is an individual portion of the cosmic mind bestowed in the local universe by a Creative Mother Spirit. The Infinite Spirit is the perfect expression of the mind of the Creator to all creatures, just as the Supreme Being is the evolving expression of the minds of all creatures to the Creator.

The Conjoint Actor coordinates all levels of universe actuality through the phenomenon of universe reflectivity. He has the power to see, hear, sense, and know all things as they transpire, and to reflect this knowledge to any desired point. Reflectivity is the most complex interassociation of phases of existence in creation. There is a unique unification of spirit, energy, and mind in reflectivity which enables the universe rulers to know about remote conditions throughout the universes instantaneously. Reflectivity appears to be omniscient within the limits of the experiential finite. It may represent the emergence of the consciousness of the Supreme Being.

The Infinite Spirit transmits many of his powers to subordinate personalities, including the Seven Master Spirits of Paradise and the local universe Creative Spirits. The Third Source is further represented in the universes by a vast array of spirits, messengers, teachers, adjudicators, helpers and advisers. This vast family of the Infinite Spirit is dedicated to administering the love of God and the mercy of the Son to all intelligent creatures in time and space. These spirit beings constitute the living ladder whereby mortals climb from chaos to glory.

The Father upholds, the Son reveals, Paradise stabilizes, and the Spirit unifies.

10—THE PARADISE TRINITY

The existence of the Paradise Trinity is the one inescapable inevitability in universe affairs. The concept of Trinity combines the absolute unity of Deity with the voluntary liberation that is inherent in God's threefold personalization.

The Universal Father delegates everything possible to other Creators or creatures, in every way, in every age, and in every place except in the central universe of his own indwelling. God has reserved for himself only those powers and authorities which seem impossible to delegate: absolute fatherhood and absolute volition.

By bestowing absolute personality on the Original Son, the First Source and Center became the Universal Father and escaped the fetters of personality absolutism. The creation of the Infinite Spirit was a joint effort of the Father and the Son. The Father has no ancestral precedents, but is parent to both the Son and the Spirit. The Son is son to the Father and parent to the Spirit, and the Spirit is the son of both the Father and the Son.

The Universal Father, the Eternal Son, and the Infinite Spirit are unique persons. None is duplicate, each is original, yet all are united. They can act personally and collectively in seven possible combinations: Father alone, Son alone, Spirit alone, Father-Son, Father-Spirit, Son-Spirit, and Father-Son-Spirit. The seven available arrangements of divinity make it inevitable that the universe appears in seven variations of values, meanings, and personalities.

The First Source performs multiple functions outside of Havona. He acts as creator through the Creator Sons, and as controller through the gravity of Paradise. Through the Eternal Son he functions as spirit, and through the Conjoint Actor he functions as mind. He maintains parental contact with all creatures by means of his personality circuit. He acts directly as a person through his divine fragments, the Thought Adjusters. Only within the Paradise Trinity does the First Source function as total Deity.

The Trinity is an association of persons functioning in a nonpersonal way, somewhat like the way a corporation functions as a nonpersonal entity subject to the personal will of its officers. Functions of the Paradise Trinity include justice administration, coordinate actions, and cosmic overcontrol. The Trinity is not merely the sum of the attributes of the Father, Son, and Spirit. All associations, including families, social groups, and the Trinity, enjoy a group potential far in excess of the sum of the component individuals.

God *is* law. Law originates in the First Source and Center. The administration of law inheres in the Second Source and Center. The revelation of law is the function of the Third Source and Center. The application of law—justice—is carried out by the Trinity. Justice is inherent in the sovereignty of the Paradise Trinity; it is the Trinity's response to the attributes of the Father's love, the Son's mercy, and the Spirit's ministry. Justice is always a group function, never a personal one.

Judgment, the application of justice, is the work of the Stationary Sons of the Trinity: Trinitized Secrets of Supremacy, Eternals of Days, Ancients of Days, Perfections of Days, Recents of Days, Unions of Days, Faithfuls of Days, Perfectors of Wisdom, Divine Counselors, and Universal Censors. These children of the Trinity are specifically designed to represent the collective attitude of Deity in the domains of justice.

The Supreme Being appears to reflect the attitude of the Trinity, but he is something less than the Trinity functioning in the finite universes. The overcontrol of the Supreme is not wholly predictable. Some events—accidents, disasters, illnesses—may or may not be correlated with the workings of the Supreme Being, but it is certain that all difficult situations inevitably accrue to the welfare and progress of the universes. As things appear to mortals, the Paradise Trinity, like the Supreme Being, is concerned only with the total planet, the total universe, the total super-universe. Human beings will not always be able to understand how the acts of the Trinity work for the good of individual mortals.

No single person of the Paradise Deities fills all Deity potential, but all three collectively do. The three divine persons activate the prepersonal and existential potential of total Deity—the Deity Absolute. The First, Second, and Third Persons of Deity are equal to each other, and they are truly and divinely one.

11—THE ETERNAL ISLE OF PARADISE

Paradise is the dwelling place of Deity and the eternal center of the universe of universes. It is the largest organized body of cosmic reality in the master universe; it is material as well as spiritual. The streams of life, energy, and personality flow outward from God in Paradise to every corner of the universe.

The Eternal Isle is essentially a flat ellipsoid divided into three geographic domains: upper Paradise, peripheral Paradise, and nether Paradise. Paradise is the original non-spiritual expression of the First Source and Center and is created of a substance found nowhere else in the universe. Paradise is nonspatial; it exists without time and has no location in space. Space seems to originate just below nether Paradise, and time from just above upper Paradise.

The three spheres of activity on upper Paradise are the Deity presence, where the Three Persons dwell; the Most Holy Sphere, which is wholly spiritual; and the Holy Area, which is the residential area of Paradise Citizens, Havona natives, and ascendant creatures from the seven superuniverses. The staggering number of residential areas on Paradise currently occupy less than one per cent of the total residential area available.

The peripheral surface of Paradise contains landing and dispatch fields for spirit personalities. The Seven Master Spirits maintain headquarters on the Paradise periphery. Here, the Seven Supreme Power Directors mark the locations of stations that disperse Paradise energy into the seven superuniverses. Peripheral Paradise is also the location of enormous historic and prophetic exhibit areas dedicated to the local universes of time and space.

All physical-energy and cosmic-force circuits have their origin in nether Paradise. One zone of the force center of nether Paradise seems to act as a gigantic heart whose pulsations direct and modify force-energy currents to the outermost borders of physical space. The nether Paradise space presence is entirely impersonal, notwithstanding that in some manner it seems to be indirectly responsive to the Trinity. Personalities do not travel to nether Paradise.

All forms of force and energy appear to be encircuited, traveling out throughout the universes and returning by defined routes. The emanations seem to be either outgoing or incoming; they never occur simultaneously. All force-energy originates from nether Paradise and eventually returns thereto. Material organizations of the universes do not, however, all come from nether Paradise; space itself is the womb of several forms of matter and pre-matter. All physical force, energy, and matter are one.

Space alternatively contracts and expands, but we do not know the mechanism of this space respiration.

Space does not exist on any surface of Paradise, neither does it touch Paradise. Paradise is the motionless nucleus of the quiescent zones existing between pervaded and unpervaded space.

Pervaded space extends from nearly peripheral Paradise through the fourth space level and beyond. The relatively quiet zones between the moving space levels act as buffers, stabilizing the alternate clockwise and counterclockwise flow of the galaxies. Space levels function as elliptical regions of motion, surrounded on all sides by relative motionlessness.

Gravity is the all-powerful grasp of the physical presence of Paradise. Space, while nonresponsive to gravity, acts to equalize gravity. The center of absolute material gravity is the central Isle. Absolute gravity is Paradise gravity; linear gravity pertains to energy or matter. Linear gravity operates in the central universe, superuniverses, and outer universes wherever suitable materialization has taken place.

Paradise is unique because it is both the origin and the destiny of spirit personalities. Paradise is the geographic center of infinity. It is not part of universal creation, nor even a part of the eternal Havona universe. When the Father gave infinite personality to the Son, simultaneously, he revealed the infinite potential of his nonpersonal aspect as Paradise. Non-personal, non-spiritual Paradise appears to be an inevitable repercussion of the Father's act which eternalized the Son. God projected reality in two phases: personal and non-personal, spiritual and non-spiritual. The tension between the two gave existence to the Conjoint Actor and the central universe of material worlds and spiritual beings.

Paradise is the absolute of patterns. Everything which has been, now is, or will be, has come, now comes, or will come from this eternal home of God.

12—THE UNIVERSE OF UNIVERSES

God is spirit, but Paradise is not. The material universe is the arena wherein spiritual activities take place; spirit beings and spirit ascenders live and work on physical spheres of material reality. The universe of universes may seem boundless to finite minds, but it has definite dimensions. The total aggregate of material creation functions with predictable behavior as an organized whole.

The universe of universes is a series of elliptical space levels separated by quiet zones, all of which continuously move through the great circuits of space. The first of six ellipses encircling Paradise is Havona, the central universe. Havona has existed eternally and consists of one billion perfect spheres. Together with Paradise, this system forms the nucleus of the master universe.

The grand universe consists of the Paradise-Havona system combined with the seven superuniverses. The superuniverses are geographic clusters, each containing approximately one-seventh of the organized creation outside of Havona. The superuniverses are not yet fully inhabited. Our local universe of Nebadon is one of the newer creations within Orvonton, the seventh superuniverse.

One-half million light years beyond the seven superuniverses, an unbelievably vast creation of force and energy is assembling in the first outer space level. Fifty million light years beyond the first outer space level, past a quiet zone, even greater activity heralds the advent of the second, third, and fourth outer space levels. The almost countless collection of universes evolving beyond the borders of the grand universe constitutes the domains of the Unqualified Absolute.

All forms of energy—material, mindal, and spiritual—are subject to gravity. Ninety-five per cent of the physical gravity of the Isle of Paradise is now engaged in controlling systems beyond the borders of the grand universe. However, virtually all of the spirit gravity pull of the Eternal Son is presently functioning within the grand universe. The universes evolving in outer space are, as yet, non-spiritual. Eighty-five per cent of the mind-gravity of the Conjoint Actor takes origin in the existing grand universe, which suggests that mind activities are involved with the physical activities progressing in outer space.

Space from the human viewpoint seems to be nothing, but space is real. Space contains and conditions motion, and space itself moves. The alternating direction of movement from one space level to the next contributes to the equalization of space tensions in the universes. The universes are not static. The stability of the universes is the product of balanced energies, cooperative minds, spirit overcontrol, and personality unification. Stability is wholly proportional to divinity.

Time is a result of motion. The absolute limit of time is eternity, but the absolute limit of space is unknown.

The will of God rules the universe of universes, even though it does not always prevail in the heart of each person. God loves each individual as a child without duplicate in infinity, as a creature irreplaceable in all eternity. The universality of God's love creates the universal brotherhood, which includes every personality in existence.

All original energy proceeds from Paradise. Its journey through the universe is obedient to the ever-present pull of the eternal Isle. Physical energy steadfastly obeys universal law; only in the realms of creature will has there been deviation from the divine plans.

Mind alone can mediate the material and spiritual levels. As the mind of any personality becomes more spiritual, it simultaneously becomes less responsive to material gravity. Liaisons between the spiritual and material realms are phenomena of mind caused by acts of the Infinite Spirit. Mind is the technique whereby creature personalities experience spirit realities.

Mind, matter, and spirit are equally real, but they are not of equal value to personality in the attainment of divinity. Matter is organized energy subject to physical gravity. Mind is organized consciousness modified by spirit, and is not wholly subject to material gravity. Spirit, the highest personal reality, is immune to physical gravity. Spirit eventually becomes the motivating influence over every evolving energy system bestowed with personality.

The sum of two or more things is often something more than the predictable consequence of their union. The human mind is a personal-energy system surrounding a divine center, functioning in a material environment. Mortal man has a spirit nucleus. It is this living relationship of personal mind and divine spirit that creates the potential for eternal personality.

13—THE SACRED SPHERES OF PARADISE

Three eternal seven-world circuits belonging to the Father, the Son, and the Spirit exist between the Isle of Paradise and the innermost Havona planets.

Each of the seven spheres of the Father manifests a special aspect of the Deities of the Paradise Trinity. Divinington holds the secret of the bestowal and mission of Thought Adjusters. Sonarington contains the secret of the incarnation of the divine sons. Spiritington is the sphere that holds the mysteries of reflectivity. Vicegerington includes the secrets of trinitization. Solitarington is the rendezvous point of numerous unrevealed orders of beings. Seraphington is the planet where the secrets of seraphic transport are held. Ascendington is the receiving sphere for pilgrims of time who pass through Havona on the way to Paradise. The secrets of Ascendington include one of the most perplexing mysteries in the universe—how the mind of a mortal creature can evolve an immortal soul. Throughout all of eternity, mortals will regard Ascendington as their home.

The seven spheres of the Eternal Son are worlds of pure-spirit existence. There is little concerning these worlds that can be revealed to material personalities.

The seven executive worlds of the Infinite Spirit are inhabited by various beings, including offspring of the Spirit, trinitized sons of created personalities, and other unrevealed beings. The Seven Master Spirits conduct work pertaining to the operations of the grand universe from these planets, the Paradise headquarters of the seven superuniverses. The Master Spirits control the flow of the spirit presence of Deity into the realms of the superuniverses.

Physical reactions are uniform and unvarying throughout the universe, but the availability of the spiritual presence of the Deities is conditioned by the decisions, choices, and attitudes of will creatures. God is ever faithful in satisfying the sincere desire of created beings for his presence in their lives.

14—THE CENTRAL AND DIVINE UNIVERSE

The billion worlds of Havona are arranged into seven concentric circuits surrounding the three circuits of Paradise satellites. Circling on the outskirts of this central universe are a large number of enormous dark gravity bodies. Since these dark gravity bodies neither reflect nor absorb light, they serve to hide Havona from the view of nearby inhabited universes.

Time is not reckoned on Paradise, but each Havona world observes its own time as determined by its position in the circuit around Paradise. The Paradise-Havona day is based on the length of time the inner

Havona circuit takes to complete one revolution around the Isle of Paradise—in earth years, just seven minutes less than one thousand years.

The substance of the Havona worlds is different from the material organization of the planets in the seven superuniverses. Havona material consists of one thousand basic chemical elements. The energy of Havona is threefold, as compared to the twofold energy charge of the superuniverses. Havona natives respond to forty-nine sensory stimuli. Citizens of the central universe would not be visible to a person from Urantia; neither would our current senses react to any of the physical stimuli of Havona worlds.

Havona is spiritually perfect and physically stable. No sin has appeared in any ascending creature who has arrived there, and the freewill natives of Havona have never been guilty of transgressing the will of Deity. Life in the central universe is so rich and replete that it transcends human comprehension. Each planet of the central universe is a matchless, unique, and perfect creation.

Havona citizens enjoy the ideal of true self-government. The billion Havona spheres are training worlds for the natives of Paradise and Havona, and are the final proving grounds for ascending creatures of the worlds of time. Only about one per cent of Havona's capacity relative to the mortal ascension plan is currently being used.

There are seven types of beings in the central universe: material, morontial, spiritual, absonite, ultimate, co-absolute, and absolute. Havona natives are the offspring of the Paradise Trinity. They are non-reproducing beings. As mortals strive to do the will of the Father, so Havona natives live to fulfill the ideals of the Paradise Trinity. By nature, they *are* the will of God. All beings in all universes are created after a pattern of some creature living on one of the billion Havona worlds.

Havona serves many purposes. The central universe compensates for the time-space delay of the Father's urge for infinite expansion. It is his perfect pattern for all evolving universes, a revelation of spirit reality, the power nucleus for future universe expansion, and a worthy goal for ascending beings. Havona gives the Eternal Son a base for ever-expanding spirit power and a foundation for his spirit-gravity control. The Infinite Spirit finds in Havona a laboratory for the creation of mind, a place to rehearse ministry, and a venue where he can participate in universe administration. Havona also serves as a pattern of the potential of the Supreme Being, the training ground for the Creator Sons and the

Universe Mother Spirits, the destiny of every ascending mortal, and the starting place for finaliters as they begin their exploration of the infinity of the Universal Father.

15—The Seven Superuniverses

The seven superuniverses travel counterclockwise in an orderly elliptical procession around the home of the First Great Source and Center. Imagine the grand universe as a wheel, the hub being Paradise, the spokes as the radiations of the Seven Master Spirits, and the rim being the outer perimeter of the superuniverses. Our local universe of Nebadon belongs to the seventh superuniverse, Orvonton. Our planet, Urantia, is near the outermost border of Nebadon, which travels along the periphery of Orvonton.

The seven superuniverses are divided into ten major sectors, each of which encompass one hundred minor sectors, which each contain one hundred local universes. One local universe holds one hundred constellations. Each constellation consists of approximately one hundred thousand inhabitable worlds.

The Milky Way is the central nucleus of our superuniverse; nearly all of the stars visible to the naked eye on Urantia are within Orvonton. When we look through the thickest area of the Milky Way, we are looking toward the central universe, the center of all things. The rotation point of our minor sector is located in the dense star cloud of Sagittarius.

Paradise force organizers transform space potency into primordial force. They evolve this potential material into the primary and secondary energy manifestations of physical reality. Paradise force organizers originate nebulae, the mother wheels which give origin to suns and solar systems. Some of the larger nebulae of outer space are capable of generating one hundred million suns. The bulk of the mass contained in the suns and planets of the superuniverses comes from the nebular wheels.

There are five major classifications of the spheres of space: suns, dark islands, minor space bodies, planets, and architectural spheres. Suns serve as local accelerators of energy circulation and act as power-control stations. Dark islands of space are dead suns and other large aggregates of matter without heat or light; they exert a powerful influence in universe equilibrium and energy manipulation. Planets are the larger masses of matter orbiting around a sun or other space body. Minor space bodies are comets, meteors, and other small particles of matter.

Three planets in our solar system are presently suited to harbor life.

Architectural spheres are the only planets without evolutionary origins. Architectural worlds are specifically constructed to serve as headquarters for universe administration. Headquarters worlds also function as power-energy regulators and serve as focal points for directing energy into the local universes. The grandeur of Uversa, the architectural world that is Orvonton's capital, surpasses anything known in the time-space creations.

Universe Power Directors are responsible for maintaining equilibrium between matter and energy. They can condense and expand energy, and can make, unmake, and remake matter in the endless metamorphoses of the universes. Orvonton seems now to be winding down, but it is not so; nebulae may disperse, suns burn out, systems vanish, and planets perish, but the universes do not run down.

Four circuits of Paradise pervade the seven superuniverses: personality gravity, spiritual gravity, mind gravity, and material gravity. Superuniverse circuits include the cosmic-mind circuit of the Master Spirits, reflective-service circuits of the Reflective Spirits, circuits of the Mystery Monitors, and circuits of the power centers. The local universe circuits are the Spirit of Truth, the Holy Spirit, and the intelligence-ministry circuit.

The present scheme of administration of the seven superuniverses has existed nearly from the beginning of time. The executive branch of superuniverse government includes three Ancients of Days, three groups of the children of the Paradise Trinity, and three groups of perfected mortals ascended from the evolutionary worlds. When a local universe is settled in light and life, it becomes a member of the superuniverse confederation of perfected creations and is eligible for admission into the councils of the Ancients of Days.

The legislative council of each superuniverse capital is known as the deliberative assembly. The seven houses of this council consist of elected representatives from each of the local universes belonging to the superuniverse confederation.

The judicial branch of government in the superuniverses is made up of personnel from the executive branch. The courts of the Ancients of Days are the high tribunals for the spiritual adjudication of the universes. Sentences involving the extinction of will creatures are always executed from the headquarters of the superuniverse; only the Ancients of Days can sit in judgment on issues of eternal life and death. Courts of the Perfections of Days deal mainly with decisions about the intellectual status of the major sectors. Minor sector governments, ruled by three Recents of Days, are concerned with physical control and stabilization of the local universes.

Each superuniverse has a special function arising from its unique nature. Orvonton demonstrates a combination of love and mercy, and also seems to be weaving the unique purposes of the six other super-universes into a "meaning-of-the-whole" in the seventh superuniverse.

Urantia is the 606th planet of the system of Satania, the twenty-fourth system in the constellation Norlatiadek. Norlatiadek is number seventy of the constellations belonging to Nebadon, which is the eighty-fourth local universe in the minor sector of Ensa. Ensa is the third minor sector of the major sector of Splandon, the fifth major sector in the seventh su-per-universe. Our planet is one of trillions in the cosmos, but it is just as lovingly administered as if it were the only inhabited world in existence.

16—THE SEVEN MASTER SPIRITS

The Seven Master Spirits of Paradise are the primary personalities of the Infinite Spirit. While the Infinite Spirit is personally present within the Paradise-Havona system, his presence is revealed to the rest of the grand universe through the Seven Master Spirits. Individual differences between the Seven Master Spirits appear because each of them repre-sents one of the seven possible Deity combinations.

Master Spirit Number One presides over the first superuniverse, and is a manifestation of the power, love, and wisdom of the Universal Father.

Master Spirit Number Two portrays the character of the Eternal Son as he directs the destinies of the second superuniverse.

Master Spirit Number Three is in charge of the third superuniverse and resembles the Infinite Spirit.

Master Spirit Number Four displays the combined natures of the Fa-ther and the Son as he fosters the fourth superuniverse.

Master Spirit Number Five directs the fifth superuniverse and blends the characters of the Father and the Spirit.

Master Spirit Number Six portrays the combination of the Son and the Spirit in the sixth superuniverse.

Master Spirit Number Seven portrays the personal natures of the Father, Son, and Spirit and his domain is the seventh superuniverse. He represents the personal attitude of God the Supreme, discloses the deity attitude of the Paradise Trinity, and sponsors the progress of ascension candidates from the worlds of time and space.

As a group, the Master Spirits function on every universe level of reality except the absolute level. They are efficient supervisors of all phases of administrative affairs in the superuniverses. They create the Universe Power Directors, who organize and regulate the physical energies of the grand universe. The Master Spirits assist Creator Sons as they shape and organize the local universes. They are the sevenfold source of cosmic mind, which provides the intellectual potential of the grand universe and of the individuals who inhabit evolutionary worlds. It is postulated that Orvonton's Master Spirit is involved with Life Carriers, adjutant mind-spirits, reflectivity mechanisms, and the bestowals of the Holy Spirit and the Spirit of Truth.

Each segment of the grand universe enjoys the benefits of the united wisdom of all seven Master Spirits, but receives the personal attention of just one. Every human and angel created in the superuniverses bears the characteristic stamp of one of these seven Paradise Spirits.

All will creatures are endowed with an innate response to three domains of universe realities: Causation, duty, and worship. Causation, the domain of physical reality, is the factual, mathematical, or scientific form of cosmic discrimination. Duty is the domain of morality, the arena in which right and wrong are judged. Worship is the spiritual domain of divine fellowship, spirit values, and the assurance of eternal survival. These innate cosmic intuitions make it possible for humans to function rationally as self-conscious personalities in the realms of science, philosophy, and religion. It is the purpose of education to develop these innate endowments, of civilization to express them, of life experience to realize them, of religion to ennoble them, and of personality to unify them.

Man's moral and religious nature distinguishes him from the rest of the animal world. Virtue is righteousness—conformity with the cosmos. Virtue is realized by the consistent choosing of good over evil, and such choosing is evidence of moral nature. Morality cannot be advanced by law or force; it is a personal choice that spreads through contact with moral persons. Mortals can ascend to the level of moral beings because they are endowed with personality.

Creature personality is distinguished by two phenomena: self-consciousness and relative free will. Self-consciousness is the awareness of personal actuality. It includes the ability to recognize the reality of other personalities and indicates a capacity for individual experience with cosmic reality. Free will is involved in moral decisions, spiritual choices, brotherly service, group loyalty, cosmic insight, devotion to God's will, and worship.

Once a personality begins the realization of Deity kinship, such a self, indwelt by a fragment of God, is in truth a spiritual child of God. A human being can never become as absolutely certain of a fellow human being's reality as he can be sure of the reality of the presence of God living within him. The recognition of God is inalienable and constitutive in all mortals. Self-consciousness is essentially a communal consciousness of God and man, Parent and child, Creator and creature. We become conscious of the brotherhood of man because we first become conscious of God as our Father. We worship God because he is, then, because he is in us, and last, because we are in him.

17—THE SEVEN SUPREME SPIRIT GROUPS

The work of the Master Spirits in the grand universe is carried out by the subordinate personalities of the Supreme Spirit groups. Together, the seven groups of Supreme Spirits constitute the nucleus of the functional family of the Third Source and Center. They unify the descending administrative levels in the central, super, and local universes and are classified as:

The Seven Master Spirits

The Seven Supreme Executives carry out all executive matters—rulings, regulations, and administration—and are in essence the board of directors of the post-Havona creation. They direct all things physical, intellectual, and spiritual; they see all, hear all, and know all that transpires in Havona and the seven superuniverses.

The Reflective Spirits are the offspring of the Paradise Trinity and the Master Spirits. They are led by Majeston, the personal center of reflectivity in the seven superuniverses. Each one of the Reflective Spirits reveals the nature of one of the seven combinations of divinity. One set serves on each super-universe headquarters, gathering news, disseminating decrees, and recording everything of true spiritual value. A mystery attends their existence: neither the Master Spirits nor the Paradise Deities demonstrate powers of reflectivity, yet together they have created reflective beings.

The Reflective Image Aids. Each Reflective Spirit creates one Reflective Image Aid, a virtual reproduction of the parent Reflective Spirit without his power of reflectivity. Image Aids function as channels of communication between the Reflective Spirits and the superuniverse authorities.

The Seven Spirits of the Havona Circuits enable the Master Spirits to provide unified spiritual supervision in the central universe. Each one of the Spirits of the Circuits permeates a single Havona circuit. Circuit Spirits are related to the native inhabitants of Havona much as Thought Adjusters are related to mortals.

The Local Universe Creative Spirits experience several stages of existence. When a Creator Son is first personalized, the simultaneous birth of his complementary Creative Mother Spirit occurs within the Infinite Spirit. While the Michael Son is training, his future consort further develops as an entity. Next, the Creative Spirit differentiates from the Infinite Spirit and becomes a part of the appropriate Master Spirit, with whom she remains until the Creator Son takes her into space to begin the adventure of universe creation.

The Adjutant Mind-Spirits are are the sevenfold mind bestowal upon the living creatures of joint creation of such a Creative Spirit and a Creator Son.

18—THE SUPREME TRINITY PERSONALITIES

Seven categories of Supreme Trinity Personalities are created by the Paradise Trinity to represent the justice of the Trinity in the superuniverses.

Ten *Trinitized Secrets of Supremacy* preside over each of the seven innermost Paradise worlds of the Universal Father.

One *Eternal of Days* permanently rules over each of the billion worlds of Havona. The Eternals of Days also preside over planetary conclaves.

The *Ancients of Days* are the rulers of the superuniverses. They possess individuality, but do not differ from each other as the Master Spirits do. Three Ancients of Days oversee the administration of each of the superuniverses.

Three *Perfections of Days* are assigned to each of the major sector headquarters. Their work is mostly concerned with intellectual matters, and they earn their name because they are perfect in the mastery of administrative detail.

Three *Recents of Days* rule over each minor sector, attending to the physical problems of the universes.

The *Unions of Days* serve as observers for the Paradise Trinity in the local universes. They coordinate all administrative activities of the universe government, from the local universes through the superuniverse levels. They report intellectual matters to the Perfections of Days and spiritual matters to the Ancients of Days.

The *Faithfuls of Days* are Paradise advisers to the constellations. Faithfuls of Days act only as counselors and never participate in administrative roles except by invitation of the constellation authorities. They report to the Unions of Days of the local universes.

19—THE COORDINATE TRINITY-ORIGIN BEINGS

Seven groups of beings are classified as Coordinate Trinity-Origin Beings. These beings are brought into existence by the Paradise Trinity. Although endowed with free will, no Coordinate Trinity-Origin Being has ever defaulted in his duties.

Trinity Teacher Sons serve throughout the central and super-universes, even on individual planets. Sometimes known as Daynals, Teacher Sons have the distinction of also being classified as Paradise Sons of God. Trinity Teacher Sons are educators devoted to the spiritual enlightenment of mortals and seraphim.

Perfectors of Wisdom personify the wisdom of divinity in the super-universes. They do not reflect the wisdom of the Trinity; they *are* that wisdom. One billion Perfectors of Wisdom are assigned to each of the superuniverses where they engage in the revelation of truth to ascending creatures.

Divine Counselors are the counsel of Deity to the superuniverse realms. Three billion serve in each superuniverse. When teamed with one Perfector of Wisdom and one Universal Censor, seven Divine Counselors constitute the highest mobile tribunal in time and space. The united counsel of seven Divine Counselors in liaison with a trio of perfected evolutionary beings approaches nearly-Paradisiacal attainment of the complete attitude of Deity toward any situation in the superuniverses.

Universal Censors, eight billion in number, are the judgment of Deity. One Censor serves on each of the billion planets of the central universe, and one billion are assigned to each of the seven superuniverses. When thousands of witnesses have testified, when the voice of wisdom has spoken, and when the counsel of divinity has been recorded, then the Universal Censor reveals an unerring total of all that has transpired. It appears that Censors form new meanings and values from the association of the facts and truths presented to them. Once a Censor has spoken, there is no appeal.

Inspired Trinity Spirits are one of the few wholly secret orders in existence. They belong to the category of super-personal spirits. Trinity Spirits appear to act independently of time and space, and may be related in some manner to the Thought Adjusters. It is conjectured that their work is to enlighten universe creatures by superconscious techniques; perhaps they are engaged in the communication of the vast body of essential spiritual knowledge that cannot consciously be received.

Havona natives are superb beings directly created by the Paradise Trinity. Havoners are destined to develop deep eternal friendships with ascending mortals. Mortals need to compensate for inherent spiritual impoverishment while Havona natives seek to overcome the experiential handicap of divine perfection.

Paradise citizens are not directly concerned with the ascension plan for will creatures; therefore their functions are not revealed to mortals. More than three thousand orders of this classification of intelligent personalities reside on Paradise.

20—THE PARADISE SONS OF GOD

The three classifications of Sons of God are: Descending Sons, Ascending Sons, and Trinitized Sons.

Descending Sons of God who take origin in the Paradise Deities are known as Paradise Sons of God. Paradise Sons are creators, servers, bestowers, judges, teachers, and truth revealers in the systems of time and space. They embrace three orders: Creator Sons reveal the Father, Magisterial Sons reveal the Son, and Trinity Teacher Sons reveal the Infinite Spirit.

Creator Sons are the subject of the subsequent essay.

Magisterial Sons, also known as Avonals, are planetary ministers and judges. There are nearly one billion unique Magisterial Sons. They serve in judicial, magisterial, and bestowal missions on the evolutionary worlds. Avonals preside over the dispensations of planetary ages and the awakenings of sleeping survivors.

When Magisterial Sons perform judicial actions they usually arrive as a spiritual being rather than through incarnation. During his initial magisterial mission on an evolutionary world, an Avonal appears as an adult male. During bestowal missions, the Paradise Son is always born of a mortal woman. The bestowal process is a necessary part of a Magisterial Son's education. The Spirit of Truth comes to an evolutionary planet only after a successful bestowal, and Thought Adjusters cannot come en masse to a planet until the Spirit of Truth has been poured out. There has never been a failure of a Magisterial Son during a bestowal mission.

Trinity Teacher Sons, the Daynals, are constantly increasing in number. They are the moral and spiritual educators of the universes, and their ministry is interrelated with that of the personalities of the Infinite Spirit. Teacher Sons are the embodiment of service and wisdom. They begin their work in the local systems and advance inward through their home constellation teaching mortals and angels. When a planet is ready to embark on a spiritual age, the Daynals volunteer for one thousand years of planetary service. Trinity Teacher Sons attempt to create spiritual counterparts for the temporal wisdom and material knowledge of their students.

21—THE PARADISE CREATOR SONS

Creator Sons, also known as the Michael Sons, are of dual origin. Springing from God the Father and God the Son, they embody characteristics of both. They are the designers, creators, and administrators of the local universes of time and space. Each unique Michael Son is accompanied in his local creation by a Creative Daughter of the Infinite Spirit. A Creator Son pledges to uphold, protect, defend, and, if necessary, retrieve his local universe. There is no experience of the children of time and space in which some Michael has not personally participated.

A Michael Son cannot assume supreme sovereignty in his local universe until he completes seven bestowal missions. Jesus of Nazareth, the Creator Son of our local universe, died on the cross two thousand years ago. His last words, "It is finished," applied not only to his human life but also to his sevenfold bestowal career.

Once his seventh bestowal is completed a Creator Son is considered a Master Michael. Master Sons enjoy perfect connection with the Eternal Son and, through the Spirit of Truth, with every bestowed world in their realm; thus Master Sons serve as a link between the lowest and highest intelligent creatures in the universe.

22—THE TRINITIZED SONS OF GOD

Trinitized Sons of God are divided into three groups:

1. Deity-trinitized Sons are an unrevealed order.

2. Trinity-embraced Sons:

Mighty Messengers are ascendant Adjuster-fused mortals who function loyally in the face of insurrection. One trillion of them are commissioned on Uversa, and it is believed that there are one trillion in each of the seven superuniverses. They serve as observers for the Ancients of Days on individual planets and the headquarters worlds, and take part in all phases of mortal progression.

Those High in Authority are perfected mortals who exhibit superior administrative ability. They are chosen to serve as executives for the Ancients of Days on the inhabited worlds.

Those Without Name and Number comprise over one hundred million ascendant Adjuster-fused mortals with minds of superior spiritual capacity who function as the supreme jurors of Orvonton.

Trinitized Custodians are selected from ascendant seraphim and translated midway creatures who have shown valiant cooperation with an ascendant mortal member of the Corps of Finality. Currently about ten million Custodians administer group projects in Orvonton.

Trinitized Ambassadors are Son-fused and Spirit-fused mortals selected for the Trinity embrace as emissaries of the Ancients of Days. They are assigned to assist in the administration of Son-fusion and Spirit-fusion worlds. There is nothing on Urantia that is analogous to the activities of these beings.

3. Creature-trinitized Sons. Paradise-Havona personalities and some members of the finaliter corps can engage in creature-trinitization. This process creates an entirely new being who is the personification of some previously unexpressed concept, idea, or ideal. Trinitization can be achieved between two Paradise-Havona citizens, or two finaliters, or one of each. On the advice of the Trinity Teacher Sons, creature-trinitized beings may be embraced by the Trinity, thereby becoming twice-trinitized.

Celestial Guardians are those of lower service and number almost one billion in Orvonton.

High Son Assistants are those of higher service, and about one and one quarter million are in constant circulation, traveling wherever they are needed to further the work of the Paradise Trinity.

23—The Solitary Messengers

The Solitary Messengers were created in a single act by the Infinite Spirit. At last report 7,690 trillion Solitary Messengers were in service in Orvonton, which is apparently less than one seventh of their total number. Solitary Messengers begin at the center of all things and move outward. They crave remote assignments, even into the outer space levels. They are an important part of the Infinite Spirit's personal contact with the creatures of time and space. Solitary Messengers are capable of tuning into the universe broadcasts wherever they travel, and can detect the presence of Thought Adjusters and Inspired Trinity Spirits. They contribute much to the development of kinship between spiritual beings. Solitary Messengers are distinguished by services they perform.

Messengers of the Paradise Trinity are involved with the unrevealed policies and future conduct of the Deities. Since they are perfect, they never divulge secrets or betray confidences.

Messengers of the Havona Circuits enjoy close, personal communion with Havona natives.

Messengers of the Superuniverse can be dispatched with messages from the headquarters of one superuniverse to another. This is an advantage they enjoy over all other personalities, who must pass through Havona and the executive worlds of the Master Spirits before traveling to other superuniverses. A wide range of services are provided by Solitary Messengers in this capacity. They most delight to serve in Orvonton, because the opportunities for heroic effort are greatest in the youngest universe.

Messengers of the Local Universe reveal the motives and intent of the local universe Mother Spirit.

Explorers of Undirected Assignment are thrilled to be assigned to the task of exploring and charting new worlds and universes in the unformed parts of the universes.

Revelators of Truth are frequently attached to commissions sent to enlarge the revelation of truth to worlds and systems.

Ambassadors and Emissaries of Special Assignment represent one local universe to another until a native ambassador can be transported by seraphim to her assignment. Seraphim can carry a person at a speed of 550,000 miles per second, but Solitary Messengers are very nearly capable of defying time and space. The distance a seraphic transport travels in two hundred years can be completed by a Solitary Messenger in sixty-nine minutes. Faster beings exist, but they are not persons.

24—HIGHER PERSONALITIES OF THE INFINITE SPIRIT

There are seven divisions of the Higher Personalities of the Infinite Spirit:

The Solitary Messengers.

Universe Circuit Supervisors. The vast power currents of space and the circuits of spiritual energy are subject to intelligent supervision by four orders of this group: One supreme circuit supervisor is stationed at each of the seven pilot worlds of the Havona circuits; one associate circuit supervisor is in charge of the circuits of the seven superuniverses; secondary circuit supervisors on the headquarters of each superuniverse oversee energy circuits for the local universes; and tertiary circuit supervisors serve within each local universe. Circuit supervisors serve eternally at the same assignment, directing personality transits and transmissions of spiritual messages. If a system is in rebellion, it is they who isolate the worlds in spiritual quarantine.

Census Directors are immediately aware of the birth and death of every will creature in every part of the grand universe. They are personally sensitive and responsive to intelligent will. Orvonton contains 100,000 Census Directors who are overseen by Usatia, superuniverse chief of census directors.

Personal Aids of the Infinite Spirit travel through space like Solitary Messengers. Only the Infinite Spirit relates to them as persons; they emit no spiritual presence, and we do not meet them on the way to Paradise.

Associate Inspectors, 700,000 in number, observe the affairs of the local universes and report to the Seven Supreme Executives.

Assigned Sentinels, seven billion in total, keep the Associate Inspectors informed of the affairs of the systems of the local universes.

Graduate Guides are in charge of the university of technical instruction and spiritual training for mortal ascenders. A Graduate Guide greets each mortal as they arrive in Havona and accompanies them throughout their entire billion-world journey.

25—The Messenger Hosts of Space

Midway between the highest and lowest personalities of the Infinite Spirit are the Messenger Hosts of Space.

Havona Servitals are the offspring of the Seven Master Spirits and the Supreme Power Directors. They are created in groups: 250 semimaterial Servitals for every 750 true spirit types. These versatile beings train ascenders on the study worlds surrounding the headquarters of the superuniverses.

Universal Conciliators are the embodiment of supreme justice. One Universal Conciliator appears in each of the superuniverses as a response to the creation of each Havona Servital. The Conciliators collectively manifest forty-nine experiential viewpoints in the superuniverses, insights which together are mutually compensatory. They serve in quartets, consisting of one Judge-Arbiter, one Spirit-Advocate, one Divine Executioner, and a Recorder. Conciliators keep the universes running smoothly. Less experienced Conciliators begin as Conciliators to the Worlds, assisting the supervisors of individual planets. As they ascend inward from the local universe, they evolve from arbiters of differences to explainers of mysteries. At the superuniverse levels Conciliators become wise teachers of the ascending pilgrims of time and space. At last count, eighteen trillion quartets of Conciliators served in Orvonton.

Technical Advisers serve in groups of seven as the legal and technical minds of the spirit world, the living law libraries of time and space. There currently are more than sixty-one trillion Technical Advisers in Orvonton. Technical Advisers help Universal Censors, Melchizedeks, Life Carriers, and the rulers of systems, constellations, universes, and universe sectors; they do not directly deal with material creatures. No Adviser has ever been known to go astray.

Custodians of Records on Paradise are chosen from the tertiary supernaphim in Havona to keep the formal written archives of Paradise.

Celestial Recorders serve by keeping the records of the superuniverses. Using their ability to manipulate both spiritual and material energy, they make original spirit recordings and simultaneously create semimaterial copies for the superuniverses. Through their work, ascending mortals learn the history and traditions of each sphere.

Morontia Companions are children of the local universe Mother Spirits. They are gracious hosts during an ascender's morontia career, ensuring that time in rest and play is well spent.

Paradise Companions are angels selected to befriend any being who comes alone to Paradise. They work mostly with ascendant beings who reach Paradise without either a close associate or seraphic guardian. They are sympathetic and intriguing companions. If, during the course of the Havona adventure, a lone ascender fails in the Deity adventure and must be sent back to the universes of time, a Paradise Companion follows to comfort and cheer him.

26—MINISTERING SPIRITS OF THE CENTRAL UNIVERSE

Angels who serve in the central universe are known as Supernaphim, the highest order of the angelic hosts. Supernaphim are created in three categories: primary, secondary and tertiary. Primary supernaphim are so unique that they will be separately discussed in the subsequent essay.

Tertiary Supernaphim are specialists who serve ascending pilgrims of time and descending pilgrims of eternity in Havona. They originate in the Seven Spirits of the Circuits, and serve in seven classifications.

Harmony Supervisors contribute to mutual understanding between the ascenders and descenders on Havona.

Chief Recorders record every important matter in triplicate—one copy for Havona, one for Paradise, and one for their own files.

Broadcasters receive and send broadcasts of Havona and space reports of Deity phenomena on Paradise.

Messengers bear messages requiring personal transmission throughout the Paradise-Havona system.

Intelligence Coordinators are the "living newspapers" of Havona, able to assimilate as much information in one hour as the fastest telegraph can record in a thousand years.

Transport Personalities carry various beings within Havona and also between Havona and the universes of time.

The Reserve Corps are capable of performing any of the services of their order.

Secondary Supernaphim are created by the Seven Master Spirits. They work in the central universe tutoring Paradise citizens and ascending mortals. When ascenders arrive on Havona they will possess a single aspect of perfection—perfection of purpose. On Havona, mortals begin to develop the comprehension necessary for Paradise perfection of personality. Seven groups of Secondary Supernaphim help mortals in this work.

Pilgrim Helpers provide detailed instruction to ascenders in three areas: supreme understanding of the Paradise Trinity, spiritual comprehension of the Father-Son partnership, and intellectual recognition of the Infinite Spirit. Their work is done when their students spiritually recognize the Master Spirit of their superuniverse.

Supremacy Guides work on the sixth circle of the Havona worlds to help ascenders comprehend the Supreme Being. In the sixth circle, ascending creatures undergo transforming growth, integration of consciousness, and spiritualization of purpose. These changes seem to be attributed to unrevealed activity of the Supreme Being.

Trinity Guides of the fifth circle give mortals advanced instruction concerning the Trinity in preparation for the quest to achieve personal recognition of the Infinite Spirit. Intense mental effort and arduous spiritual exertion are required to discern the Infinite Spirit on Paradise.

Son Finders of the fourth Havona circuit assist ascenders in their attempt to achieve contact with the Eternal Son. In addition to continued work in the realization of Trinity, Son Finders must prepare their charges to recognize the personality of the Son and to differentiate the personalities of the Son and the Spirit. Pilgrims who attain the Spirit seldom fail in finding the Son.

Father Guides of the third circle are the most experienced of the superaphic ministers. All beings who inhabit the central universe serve as teachers in the schools and colleges maintained by the Father Guides.

Counselors and Advisers of the second circle minister to all who attempt the attainment of the Universal Father. They comfort those who fail to attain the Father, and instruct those who succeed concerning the responsibilities of the Paradise career. On Paradise, disappointment is never regarded as defeat; postponement is never looked upon as disgrace; the apparent failures of time are never confused with the significant delays of eternity.

Complements of Rest train ascenders for Paradise residence; they use the diverse residents of the final Havona circuit to further this education. Near the end of the sojourn through this inmost circle of Havona, the Instigators of Rest help prepare ascenders for the final metamorphosis as they transform into children of Paradise.

27—Ministry of the Primary Supernaphim

The seven orders of primary supernaphim are perfect servants of the Paradise Deities. Primary supernaphim serve on the Eternal Isle, of which it is said: "There shall be no night there; and they need no light of the sun, for the Great Source and Center gives them light; they shall live forever and ever. And God shall wipe away all tears from their eyes; there shall be no more death, neither sorrow nor crying, neither shall there be any more pain, for the former things have passed away."

Instigators of Rest collaborate with the Complements of Rest on Havona to produce the final sleep of mortal ascenders to Paradise. Metamorphic sleep is required between earth and the mansion worlds, from Orvonton to Havona, and from Havona to Paradise.

Chiefs of Assignment preside over the self-governing orders of primary, secondary, and tertiary supernaphim.

Interpreters of Ethics assist new Paradise arrivals with the ethics needed to get along with their ever-increasing circle of universe associates.

Directors of Conduct instruct newcomers in proper Paradise conduct. They teach divine techniques for spontaneous worship and the approach of Divinity.

Custodians of Knowledge are living books of knowledge, automatic libraries for reference and verification. These brilliant beings are "the very thing you wish to know."

Masters of Philosophy conduct elaborate courses in seventy functional divisions of wisdom. They delight in their work and teach by every possible method of instruction.

Conductors of Worship direct worship experiences on Paradise. Never since the time the first ascendant mortal reached Paradise have the supernaphim been able to fully accommodate the spirit of worship on Paradise.

28—MINISTERING SPIRITS OF THE SUPERUNIVERSES

There are three types of angelic hosts in the superuniverses:

Omniaphim, who are exclusively of grand universe assignment; Tertiaphim, residents of the superuniverse capitals and not native to the local universes; and Seconaphim, the only group directly involved in ministry to mortals. They are produced in groups of seven by the seven Reflective Spirits, each group consisting of one primary, three secondary and three tertiary Seconaphim.

Primary Seconaphim are living mirrors that allow the Ancients of Days to instantly communicate with beings hundreds of light-years away. They are categorized by the type of service they perform: Voices of the Conjoint Actor, Voices of the Seven Master Spirits, Voices of the Creator Sons, Voices of the Angelic Hosts, Broadcast Receivers, Transporters and reserves.

Secondary Seconaphim come in seven classes and assist Perfectors of Wisdom, Divine Counselors, and Universal Censors: The Voices of Wisdom are in perpetual liaison with the living libraries of Paradise; Souls of Philosophy create connections with the Masters of Philosophy on Paradise; the Unions of Souls reveal the knowledge of Interpreters of Ethics; Hearts of Counsel are reflective of the intelligence and counsel of all beings, high and low; The Joys of Existence improve appreciation for humor and demonstrate the inherent joy in freewill existence; Satisfactions of Service are reflective of the directors of conduct on Paradise, doing much to illuminate the deferred rewards inherent in unselfish service; Discerner of Spirits inform Universal Censors about the true motives, natures, and purposes of any individual in their universe, allowing the Censors to see the very soul of the reflected individual.

Tertiary seconaphim serve the Mighty Messengers, Those High in Authority and Those Without Name and Number. Significances of Origins are living genealogical references. Memories of Mercy are living records of the mercy which has been extended to individuals and races by children of the Infinite Spirit. Imports of Time instruct ascenders in the best use of time for rest and work. Solemnities of Trust reveal the sacredness of trust to ascending creatures and reveal the trustworthiness of any creature to the Trinitized Sons of Attainment. Sanctities of Service bare the motives of human hearts and angelic minds to determine their trustworthiness in service. The Secrets of Greatness and Souls of Goodness are two types of angels who function in tandem because greatness and goodness cannot be separated.

29—The Universe Power Directors

The Universe Power Directors are one of the three groups of living beings concerned with force control and energy regulation. Power Directors embrace four major divisions.

Seven Supreme Power Directors are stationed on peripheral Paradise. Their creation by the Seven Master Spirits is the first recorded instance of semimaterial beings being derived from spirit ancestry. They are, along with the Seven Master Spirits, ancestors of the vast host of the Power Centers and Physical Controllers throughout the superuniverses.

Supreme Power Centers possess exquisite intelligence; they are the intellect of the power systems of the grand universe. Power Centers are inherently perfect and are always on duty. They do not originate power, but they modify, manipulate, and directionize it. Power Centers are living and personal, and are closely associated with the cosmic overcontrol of the Supreme Being. Seven groups of Power Centers regulate the master energy circuits of the grand universe from nether Paradise through Havona and down into the inhabited worlds.

Master Physical Controllers serve throughout the grand universe and are able to traverse local space at speeds approaching that of Solitary Messengers. They are chiefly concerned with the adjustment of basic energies undiscovered on Urantia, and their numbers include seven distinct groups: Associate Power Directors, Mechanical Controllers, Energy Transformers, Energy Transmitters, Primary Associators, Secondary Dissociators, and Frandalanks.

Master Force Organizers are residents of Paradise but generally commute to unorganized space for their work. They are under the supervision of the Architects of the Master Universe. Primary Master Force Organizers create nebulae.

30—Personalities of the Grand Universe

The enormous numbers of living beings are classified differently in the grand universe than on Paradise. Living beings on Paradise are classified according to inherent and attained relationship with the Paradise Deities: Triune Origin Beings, Dual-Origin Beings, Single-Origin Beings, Eventuated Transcendental Beings, Fragmented Entities of Deity, and Superpersonal Beings. Registries on the superuniverse headquarters of Uversa include seven grand divisions of personalities: Paradise Deities, Supreme Spirits, Trinity-Origin Beings, Sons of God, Personalities of the Infinite Spirit, Universe Power Directors, and the Corps of Permanent Citizenship.

Evolutionary mortals pass through seven stages of universe development.

Planetary mortals are animal origin beings of ascendant potential.

Sleeping survivors are those who have not attained the level of intelligence and spirituality required to go directly to the mansion worlds after death. Such surviving souls remain unconscious until a new dispensation on the planet of their origin releases them for resurrection on the mansion worlds.

Mansion world students reawaken on the mansion worlds. Personality resurrection on the mansion worlds provides a new morontia form for the indwelling soul.

Morontia progressors strive for the advancement of intellect, spirit, and personality throughout their ascension through the local universe.

Superuniverse wards are accredited evolving spirit beings who have embarked upon an individualized course of study on the worlds of the minor sectors, major sectors, and superuniverse headquarters.

Havona pilgrims have completed their spiritual development and have begun personalized instruction in the perfect worlds of the central universe.

Paradise arrivals are ascenders who have earned residency on Paradise.

31—THE CORPS OF THE FINALITY

The Corps of Mortal Finaliters is one of seven finaliter corps whose destiny is assumed to be service in the outer space realms. During the present universe age, finaliters serve in all of the superuniverses; however, they do not return to their native superuniverse until they have served in all the others. Mortal finaliters are always in service on Urantia. Finaliters are self-governing, bearing allegiance only to the Paradise Trinity. They are forever secure against sin. Finaliter corps are composed from six groups of beings:

Havona Natives serve as teachers in the training schools of the central universe, and may become greatly attached to the ascending mortals in their care. Only one perfect Havona native is mustered into each thousand-member finaliter corps.

Gravity Messengers are personalized Adjusters who hail from Divinington and are able to transcend time and space. They are superspirit beings—divine, intelligent and touchingly understanding. Gravity Messengers and glorified mortals have a profound affection for one another, one being a personalization of a fragment of the Father and the other an immortal soul fused with a Father fragment.

Glorified Mortals make up the bulk of each finaliter company. It is conjectured that the lengthy universe training ascendant mortals receive is designed to qualify them for greater tests of future service. Glorified mortals have not yet achieved final spirit status, final creature service, or experiential Deity attainment. They have ascended through every step of possible intelligent existence, and have been trained in every possible detail of administration of the superuniverses.

Adopted Seraphim are seraphic guardians who have gone through the ascendant career. Many join the corps after becoming Father-fused.

Glorified Material Sons and Daughters may elect to humanize and re-ceive adjusters after their planet settles in light and life. If they join a finaliter company, they are invariably chosen as its leaders.

Glorified Midway Creatures released from permanent citizenship at the onset of the age of light and life on their home planet are destined for the finality corps. Secondary midwayers are eventually Adjuster-fused and may be accepted into the mortal corps.

The Architects of the Master Universe oversee all seven corps of final-ity: Mortal Finaliters, Paradise Finaliters, Trinitized Finaliters, Conjoint Trinitized Finaliters, Havona Finaliters, Transcendental Finaliters, and the Unrevealed Sons of Destiny. These seven finaliter corps are destined to serve the future needs of the undeveloped vast new system of uni-verses now organizing in the domains of outer space.

PART II

THE LOCAL UNIVERSE

Part II
The Local Universe

32—The Evolution of the Local Universe

Once a material creation has been planned by the Architects of the Master Universe, the Master Force Organizers manipulate primordial energy until it becomes responsive to gravity. When gravity response exists, Power Directors mobilize the energy to produce suns and material spheres. When energy-matter reaches a certain stage of materialization, the Creator Son arrives with the Creative Spirit, and construction of the headquarters sphere begins.

It took over one billion years to construct Salvington, the local universe headquarters. Salvington is located at the exact center of the local universe of Nebadon, which is a young cluster of stars, with 3,840,101 inhabited planets at last count. Our system of Satania has more than six hundred inhabited worlds in over five hundred physical subsystems. Forty-six subsystems in Satania have two inhabited worlds, four systems have three, and one has four inhabited planets. Satania is on the edge of Nebadon, which itself is well out toward the edge of Orvonton.

Gabriel, the Bright and Morning Star, was the first offspring of the Creative Spirit and Creator Son and is the chief executive of Nebadon. Immediately after Gabriel's creation, the Creator Son and Spirit began the production of a vast and wonderful array of diverse creatures—the sons and daughters of the local universe.

Will creatures of evolutionary nature ascend the scale of life by progressively translating from life to life and sphere to sphere. The acquired perfection of the creatures of time is a true personality possession, the result of individual effort and experience. God could have created all of his children in perfection, but doing so would have deprived mortals of the valuable inward climb to perfection. Perfect beings and perfected beings are co-ordinate and dependent. Each type requires the other to achieve completion of function, service, and destiny.

Human beings are part of an immense plan. The struggle of material existence is a transient bridge to eternal spiritual reality. Humans are virtually unable to comprehend eternity—that which is never-beginning and never-ending—because everything familiar to mortals has an end. Death seems to represent an ending, but it is the only method other than fusion by which mortals can escape the fetters of time and the bonds of the material world.

33—THE ADMINISTRATION OF THE LOCAL UNIVERSE

The Creator of our local universe, Michael of Nebadon, is 611,121st in a line of Creator Sons created by the Universal Father and the Eternal Son. Michael personifies the Paradise Father and the Eternal Son; his consort, the Mother Spirit, represents the Infinite Spirit. Michael's bestowal experience also qualifies him to portray the divinity of the Supreme Being. These multiple aspects of deity personification give Michael unique qualifications for sovereignty. For all practical purposes, Michael *is* God in the local universe.

The Mother Spirit and Michael are concerned with three occupations: creation, sustenance, and ministry. The Son and the Spirit function with the counsel and approval of the other. The Creator Son functions as a father, and the Creative Spirit ministers as a mother. This arrangement is the pattern for family organization and government throughout all of Nebadon.

Gabriel, chief executive of the local universe, is capable of broad and sympathetic contact with seraphic hosts and evolutionary will creatures. He and his staff are administrators, never departing from this work except during Michael's creature bestowals. Gabriel supervises Nebadon's judicial system.

Personalities from the central universe and Paradise are present in every local universe. At the head of Nebadon's Paradise group is Immanuel of Salvington, a Union of Days. He is the only personality in Nebadon who does not acknowledge subordination to Michael. Immanuel functions as an advisor to Michael and as supervisor to the Faithfuls of Days.

There are seventy court branches in Nebadon. Courts and assemblies of universe administration focus on spiritual transactions, and are thus very different from corresponding activities on Urantia. The universe courts cannot rule on matters involving questions of eternal life, defections of Local Universe Sons, or the spiritual status of any part of a local universe in spiritual isolation. In all other matters, the courts of Salvington are supreme; there is no appeal to their decisions.

Salvington has research and advisory councils but no true legislative bodies. Legislative assemblies are located in the headquarters of the one hundred constellations, and administration of the local creations is largely handled within the system headquarters.

34—THE LOCAL UNIVERSE MOTHER SPIRIT

When a Creator Son is ready to create life in a local universe, a new local universe Mother Spirit is personalized. The Mother Spirit, also known as the Divine Minister or the Creative Spirit, possesses all the physical-control attributes of the Infinite Spirit including antigravity and mind gravity. There is a basic uniformity of spiritual character in all Universe Mother Spirits; there is also diversity caused by the influence of one of the seven Master Spirits.

The Creative Spirit and the Creator Son produce, uphold, and conserve every creature in their realms. In personal prerogatives, the Creative Spirit is independent of space but not of time; she is equally present throughout her entire local universe. The Creator Son is usually independent of time, but not always of space. Michael cannot be in two places at once. When working together, the Creative Spirit and the Creator Son are essentially independent of both time and space.

Three distinct spirit circuits function in Nebadon: the Spirit of Truth, the Holy Spirit, and the intelligence-ministry circuit of the adjutant mind-spirits. The Spirit of Truth is the spiritual force that draws all truth seekers towards Michael. It derives from the Creator Son, but functions from within the Divine Minister. The Holy Spirit of the Mother Spirit is active only in her personal presence. By maintaining residence on Salvington, the Creative Mother Spirit serves as the universe focus of both the Spirit of Truth and the Holy Spirit.

The Spirit of Truth and the Holy Spirit work as one, hovering over the worlds, seeking to enlighten the minds of ascending creatures. The

Spirit of Truth is limited by man's personal reception of the mission of the bestowal Son. The Holy Spirit is partially independent of human attitude, but is most effective in those mortals who most fully obey divine leadings. As individuals we do not personally possess a portion of these spirits, but our indwelling Thought Adjusters work in perfect harmony with the combined spirits of the Creator Son and the Creative Spirit. As mortals progress in spirit perception, the multiple spirit ministries become more and more co-ordinate.

Adjutant mind-spirits endow human and sub-human orders of life. The seven adjutant mind-spirits—the spirits of wisdom, worship, counsel, knowledge, courage, understanding, and intuition—are created by the Divine Minister. The Creator Son and the Mother Spirit work on the evolutionary worlds first with lifeless material, then vegetable life, then animal organisms, then early humans, then will creatures. The seven adjutants, by leading the races of mankind toward higher ideals, are largely responsible for this progression. Mortal man first experiences the ministry of the Holy Spirit when he develops receptivity for the adjutants of worship and wisdom.

A conspiracy of spiritual forces increasingly subjects mortals to the leadings of the Spirit. When such guidance is freely accepted, the human mind gradually develops consciousness of divine contact and assurance of spirit communion. This consciousness of spirit domination attends an increasing exhibition of the fruits of the spirit: love, joy, peace, long-suffering, gentleness, goodness, faith, meekness and temperance.

On normal worlds, mortals do not experience conflicts between the spirit and the flesh as acutely as Urantians do, but even on the most ideal planets, people must put forth positive effort to ascend. On Urantia, the Calagastia betrayal robbed subsequent generations of the moral assistance of a well-ordered society. The Adamic default deprived the races of a physical nature that would have been more responsive to spiritual aspirations. In spite of these handicaps, mortals who enter the spirit kingdom enjoy comparative deliverance from bondage in the flesh. Faith sons work on levels far above the conflicts produced by unrestrained or unnatural physical desires.

The love of God is shed abroad in all hearts by the presence of the divine Spirit. In every dark hour, at every crossroad in the forward struggle, the Spirit of Truth will always speak, saying, "This is the way."

35—The Local Universe Sons of God

Melchizedeks, Vorondadeks, and Lanonandeks are orders of local universe Sons of God created jointly by the Creator Son and Creative Spirit.

The firstborn of the Melchizedek order, the Father Melchizedek, collaborates with the Creator Son and Creative Spirit in the creation of the rest of the Melchizedek group. The Father Melchizedek is the first executive associate of Gabriel. Gabriel presides over regular tribunals and councils of Nebadon, while Father Melchizedek presides over special and emergency commissions.

Melchizedeks are a self-governing order. They are the first order of divine Sons that are close enough to humans to minister directly to them. Melchizedeks are understanding friends, sympathetic teachers, and wise counselors to all forms of intelligent life. They often win whole worlds to the recognition of the Creator Son and the Paradise Father. Melchizedeks are nearly perfect in wisdom but are not infallible in judgment.

Generally, Melchizedeks devote themselves to education and training, but can also function in unusual assignments. On Edentia, they are known as emergency Sons. Melchizedeks render assistance when local universe plans are threatened, and sometimes act as temporary custodians of wayward planets. In Nebadon, a Melchizedek has appeared seven times in the likeness of mortal man.

Vorondadek Sons are commissioned by Gabriel to rule in the constellations. They do not possess the versatility of the Melchizedeks, but are more efficient as rulers and administrators. Vorondadeks serve as ambassadors, legislators, historians, and consuls. They rarely fall into error and have never rebelled. Twelve Vorondadek Sons presently administer our constellation of Norlatiadek.

Lanonandek Sons serve as Universe Coordinators, Constellation Counselors, System Sovereigns, Planetary Princes, Messenger Corps, Custodians, Recorders, and Reserves. Lanonandeks are able and versatile local universe administrators. Because they are a lower order of sonship, they are of greater service to the lower creatures than either Melchizedeks or Vorondadeks, but they also stand in greater danger of going astray. In Nebadon, seven hundred Lanonandeks rebelled against the universe government, precipitating confusion and spiritual isolation in several systems.

36—THE LIFE CARRIERS

Life Carriers bring life into the inhabitable worlds. The Life Carriers are the offspring of three personalities: the Creator Son, the Universe Mother Spirit, and one Ancient of Days. One hundred million Life Carriers live in Nebadon in three divisions: senior Life Carriers, assistants, and custodians.

Life Carriers are devoted to the study of universe life. They are involved in new life design, life preservation, evolution of creature life, life associated with mind, the correlation of mind with spirit in living organisms, and in unrevealed domains of evolutionary creature life. The Life Carriers are living catalytic presences that agitate, organize, and vitalize otherwise inert material.

A commission of Life Carriers can either carry life plasm onto a new world or organize life patterns after they arrive. Once physical patterns are arranged, the Universe Mother Spirit supplies the vital spark of life; inert patterns become living matter. Life Carriers may spend five hundred thousand years to establish life on an evolutionary world. Once they have succeeded in producing a moral being, the Life Carriers' work ends. Life Carriers are forbidden to interfere with will creatures.

The central lodgments of the seven adjutant mind-spirits are on the headquarters world of the Life Carriers. The adjutants send forth their influence into all inhabited worlds. The first five adjutant mind-spirits—intuition, understanding, courage, knowledge, and counsel—function in the animal orders. The adjutants' experience in relationship to animals makes them more effective in their ministry to human beings. The final two mind-spirits, worship and wisdom, function only in mortal candidates for spiritual ascension. The adjutant mind-spirits are not directly related to the function of the Holy Spirit, but they help prepare mortal minds for the appearance of this Spirit.

The survival of mortal creatures is wholly dependent on the evolution of an immortal soul within the mortal mind. The life bestowed on plants and animals possesses neither identity nor personality; it survives only as a part of the cosmic forces of the universe. Life is neither energy nor force; it is the animation of material, mindal, and spiritual systems of energy. Life flows from the Father, through the Son, by the Spirit.

37—PERSONALITIES OF THE LOCAL UNIVERSE

Long-term and permanent residents of the local universe include the Brilliant Evening Stars, Archangels, Most High Assistants, High Commissioners, and Celestial Overseers.

Brilliant Evening Stars are planned by the Melchizedeks and created by the Creator Son and the Mother Spirit. They chiefly serve as liaison officers for Gabriel, representing him at every constellation and system capital in Nebadon. *Brilliant Evening Stars* are a twofold order—some are specifically created to serve in this position and others attain service. They accompany Avonal Sons on their bestowal missions and may be assigned as liaisons for Trinity Teachers Sons in the mortal realms.

Archangels are created by the Creator Son and the Mother Spirit, and serve under the jurisdiction of Gabriel. Nearly eight hundred thousand archangels dedicate themselves to mortal survival and ascension in Nebadon. Archangels serve the Avonal orders and preserve mortal personality identification records between mortal death and resurrection.

Most High Assistants originate outside the local universe and volunteer in the local creations. They help local universe natives come to fuller harmony with the ideals of Paradise. They are supervised by the Union of Days. Most High Assistants are assigned to administrative, executive, and educational activities.

High Commissioners are Spirit-fused ascendant mortals. Souls of this order attain immortality by fusing with a fragment of the Universe Mother Spirit. High Commissioners begin their service as race commissioners, portraying the viewpoints and needs of various human races. They may serve at tribunals, with messenger hosts, with ministering spirits of time, at universe assemblies, or with bestowal missions. High Commissioners provide a continuity that enhances and stabilizes local universe administration.

The Nebadon education system is maintained by the *Celestial Overseers.* More than three million recruited Overseers currently oversee the education of ascending mortals, from the nativity worlds up through local universe headquarters. Their divine education provides for the intimate association of work and instruction.

Certain high-origin spirits of the family of the Infinite Spirit are on permanent assignment to the local universes. These include Solitary Messengers, Universe Circuit Supervisors, Census Directors, Associate Inspectors, Assigned Sentinels, Universal Conciliators, Technical Advisers, Celestial Recorders, and Morontia Companions.

Material Sons of God, created solely by the Creator Son to express his dual origin, serve as the original Adam and Eve of each local system in Nebadon. Their children are the permanent citizens of the system capitals.

Midway Creatures are difficult to classify. They arise from unusual circumstances involving transactions of superhuman beings on evolutionary planets. Midway Creatures are the permanent residents of the evolutionary worlds, providing continuous planetary administration despite ever-changing celestial ministries and shifting mortal inhabitants.

38—MINISTERING SPIRITS OF THE LOCAL UNIVERSE

Seraphim are created by the universe Mother Spirit. Seraphim are just outside the mortal range of vision, and appreciate human efforts in music, art, and humor. Once they complete their training, seraphim are commissioned as ministering spirits of time. They gather in groups of 24, companies of 288, battalions of 3,456, units of 41,472, and legions of 497,664. Twelve legions constitute a host and twelve hosts make an army of 71,663,616 angels.

Cherubim and sanobim are slightly lower than the seraphim spiritually. They assist the seraphim in routine spiritual matters on individual worlds but never attend to human beings. Every fourth cherub is nearly material. These quasi-material types are able to perform many indispensable tasks. Cherubim and sanobim may become ascension candidates; some achieve full seraphic standing.

Midway creatures appear on most inhabited worlds and all decimal planets. Primary midwayers, the more spiritual type, are progeny of the mortal staff of the Planetary Prince. They resemble angels more than mortals. On a normal world, primary midwayers are the intelligence corps of the Planetary Prince. Secondary midwayers are a more material group and are quite similar to human beings. There are twenty-four diverse techniques by which secondary midwayers can be created. If midwayers remain faithful to their trust, they eventually enter into the ascension plan alongside their mortal brethren.

Beings descending from the Father and the Son are spoken of as sons, while children of the Spirit are referred to as daughters. For this reason, all mortals are considered sons of God, even if they are female, and all angels are referred to as daughters of God.

39—The Seraphic Hosts

Although seraphim do not experience childhood as we know it, they are experiential creatures. They augment their divine endowments by acquiring skill in the various seraphic services. The higher the inherent function of an angel, the more she seeks assignment to the lower orders of service. Seraphim crave to serve at the lowest possible levels to achieve the highest range of experience. There are seven distinct groups of seraphim.

Supreme Seraphim may serve as Son-Spirit Ministers, Court Advisers, Universe Orientors, Teaching Counselors, Directors of Assignment, or Recorders. *Superior Seraphim* are Intelligence Corps, Voices of Mercy, Spirit Coordinators, Assistant Teachers, Transports, and Recorders. *Supervisor Seraphim* serve in the constellations as Supervising Assistants, Law Forecasters, Social Architects, Ethical Sensitizers, Transporters, and Recorders. *Administrator Seraphim* serve in the systems as Administrative Assistants, Justice Guides, Interpreters of Cosmic Citizenship, Quickeners of Morality, Transporters, and Recorders.

Planetary Helpers are assigned to serve the Planetary Adams. They include the Voices of the Garden, Spirits of Brotherhood, Souls of Peace, Spirits of Trust, Transporters, and Recorders. *Transition Ministers* serve on the mansion worlds. *Seraphim of the Future* are not directly concerned with the mortal ascension plan.

There are hundreds of paths by which seraphim may attain Paradise, but their preferred career choice is that of guardian angel to an evolutionary mortal. Only the most experienced seraphim are chosen to be guardians of mortal destiny.

40—THE ASCENDING SONS OF GOD

There are seven classes of ascending sons. The non-mortal classes include evolutionary seraphim, ascending Material Sons, translated midwayers, and Personalized Adjusters. The mortal classes of ascending sons are Father-fused mortals, Son-fused mortals, and Spirit-fused mortals.

Mortals are also classified according to their type of Adjuster. Series one mortals are indwelt with transient Adjusters. This is a temporary series, appearing during the early eras of some inhabited worlds. Series one Adjusters contribute much to the advancement of primitive men but are unable to achieve union with them.

Series two mortals are also unable to attain eternal union with Adjusters. Many non-breathers belong to this series, along with many other groups who do not usually fuse with Adjusters. These mortals are often indwelt by virgin Adjusters. It is unknown why these beings cannot fuse with the Father fragments.

Series three are mortals of Adjuster-fusion potential. They are all of animal origin, and may be one-brained, two-brained, or three-brained. Nearly all surviving mortals fuse with their Adjusters during their sojourn on the mansion worlds, thereby entering a career of nearly limitless universe service. Since Thought Adjusters take origin in the Father, they do not cease striving until the mortal of their indwelling stands face to face with God.

Mortals who fail to attain fusion with their Adjuster may become fused with a fragment of the spirit of the Creator Son. These Son-fused mortals are rare, numbering less than one million in Orvonton. They usually live permanently in the superuniverse of their birth. The wisdom of Son-fused mortals is a vital factor in the settling of a universe.

Spirit-fused mortals are those who fuse with the spirit of the Third Source and Center. When they arrive in the resurrection halls of the morontia spheres they are like newly created beings, without human memory. Spirit-fused mortals are permanent citizens of the local universes.

God loves each of his sons alike, and his love utterly eclipses all other facts. All souls of every possible phase of mortal existence will survive, provided they cooperate with their indwelling Adjusters and desire to find God and to attain divine perfection.

41—Physical Aspects
of the Local Universe

The physical boundaries of the local universes are not easily identified, although the major and minor sectors of Orvonton are clearly distinguishable. What separates one local universe from all others is the presence of a local universe Creative Mother Spirit.

Nebadon sprang from Andronover and other nebulae. Today it travels in an increasingly settled orbit around the Sagittarius center of our minor sector. Our system of Satania is one of one hundred systems in the constellation Norlatiadek.

There are more than two thousand suns in Satania. Suns serve as way stations for concentrating the energy circuits of the material creations. Some larger suns may break up or split into double stars. Some are solid, especially the older ones, and their density may be so great that one square inch weighs three tons. Urantia's gaseous sun has a density of about one and a half times that of water.

Suns generate light and x-rays. Light is real; it can be highly explosive. Energy, including light, moves through space in straight lines and is responsive to other forces and energies. Large suns maintain such gravity control over their electrons that light escapes only with the aid of powerful x-rays. These rays penetrate all of space, and contribute to the maintenance of ultimatonic energy associations. Atoms and electrons are subject to physical gravity, but ultimatons are obedient only to Paradise gravity.

Our sun's surface temperature is about six thousand degrees Fahrenheit; the interior temperature can approach thirty-five million degrees. Sources of this enormous energy include annihilation of atoms, transmutation of elements, accumulation of space energies, and solar contractions. A regulating blanket of hot gases envelops the sun and acts to stabilize solar heat loss. The heat given out by the sun each second is enough to boil all the water in all of Urantia's oceans, instantly.

Earth's sun is six billion years old and will continue to function in its present state of efficiency for another twenty-five billion years. It currently radiates almost one hundred billion tons of matter annually.

42—ENERGY—MIND AND MATTER

The foundation of the universe is material, but the essence of life is spirit. All energy is under God's control. Energy and matter are manifestations of the same cosmic reality, a phenomenon inherent in the Universal Father. The first measurable form of energy, the ultimaton, has Paradise as its nucleus.

The river of energy and life pours out from the Deities, pervading all creation. The force organizers modify space-force into energy, the power directors transmute energy into matter, and the material worlds are born. Energy is indestructible. It may be subject to endless transformation, but having originated in Paradise, energy will ultimately return there.

Energy denotes motion, action, and potential. Force is pre-gravity; power is post-gravity.

Space potency refers to a pre-reality known as absoluta on Uversa. Primordial force is pure energy. It is the first basic change from space potency and is known as segregata. Emergent energies are two forms of primordial force known on Uversa as ultimata. Havona energy, triata, is characteristic of the triune energy systems of the central universe. Transcendental energy operates only with absonite beings, and is known as transota. Monota is the living non-spirit energy of Paradise.

There are ten divisions of matter: ultimatonic, subelectronic, electronic, subatomic, shattered, ionized, atomic, molecular, radioactive, and collapsed. Matter is identical in every universe except Havona. Power centers manipulate the basic units of materialized energy—ultimatons—into electrons. The metamorphosis of energy and matter is influenced by gravity, temperature, velocity, revolution, energy currents, distance, and the presence of force organizers and power directors.

In Orvonton one hundred octaves of energy behave with wavelike tendencies. Sixty-four of these octaves are recognized on Urantia, including electronic energy, gamma rays, X-rays, ultraviolet, visible light, infrared rays, and radio waves. The human eye reacts to just one octave, the visible white light of sunlight.

The formation of matter resembles the solar system: a relatively stable energy nucleus surrounded by whirling energy units. There are one hundred stabilized atomic elements in Nebadon.

Material mind systems are non-spiritual energy systems. These include the mechanical mind, adjutant-spirit minds, evolving morontia minds, and the cosmic mind—the mind of time and space as ministered by the Master Spirits. Mind always connotes the presence of living ministry plus various energy systems. The universe is neither mechanical nor magical; it is planned and administered by the spirit-mind of the Creator.

Nearly every being in the superuniverses has a form. Humans think of a body as having a spirit, but spiritual beings regard spirit as having a body. The spirit is the architect, the mind is the builder, and the body is the material building.

43—The Constellations

Norlatiadek's government worlds are ten satellites surrounding each of seventy major spheres surrounding the capital, Edentia. Edentia contains thousands of lakes and interconnecting streams. Edentia is the home of the resurrection halls and two Melchizedek schools.

Edentia's sea of glass, an enormous circular crystal one hundred miles in diameter and thirty miles deep, is used as a landing zone for transport angels and as a reflectivity surface.

Constellation administration is autonomous and is concerned primarily with legislative functions. The rulers of the constellations are Vorondadek Sons, also known as the Most Highs. A minimum of three Vorondadeks rule on each constellation.

The capitals of the constellations are the acme of morontia activities and botanical artistry. These architectural worlds are called 'the Gardens of God' because of the exquisite beauty of the gardens of the Most High. Architectural worlds have ten forms of material life: three animal, three vegetable, and four unrevealed types. The animals are intelligent, serviceable herbivores. The plant life tends to be purple instead of green.

A mortal's time on the worlds of Norlatiadek is spent primarily in the mastery of group ethics—pleasant interrelationship with other personalities. We will achieve real socialization of our evolving personalities by learning to live and cooperate with fellow morontians as well as univitatia, the permanent citizens of Edentia. Time spent on the constellation training worlds is the most stable phase of the morontia career.

44—The Celestial Artisans

Celestial artisans devote themselves to embellishment and beautification throughout the grand universe. Celestial artisans are selected from Havona natives, ascending mortals, and other celestial groups. They work with morontial and spiritual reality, since to spirit beings, the material world is almost entirely unreal. There are seven divisions of celestial artisans:

Celestial Musicians manipulate spiritual forces of sound, light, energy, color, thought, music, and orders of beings to produce celestial harmony. Harmony is the universal code of spirit communication; it is the speech of Havona.

Heavenly Reproducers work in areas that are mostly unknown to us. They can present dramas using one million actors and one thousand scenes. They are able to re-enact an entire age, or portray the eternal values of the spirit world.

Divine Builders create homes, industrial buildings, recreational facilities, temples of worship, schools, and public buildings.

Thought Recorders preserve thoughts, idea patterns, oratory, broadcasts, rhythm, poetry, and something like group photographs.

Energy Manipulators include physical energy manipulators, mind energy manipulators, and spiritual energy manipulators. Compound manipulators work with all three energies in their attempt to discover God the Supreme, in whom occurs the unification of divine energy.

Designers and Embellishers work with color, sound, emotion, odor, and taste.

Harmony Workers deal with forces and energies that are unrecognized by mortals.

45—The Local System Administration

The chief executive of any local system is a primary Lanonandek Son. The System Sovereign is entrusted with unusual personal prerogatives. The present system sovereign of Satania, Lanaforge, is a gracious and brilliant ruler who demonstrated his loyalty to Michael during the second outbreak of rebellion in Nebadon. Lanaforge is a frequent visitor to Urantia.

Members of the Urantia advisory council are known as the four and twenty counselors. They live on Jerusem, the administrative capital of Satania. The four and twenty counselors are the personal agents of Michael in all matters concerning mortal ascension on the isolated worlds of the system. Counselors include representatives from the Urantia races, Adam and Eve, Enoch, Moses, Elijah, Machiventa Melchizedek, John the Baptist, and 1-2-3 the First. Eight seats on this committee are being kept in reserve for future teachers and ascending mortals from Urantia.

Jerusem is surrounded by seven major satellites: the Finaliter World, the Morontia World, the Angelic World, the Superangel World, the World of the Sons, the World of the Spirit, and the World of the Father. Jerusem is the location of more than thirty educational centers maintained by the Melchizedeks.

Elective bodies on Jerusem are voted into authority by three groups: Material Sons and Daughters, seraphim and associates, and mortals. Suffrage is universal among these three groups, but votes are weighted according to each individual's mota achievement. Mota is so important that ascenders cannot leave system headquarters to begin their constellation career until they are certified for achievement of mota personality.

46—LOCAL SYSTEM HEADQUARTERS

Jerusem, the capital of Satania, is nearly perfect materially, morontially, and spiritually.

One day on Jerusem is a little less than three Urantia days. There are no days, nights, or seasons. Jerusem is not luminous in space, and would not be visible from Urantia even if it were near us.

Jerusem has no mountain ranges, no earthquakes, and no storms. There are thousands of small lakes but no rivers or oceans. The atmosphere is a mixture of three gases. On Jerusem there are no conflicting forms of life, no survival of the fittest, no struggle for existence. Jerusem so transcends the things of Urantia that comparison is almost grotesque.

Mount Seraph, 15,000 feet high, is the point of departure for seraphic transports. Transports arrive on the planet on the "sea of glass," a crystal field that also serves as a receptor of the universe broadcasts. This broadcast-receiving station is surrounded by an amphitheater large enough to hold five billion material and morontial beings, plus innumerable spirit beings. Listening to universe broadcasts is the most popular of all leisure activities on Jerusem. Occasionally, messages come in from Paradise and the entire population gathers to enjoy the reflectivity phenomenon.

Each of the seven major groups of universe life is assigned a set of seven concentric residential circles. The circles of the Sons of God are successively elevated so that each of the outer circles overlooks the smaller inner circles. People who live in these circles are Magisterial Sons, Trinity Teacher Sons, Melchizedeks, Vorondadeks, Lanonandeks, Life Carriers, and ascending sons. The Michael memorial fills the center of the circles.

Solitary Messengers, messenger hosts, ministering spirits, administrator seraphim, planetary seraphim, transition ministers, and some unrevealed orders occupy the circles of the angels. The circles of the universe aids surround the headquarters of the Evening Stars. The circles of the Master Physical Controllers are arranged around the enormous temple of power.

The circles of the ascending mortals contain a working model of Edentia surrounded by six hundred and nineteen memorials representing the inhabited worlds of Satania. The circles of the courtesy colonies house an observatory, an art gallery, and the theater of the reversion directors. The circles of the finaliters surround a vacant, sealed temple, similar to one on every system headquarters in Nebadon.

Spornagia live within the rectangles. Spornagia, animal-type beings devoted to the material care of the headquarters world, serve all manner of universe personalities. They are the landscape gardeners of Jerusem, and use lower animals to help them in their work. Spornagia do not possess souls or personality. They can live forty to fifty thousand years. Spornagia are the only creatures in the universe who experience reincarnation when their bodies wear out.

47—THE SEVEN MANSION WORLDS

Fifty-six worlds encircling Jerusem—seven planets each surrounded by seven planets—are devoted to the transition of ascending mortals.

The mansion worlds are the seven planets surrounding transitional world number one.

Transitional world number one, also known as the finaliter world, is the location of the probationary nursery. The probationary nursery is devoted to the care of children who die on evolutionary worlds before they acquire individual status on the universe records. Parents who have growing children in the probation nursery are given every opportunity to participate in their children's training. All ascending mortals must raise children at some time during their universe careers, either on their native planets or during the afterlife.

Children who have Thought Adjusters but who have not made a final choice about the ascension career are repersonalized on the finaliter world. Once they make the choice for survival, they translate to the first mansion world and join others on the Paradise ascent.

After death, mortals resume their intellectual and spiritual training precisely at the point they were at when they died. Thought Adjusters hold human mind transcripts and memory patterns; mortal identity potentials are kept by their guardian angels. These two mortal components reassemble when sleeping survivors are restored to complete personality in the resurrection halls.

A new morontia body is acquired on each mansion world. Adjuster memory remains fully intact from one world to another. Everything in human mental life that has survival value is retained as part of personal memory throughout the ascendant career. Survivors become less material and more intellectual from one world to the next, but will continue to eat, drink, and rest.

Mansion world number one pertains to deficiency ministry—correction of the legacies of life in the flesh. Mansion world number two is devoted to the removal of intellectual conflict and disharmony. More positive educational work begins on world number three, where ascenders gain practical insight into metaphysics, cosmic meanings, and universe interrelationships.

On world number four, mortals learn about the social life of morontia creatures, which is based on mutual appreciation, mutual service, and awareness of the common destiny of divine perfection. Ascenders begin to become God-knowing, God-revealing, God-seeking, and God-finding.

The culture of the fifth mansion world corresponds to the early era of light and life on normal planets. Ascenders, having mastered the local universe language, now devote time to the perfection of the language of Uversa. They also begin to learn about the constellation study worlds. A real birth of cosmic consciousness takes place on world number five; ascenders become universe conscious. Study becomes voluntary and worship becomes spontaneous.

Time on mansion world number six is a brilliant age for ascending mortals. Fusion frequently occurs on this planet.

The last remnants of "the mark of the beast" are eradicated on mansion world number seven. Here one engages in greater spiritual worship of the unseen Father. Classes begin to form for graduation to Jerusem, where groups of ascending mortals are welcomed onto system headquarters as citizens. John the Revelator had a vision of the arrival of a class of advancing mortals on Jerusem when he said, "And I saw as it were a sea of glass mingled with fire; and those who had gained the victory over the beast that was originally in them and over the image that persisted through the mansion worlds..."

Mortal death is merely a technique of escape from life in the flesh. The mansion world experience is the transition between material existence on earth and the higher spiritual attainment of eternity.

48—THE MORONTIA LIFE

The only possible method by which mortals can transform from material beings into perfected spirits is through the transition of morontia life.

Morontia materialization is a union of material and spiritual energies made possible by the *Morontia Power Supervisors,* who provide each ascender with five hundred and seventy consecutive morontia bodies. The Power Supervisors work in close association with both the physical controllers and the seraphim. Millions of Morontia Power Supervisors coordinate the physical and spiritual energy that flows into the morontia realms.

Morontia Companions serve ascenders as companions, hosts, instructors, translators, excursion supervisors, and custodians.

Reversion Directors volunteer to help mortals rest their minds through humor. They assist ascenders in reverting memories to a former state of being by creating reminiscent jests. Reversion directors also promote the unimportance of personal anxiety and the satisfaction that all things work together for good.

Billions of *Mansion World Teachers* are recruited from the ranks of cherubim and sanobim who have completed their work as assistants to guardian seraphim. Teachers usually work in pairs in the schools of things, feelings, doing, ethics, administration, social adjustment, philosophy, divinity, and spirituality.

Transition Ministers are seraphim devoted to facilitating the transition from life in the flesh to existence on the seven mansion worlds. Since the morontia life begins at the conception of the soul, Transition Ministers begin their work on the evolutionary worlds. Transition Ministers proclaim the gospel of eternal progression and perfection attainment. They counsel human teachers about truth, righteousness, and the goodness of God. The Transition Ministers are psychologists, counselors, philosophers, instructors, and recorders. From these seraphim, ascenders learn to let pressure develop into stability; to be faithful, earnest, and cheerful; to accept challenges without complaint and difficulties without fear.

There is a divine purpose in the morontia scheme of extensive training for ascending creatures. Passage through this life will be joyous, but it also has a practical objective; the goal of transcendent service in the universes. The entire universe is a vast training school through which mortals are piloted, one by one, to their destiny as Paradise finaliters in service to new universes in the making.

49—THE INHABITED WORLDS

All worlds inhabited by mortals are evolutionary planets administered in systems of one thousand planets. Our system, Satania, is incomplete, with six hundred and nineteen inhabited worlds. Thirty-six more planets are near the life endowment stage, and nearly two hundred will be inhabitable within the next few million years.

Evolution may not always be predictable but it is never accidental. There is a precise system that determines the unfolding of life, but no two worlds are exactly alike. Life Carriers have developed seven distinct physical types of mortal life:

Atmospheric types are divided into nonbreathers, subbreathers, mid-breathers and superbreathers. Mortals on the planet Venus would be superbreathers, and on Mars, subbreathers. If mortals lived on the moon they would be nonbreathers. In Nebadon, less than three percent of all planets are inhabited by nonbreathers. Such a sphere exists in close proximity to Earth.

Elemental types may dwell on land, in the treetops, in the water, or in the air.

Gravity types are modified to adapt to a planet's gravity pull. Mortals in Nebadon average seven feet in height, with a range between two and a half feet and ten feet tall.

Temperature types come in five orders according to the surface temperature of the planet.

Electric types display ten various adjustments to electric, magnetic, and electronic energies.

Energizing types are categorized regarding nutritional intake.

Unnamed types have numerous additional unrevealed variations.

All will creatures are erect bipeds. There are three primary and three secondary races, but not all races are present on all planets. The average number of physical senses is twelve. Sex equality prevails on all advanced worlds. Agriculture is the one pursuit common to every atmospheric planet. Mortal longevity ranges from twenty-five years to nearly five hundred years.

Mortals may have different brain structures. The three-brained types are more spiritual, ethical, and worshipful than two-brained types such as Urantians, who are in turn more imaginative, adventurous, and philosophical than one-brained mortals. All three orders are equally qualified for the ascension career.

Spirit reception is influenced by mind design, specifically, by the organization of certain glands that produce differing chemical endowments. Mortal survival is dependent on the birth and evolution of the immortal soul. Some people attain sufficient spiritual progress during their mortal lives to forego mansion world training. These individuals experience the mansion world as teachers rather than students. Some mortals from advanced planets escape the world of their nativity by fusing with their Thought Adjusters. Natural death becomes increasingly infrequent on spheres long settled in light and life.

50—The Planetary Princes

A Planetary Prince is a Lanonandek Son charged with organizing and administrating an inhabited sphere. Every planet receives a Planetary Prince soon after intelligent evolutionary beings have been developed by the Life Carriers. Planetary Princes are severely tested but seldom fail.

A Prince's staff consists of personalities of the Infinite Spirit, high evolved beings, and ascending mortals. The staff organizes schools where the highest members of the evolutionary races engage in physical labor, social activity, vocational training, and spiritual culture. A keen rivalry usually develops among indigenous people seeking to gain entrance into the Prince's schools. Eventually, an uplifting and civilizing influence begins to emanate into the evolving races by way of the graduates of the Prince's training.

The progress of civilization is not alike on any two planets, but an average world passes through the following seven stages of development:

The nutrition epoch—when the quest for food is the primary focus.

The security age—when attention is paid to increasing personal and clan security.

The material comfort era—when people use their new leisure to seek personal comfort.

The quest for knowledge and wisdom—a time for the development of culture.

The epoch of philosophy and brotherhood—when people become interested in ethics and accurate judgment.

The age of spiritual striving—when people seek spiritual satisfactions and cosmic understandings.

The era of light and life—during which the blend of human accomplishments produces cosmic unity and unselfish service.

When compared to normal worlds, Urantia seems intellectually confused and spiritually retarded, but we should not imagine that life on other worlds is easy. A mortal's first life is always attended by struggle. Urantia's isolation provides a unique opportunity for faith development. Surviving Urantians will be known on Jerusem as agondonters—evolutionary will creatures who can believe without seeing, persevere when isolated, and triumph over difficulties even when alone. This distinct grouping persists even into the Corps of the Mortal Finality.

51—THE PLANETARY ADAMS

When a human race on any planet reaches its natural evolutionary limit, the System Sovereign dispatches a pair of biologic uplifters to up-step the evolutionary races. Material Sons and Daughters who serve in this capacity are usually known on the assigned planet as Adam and Eve.

Material Sons are a gift from the Creator Son to the inhabited worlds. One unique pair is produced for each local system; those who serve as Planetary Adams and Eves are descendants of the system's original pair. Materials Sons vary in height from eight to ten feet tall, are visible to humans, and glow with a radiant light of violet hue.

Adams and Eves are equal to each other, differing only in reproductive characteristics and chemical endowments. Material Sons are sustained by material food and by direct intake of cosmic energies. Created Adams and Eves are immortal, but their offspring depend on unbroken connection with the mind-gravity circuit of the Spirit for continuing life.

Material Sons are semi-material. They must dematerialize to be transported by seraphim to the planet of their assignment, where they are rematerialized. One hundred thousand angels accompany each pair. Normally, Material Sons and Daughters stay on the planet of their assignment until it attains the era of light and life.

Material Sons and Daughters dwell in a garden home. These homes are usually located in a secluded area in a near-tropical zone. Adam and Eve's offspring remain biologically segregated under the direction of the Planetary Prince until a strong violet race develops. Descendants of Adam and Eve are of two orders: physical children and secondary midway creatures. Secondary midwayers are often invisible and contribute much to the advancement of civilization.

On a normal world, the red race is ordinarily first to attain human development. The evolution of many races provides desirable variations in mortal types and contributes to the diverse expression of human potential. It is impossible to understand a normal planet's racial evolution from observing the remnants of the early races on Earth.

Slavery is typically abolished on a planet soon after the arrival of Adam and Eve. Evolutionary races are blended with the Adamic strain only after the inferior strains of each race are eliminated. Members of the violet race usually do not begin to mate with evolutionary humans until the violet race numbers one million individuals. The violet race is monogamous. Any man or woman who mates with an Adamic son or daughter must pledge to be faithful to a single spouse and to raise their children to be monogamous. The children produced from marriages between human and Adamic races are educated in the schools of the Planetary Prince before returning to the race of their evolutionary parent. Following this procreative outpouring, culture and civilization make rapid strides.

On a normal world, the centers of world culture are the Garden of Eden and the headquarters of the Planetary Prince. These two centers work together to influence progress throughout the world. The schools of the Prince are concerned with philosophy, religion, morals, and high intellectual and artistic achievements. The schools of Adam and Eve are devoted to practical arts, social culture, economic development, trade relations, physical efficiency, civil government, and fundamental intellectual training.

52—PLANETARY MORTAL EPOCHS

Urantia has not proceeded in the normal order of planetary development. Average worlds progress through seven epochs of human life, determined by the planetary missions of the divine Sons.

1. *Pre-Planetary Prince.* This age is characterized by survival of the fittest; some early races may be entirely obliterated. Primitive men are hunters and fighters. They are cave dwellers, cliff residents, or may live in treehuts. The early races learn to kindle fire, improve tools, and vanquish large animals. They use large flying animals for transportation. People usually acquire moral will when they develop early language. Some primitive people receive temporary Thought Adjusters.

2. *Post-Planetary Prince.* With the arrival of the Planetary Prince, primitive government appears and people make great social strides. The invisible Prince and his visible staff make revelations of truth to uplift the evolved religions of fear and ignorance. The races begin to develop specialized systems of religious and philosophic thought. The great social achievement of the prince's epoch is the emergence of family life, made possible by the realization of sexual equality. Domestication of animals and cultivation of the soil supplant the roving and unsettled life of the hunter. On normal worlds, the races are brought to a high state of physical perfection and intellectual strength.

3. *Post-Adamic.* When humankind has reached the apex of animal development, a Material Son and Daughter arrive. The Adamic regime moves humans completely from the hunter/herder stage to the agriculturist/horticulturist stage. This age usually completes the elimination of the unfit strains of the races. The Adamic life plasm upsteps human intellectual capacity and spiritual progress. This is an age of invention, energy control, mechanical development, and exploration. All races blend into an amalgamated race of one color, an olive shade of the violet hue. Nationalism wanes and the brotherhood of man begins to develop. Interest flourishes in art, music, literature, intellectual realities, and philosophy. Worldwide peace prompts the arrival of the age of the Magisterial Son.

4. *Post-Magisterial Son.* A Magisterial Son incarnates and sometimes rules for many generations. This age produces economic liberation. Citizens generally labor only two-and-a-half hours a day, and use their newfound leisure for self-improvement and planetary advancement. Most people are Adjuster-indwelt. Society returns to simple, natural forms of living. This age brings the flowering of art, music and higher learning. The end of this age is characterized by a worldwide spiritual enlightenment, signaling the arrival of the Bestowal Son.

5. *Post-Bestowal Son.* This age is characterized by the pursuit of moral culture and spiritual truth, and the passion for communion with spiritual reality. New systems of education and government arise. After the Bestowal Son returns to the headquarters of the local universe, he and the Creator Son send the Spirit of Truth to the planet. Along with the Spirit of Truth, Thought Adjusters arrive en masse to indwell all normal-

minded people. The average length of human life during this era is more than three hundred years. Fewer restrictive laws become necessary. The military passes away and international harmony arrives. There are many nations, but only one race, one language, and one religion.

6. *Post-Teacher Son.* Teacher Sons come in groups to effect the transition of a planet into the era of light and life. Natural death becomes less frequent as more Adjusters fuse with their subjects during mortal lifetimes. The average length of mortal life approaches five hundred years. Representative government vanishes as the world passes into the rule of individual self-control. More and more people practice justice, mercy, and joyous service to the Sons of God.

7. *Light and Life.* The Planetary Prince elevates to Planetary Sovereign when the planet enters the era of light and life.

Social brotherhood on Earth depends on the following transformations:

1. Social fraternity—international associations of travel, commerce, and competitive play; the development of a common language.

2. Intellectual cross-fertilization—an exchange of national and racial literature. Each nation must become familiar with the feelings of all nations.

3. Ethical awakening—disclosure of the immorality of intolerance and strife, development of the spiritual insight that is essential to the golden rule.

4 Political wisdom—substitution of civilized adjudication for the barbarism of war.

5. Spiritual insight—spiritual transformation, the enhancement of the soul capacity of every mortal to love every other mortal.

53—The Lucifer Rebellion

Lucifer was a primary Lanonandek Son. He was once considered one of the hundred most brilliant personalities of more than seven hundred thousand Lanonandek Sons. Lucifer now is one of three System Sovereigns in ten thousand who, by embracing sin and rejecting universe allegiance, have rebelled against the local universe government. Lucifer and his assistant, Satan, reigned on Jerusem for more than five hundred thousand years before they became traitors to the Universal Father.

It is difficult to trace the exact cause of Lucifer's rebellion. No specific conditions in the system of Satania favored the outbreak. At some point, Lucifer's evil devolved into deliberate sin; his self-pride turned into self-deception.

Several months passed before Lucifer succeeded in corrupting his assistant, but once corrupted, Satan became the primary spokesperson for Lucifer's cause on Urantia. Satan was assisted by Caligastia, the Planetary Prince; Abaddon, Caligastia's chief of staff; and Beelzebub, leader of the disloyal midwayers.

Lucifer presented his three main arguments in a manifesto known as the Lucifer Declaration of Liberty. The rebel claimed that the Universal Father was merely a myth invented by the Paradise Sons so they could maintain power in the universes. He protested the right of Michael to rule and denounced the Ancients of Days as tyrants and foreign potentates. Finally, he condemned the mortal ascension plan on the grounds that it wasted time and energy on a fictional destiny.

Lucifer's manifesto was issued at the annual conclave of Satania on the sea of glass two hundred thousand years ago. He promised that Planetary Princes who followed him would rule as supreme executives. Michael, after taking counsel with his brother Immanuel, decided to assume a position of noninterference. Lucifer was given a free hand to promote his plan, and he pointed to this apparent lack of notice as proof that the universe government was unable to stop him. The following years were a time of great testing in Satania.

Gabriel, leading Lucifer's opposition, set up headquarters in Satania and assumed command of the hosts loyal to Michael. The conflict was terrible, real, and far more deadly than material warfare on the immature worlds. Material life is lost in material conflicts, but those who choose the wrong side during heavenly rebellion forfeit their eternal lives.

The Lucifer Rebellion was system-wide. Thirty-seven Planetary Princes chose the side of the rebel; hundreds of thousands of personalities were lost. At the outbreak of the insurrection, the entire system of Satania was isolated from the universe communication circuits. No Trinitized Sons, Melchizedeks, archangels, or Brilliant Evening Stars rebelled, but a heavy loss occurred from Morontia Companions and Mansion World Teachers. All of the supreme order of seraphim remained loyal, but many superior and third order seraphim were lost. One third of the administrator angels went astray along with their associated cherubim.

Over six hundred thousand Material Sons rebelled, as did large numbers of midway creatures. Ascending mortals withstood the rebellion better than the lower spirits. Not one ascendant citizen on Jerusem was lost, which, ironically, validated the mortal ascension scheme by proving that the best security against cosmic rebellion was the experience of universe ascension.

Lucifer and Satan roamed freely until the bestowal mission of Michael was completed on Urantia. Their attack against him while he was incarnate on Urantia brought an end to any remaining sympathy for the rebel cause in Satania. Michael's bestowal terminated the rebellion throughout the system except on the thirty-seven planets that rebelled. Salvation was offered to all rebels during the early days of the insurrection; none of the leaders accepted mercy, but thousands of angels and lower orders of beings were rehabilitated.

The Ancients of Days have yet to hand down a decision regarding the disposition of Lucifer, Satan, and their associates. Lucifer and Satan are currently imprisoned on the Father's transition spheres surrounding Jerusem. For nineteen hundred years, their status has remained unchanged.

Michael's last act before leaving Urantia was to offer mercy to Caligastia and Dalagastia, but they rejected his offer. Caligastia is still free on Earth, although he has no power to enter the human mind and cannot corrupt any person unless they truly desire to be cursed with his presence. Both Caligastia and Dalagastia are powerless against Thought Adjusters and the Spirit of Truth.

The system circuits will not be reinstated as long as Lucifer lives. It is believed that all rebels who will ever accept mercy have already done so. The universe awaits the Uversa decree that will deprive these rebels of personality existence.

54—PROBLEMS OF THE LUCIFER REBELLION

Of all the problems caused by the Lucifer rebellion, none has created more difficulty than the failure of immature mortals to distinguish between true and false liberty. True liberty is related to reality and is mindful of cosmic fairness, fraternity, and divine obligations. Liberty divorced from justice, fairness, forbearance, duty, and spiritual values is suicidal. License disguised as liberty is the precursor of abject bondage.

Ever since he first formed Havona with the Son and the Spirit, God the Father has created a divine pattern of sharing. Sons and Daughters who attempt to replicate the central universe in the universes of time and space are creative partners with the Father, as is each person in every evolving universe who aspires to do the Father's will. Lucifer's crime was an attempt to disenfranchise every personality in Satania from this God-given freewill participation in the evolutionary struggle for light and life. The Lucifer manifesto, masquerading as the promotion of liberty, attempted to deprive ascenders of the privilege of participating in the creation of their own destinies.

Sin is potential whenever imperfect beings are endowed with the ability to choose between good and evil. Mortals who are puzzled as to why God permits evil and sin fail to comprehend that both are inevitable if the creature is to be truly free. Free will is not a mere philosophic concept; it is a universe reality. Wholehearted identification with sin leads eventually to non-existence, but there is always a period between the embrace of sin and the penalty thereof. The Ancients of Days do not annihilate any being until all moral values are extinct, both in the evildoer and in any related supporters.

Lucifer and Satan were permitted to work their wickedness for an extended time before they were apprehended. People who have raised children are best able to understand why Michael, the Creator-father, might be slow to destroy his sons. Immanuel, the Faithful of Days, the Supreme Executive of Orvonton, and the Divine Minister all concurred that the rebellion should be allowed to take its full natural course.

Mercy delays of time are mandated by the Creators, and there is good to be derived in the universe from patience in dealing with sinful rebels. But such delays are not interminable. Justice in a mercy-dominated universe may be slow, but it is certain. Mercy requires that wrongdoers be given sufficient time to fully choose their evil thoughts and acts. Justice will never destroy that which mercy can save.

When a father shows mercy to one of his erring children, it may bring a temporary hardship to his other children. Such risk is inseparable from the reality of being a member of a family. Each family member profits by the righteous conduct of every other member, and each suffers the consequences of the misconduct of the others. But such hardships are transient; no consequence of fraternal misbehavior can ever jeopardize the eternal prospects of another individual.

Compensation invariably accompanies the sin of rebellion. The Lucifer rebellion at first seemed to be a complete calamity, but gradually benefits began to accrue. About twenty thousand years ago, the good that had arisen from Lucifer's sin came to equal the evil incurred. The evil now has become almost stationary, while the beneficial repercussions continue to multiply throughout the superuniverse. The good that has resulted from the Lucifer rebellion is now more than a thousand times the sum of the evil created. As mortals ascend Paradiseward, they will increasingly learn how ultimate good can derive from time-limited evil.

55—THE SPHERES OF LIGHT AND LIFE

The final attainment of an evolutionary world is the age of light and life. Once attained, the era of light and life continues forever.

A morontia temple appears at a planet's entry into light and life. Morontia temples are designed on system headquarters and are built by Morontia Power Supervisors and Master Physical Controllers. Three hundred thousand seats provide for silent cosmic contemplation, revelation of spirit beings, graduation exercises, and fusion ceremonies.

A planet in the golden ages of light and life has achieved one language, one religion, and one race. Disease has not been entirely vanquished; hospitals still exist to treat accidental injuries and the infirmities of old age. Human government continues. In the advanced stages of light and life on a planet, idleness, poverty, degeneracy, insanity, and delinquency virtually disappear. Science, art, and industry flourish; economic life becomes ethical. War is known only in history; there are no armies or police forces. Government fades away in inverse proportion to morality and spirituality. Life is refreshingly simple.

Advanced mortals are taught the local universe language before fusion. Most people who live on worlds in the advanced stages of light and life do not die; they are translated directly to the morontia existence through fusion. When people gather in the morontia temples to observe the passing of a loved one to the mansion worlds, it is an occasion of great joy.

Universes also pass through stages of light and life. The first stage begins when a single planet settles in light and life; the second stage occurs when a whole system is settled; the third is the constellation stage; the fourth is the local universe stage; and the fifth and sixth stages (minor and major sectors) are relatively insignificant. It is conjectured that the seventh stage, when the entire superuniverse settles in light and life, may trigger sweeping changes throughout creation.

56—UNIVERSAL UNITY

The universe of universes is one mechanism controlled by one mind. Physical, intellectual, and spiritual realities are divinely correlated and are unified in the plans of the Architects of the Master Universe. Non-spiritual realities spring from pure energy. Divine overcontrol of all energy systems springs from pure spirit. Pure energy and pure spirit seem to be diverse phenomena, but both are centered in the Paradise Father—they are one because God is one.

Mind is the inevitable link between spiritual and material realities. At the Creator's first thought, two realities appeared: the Isle of Paradise (energy) and the Eternal Son (spirit). Mind unifies these two universe expressions of God. Mind, an endowment of the Infinite Spirit, is unified throughout time and space. From the adjutant mind spirits, to the mind of the chief executive of a universe, to the Seven Master Spirits, to the Supreme Mind—all mind ministry is perfectly correlated through the mind of the Infinite Spirit.

God is one. He reveals himself through the dual phenomena of spirit and energy. Likewise, Paradise spirit realities are one, but this single spirit is revealed through the spirit personalities of the Eternal Son and the Infinite Spirit, and through the prepersonal spirit entities of the Father. All spiritual phenomena are derived from one God.

Perfected creature existence is attained when mortal mind fuses with a fragment of spirit. When a mortal mind, created by Sons of the Eternal Son and Daughters of the Infinite Spirit, fuses with the Father's Thought Adjuster, it becomes blessed with a threefold spirit endowment. This triple endowment becomes perfectly unified in finaliters even as it was originally unified in the I AM.

Spirit ultimately becomes Trinity-unified. God is a divinely unified personality, and his ascendant children who come to Paradise by the rebound of the Thought Adjusters will also be fully unified personalities.

Personality inherently reaches out to unify all constituent realities. Through the personality circuit, each creature can maintain unbroken contact with the Father of personalities on Paradise. Philosophically, we may postulate plural Deities and Trinities, but our worshipful contact with God the Father reveals that he is one.

There are three eternal personalizations of Deity, but in the Paradise Trinity they are one undivided Deity. Divinity functions in the superuniverses through the Creator Sons and Spirits, the Ancients of Days, and the Seven Master Spirits. These first three levels of God the Sevenfold lead inward to Paradise through the coordination of the evolving Supreme Being.

In the central universe, Deity unity is a fact. In the evolving universes, Deity unity is an achievement.

Before the creation of the seven superuniverses, God the Supreme functioned only on spiritual levels. The Creators of the grand universe instigated the evolution of the power prerogatives of the Almighty Supreme. This new power of Deity coordinates with the spiritual person of the Supreme through the Supreme Mind, which sprang from the infinite mind of the Infinite Spirit. Mortals can comprehend Deity unity only as it evolves in the power-personality synthesis of the Supreme Being.

Evolution in the universes is accompanied by an increase of revelation of Deity to universe residents. Ascending mortals may experience the impersonal presence of Deity before they know these Deities on a personal level. As the creations of time and space progress, God the Supreme functions more fully and the Creator Sons and Spirits, Ancients of Days, and Master Spirits begin to withdraw.

The Supreme Being unifies divinity in time and space. He is the maximum level of Deity that mortals can comprehend. Through him, humans learn to experience absonite mind, eternal spirit, and Paradise personality. Finaliters, born in the local universes, nurtured in the superuniverses, and trained in the central universe, will have the potential to comprehend how God the Sevenfold unifies in the Supreme.

As worlds settle in light and life, the main pursuit of advancing mortals becomes the study of the comprehensible elements of Deity—truth, beauty and goodness—through philosophy, cosmology, and divinity. These qualities represent the revelation of Deity to the worlds of time and space. Eternal truth is the ministry of the Paradise Sons. Universal beauty is a reflection of the Isle of Paradise. Divine goodness is most fully shown in the ministry of the Infinite Spirit. Love, the sum of truth, beauty, and goodness, is man's perception of God as his Father. Our increasing understanding of the love of God yields the fruits of divinity: intellectual peace, social progress, moral satisfaction, spiritual joy, and cosmic wisdom.

Love is the greatest thing in the universe.

God is love.

Love is the desire to do good to others.

PART III

THE HISTORY OF URANTIA

Part iii
The History of Urantia

57—The Origin of Urantia

Nearly *one trillion years ago* an inspector from Uversa reported to the Ancients of Days that conditions were favorable for materialization in our sector of Orvonton.

Nine hundred billion years ago a permit was issued authorizing the dispatch of a force organizer and his staff, who inaugurated the energy whirl that became the Andronover nebula.

Six hundred billion years ago the Andronover nebula acquired its maximum mass. The nebula's rotational speed increased, its gravity began to weaken, and gas began to escape into two gigantic arms on opposing sides of the original mass.

Five hundred billion years ago the first sun in the Andronover system was formed.

Two hundred billion years ago the oldest inhabited planets of Nebadon were formed.

Six billion years ago our sun was born as the Andronover nebula condensed. Our solar system, Monmatia, had an unusual origin. An enormous system, Angona, drew near to Monmatia. Its gravity pulled solar gases from the sun, which evolved into planets, meteors, and space dust of our solar system. The planets now travel in the plane of the Angona system rather than around the equatorial plane of our sun. The reverse motion in the orbits of our sun's planets, which perplexes astronomers, is a result of material from the Angona system merging into our sun's gravity range. Jupiter and Saturn shone so brightly when they first formed that they were secondary suns; they remain largely gaseous today.

Three billion years ago our solar system was much as it is today. The planets were smaller; for some time the earth was not much bigger than the moon.

One and one half billion years ago volcanic activity on earth was at its height. A crust gradually formed, and atmosphere slowly began to surround the planet.

One billion years ago Urantia was officially placed on the physical registries of Nebadon. As the world cooled, the first ocean formed, covering the entire earth in fresh water one mile deep. Fifty million years later there was one great continent and one ocean. Lava flows, earthquakes, and violent storms characterized this age.

Nine hundred million years ago a scouting party from Satania recommended that Urantia be designated a decimal planet, a life- experiment world.

Six hundred and fifty million years ago the continents had separated, the seas were attaining the necessary saltiness, and Urantia was nearly ready for establishment of life in the inland seas.

58—LIFE ESTABLISHMENT ON URANTIA

Life Carriers experiment with life forms on every tenth inhabitable planet in an effort to improve types of living beings. Urantia is the sixty-first of these experimental worlds in Satania. Life Carriers chose a sodium chloride pattern of life for our planet. All life here evolved in a salt solution; human blood literally submerses every cell of the body in the essential salt solution. The Life Carriers implanted life when the ocean water became sufficiently salty, a large number of protected inland seas emerged, and atmospheric conditions became advantageous.

Five hundred and fifty million years ago the Life Carriers initiated the original life patterns of Urantia by planting them simultaneously in the ancient inland seas of three locations: Eurasia/Africa, Australia, and Greenland/America. Three identical batches of life material were planted to ensure that there would be life on each of the great land masses when the continents drifted apart. Within fifty million years, marine vegetable life was well established.

Four hundred and fifty million years ago animal life developed. The transition to animal organisms took place in sheltered tropical bays and shorelines of the separating continents. This change was inherent in the original life patterns, and came about gradually. Slime molds, classified as neither plants nor animals, are a remnant of this era.

Genetic mutations are entirely natural. From era to era, radically new species can arise; new orders of life may appear suddenly. Although there are connecting links between the most simple to the most advanced life organisms, there are none between the highest prehuman animals and the earliest humans.

59—THE MARINE-LIFE ERA ON URANTIA

The billion-year history of Urantia extends through five major eras: the Pre-Life era (Archeozoic), the Life-Dawn era (Proterozoic), the Marine Life era (Paleozoic), the Early Land-Life era (Mezozoic), and the Mammalian era (Cenozoic). At the dawn of the marine-life period, plants and animals were fairly well distributed throughout the seas and vegetation had begun to move onto the land.

Four hundred million years ago the first multicellular animals *suddenly* made their appearance. The trilobites evolved and dominated the seas for ages. Periodically, land masses would sink into the oceans and rise again. At times the American land mass was almost entirely submerged. Greenland was warmed by the Gulf Stream. Sediments of conglomerates, limestone, shale, and sandstone were deposited.

Three hundred and sixty million years ago marine life included seaweed, sponges, one-celled organisms, trilobites, and other crustaceans. Of the three thousand varieties of brachiopods appearing at the close of this period, only two hundred have survived into present times.

Three hundred and fifty million years ago saw the beginning of great flood periods on the continents. This age was characterized by enormous amounts of limestone laid down by the lime-secreting algae.

Three hundred and ten million years ago every type of marine life below the vertebrate scale was represented. Sea worms, some types of jelly-fish, corals, and sponges evolved. Cephalopods developed and have survived as the modern pearly nautilus, octopus, cuttlefish and squid. Shelled animals were single-shelled and bivalve gastropods—drills, periwinkles, snails, oysters, clams and scallops—and valve-shelled brachiopods.

Three hundred million years ago another great flood era occurred. The enormous deposits of animal and vegetable matter carried down with this land submergence provided the world with gas, oil, zinc, and lead.

Two hundred and eighty million years ago the continents had largely re-emerged. The trilobites declined. The cephalopods became masters of the seas; some of the larger mollusks grew to be fifteen feet long. Coral-reef formations multiplied. During this age primitive water scorpions evolved and soon thereafter the first air-breathing scorpions appeared.

Two hundred and fifty million years ago vertebrates suddenly appeared in the fish family. The land was rapidly overrun by new orders of vegetation. Ferns appeared suddenly and quickly spread over the face of the earth, some growing to be one hundred feet high. Leafless trees developed. The atmosphere of the earth became enriched with oxygen.

Two hundred and ten million years ago warm-water seas again covered most of North America and Europe. Out from the warm waters came snails, scorpions, and frogs. Spiders, cockroaches, crickets, locusts, and thirty-inch dragonflies soon followed.

Two hundred million years ago the most active stages of worldwide coal formation were in process.

One hundred and seventy million years ago great evolutionary changes took place. Lands rose and ocean beds sank. The earth's crust folded extensively, and inland lakes and seas evaporated. Two new climatic factors appeared—glaciation and aridity. Thousands of marine animals perished. Of the 100,000 species of life on earth during this era, less than five hundred survived. Harsh weather replaced the mild climate. Insects underwent radical changes to meet the demands of winter and drought.

This period of biologic adversity eliminated all forms of life except those that had survival value. At the close of the marine-life era, the land was largely covered with vegetation, and the atmosphere had become ideal for animal respiration. The vast oceanic nursery of life on Urantia had served its purpose.

60—URANTIA DURING THE EARLY LAND-LIFE ERA

One hundred and forty million years ago two full-fledged reptiles suddenly appeared, from which sprang crocodiles, sea serpents, flying reptiles, and dinosaurs. Early dinosaurs were egg layers and had very small brains. Several million years later the first mammal appeared and quickly failed.

One hundred and twenty million years ago dinosaurs of all sizes had evolved. The larger dinosaurs required so much food that they starved themselves into extinction.

One hundred and ten million years ago sea urchins mutated into existence. Crabs and lobsters matured, and fish continued to develop. Sea serpents infested the seas and threatened the destruction of all fishes.

Ninety million years ago angiosperms, fig trees, tulip trees, and magnolias came into existence, followed by breadfruit trees and palms.

Sixty-five million years ago plant life evolved greatly with the appearance of modern-day trees such as beech, birch, oak, walnut, sycamore, maple and modern palms. Fruits, grasses, and cereals were widespread. These seed-bearing plants were second in evolutionary importance only to the appearance of man himself. Flowering plants mutated and spread all over the world.

Sixty million years ago land turtles measured twenty feet across. Modern-type crocodiles and snakes thrived.

Fifty-five million years ago the ancestor of all bird life, a small pigeonlike creature, suddenly appeared. It was the third type of flying creature to appear on Urantia; it sprang directly from the reptilian group. This period marked the end of the continental drift and the buildup of modern mountains. Fern forests were largely replaced by pines and redwoods. By the end of this period, the biologic stage was set for the early ancestors of mammalian types.

61—The Mammalian Era on Urantia

The mammalian era covers a period of fifty thousand years, starting from the times of the origin of placental mammals to the end of the ice age.

Mammals have several survival advantages over other forms of life. They possess an ability to adapt to their environment, superior intelligence, agility, delivery of relatively mature offspring, and a tendency to nourish and protect their young.

Fifty million years ago placental mammals suddenly appeared in North America, descendants of a small, highly active, springing-type of carnivorous dinosaur.

Forty-five million years ago mammalian life was evolving rapidly. A small egg-laying type of mammal flourished. The ancestors of kangaroos existed in Australia. Small versions of horses, rhinoceroses, tapirs, primitive pigs, squirrels, lemurs, opossums and monkey-like creatures appeared. A ten-foot-tall ostrich-like bird developed which became the ancestor of the passenger birds of later times.

These early mammals lived on land, under the water, in the air and among the treetops. They had mammary glands, were covered with considerable hair, developed two successive sets of teeth, and had large brains. At this time North America was connected to every continent except Australia; the world was overrun by primitive mammals.

Thirty-five million years ago began the age of domination by placental mammals. The dinosaur species were on the decline. Various groups of mammals took origin in an amphibious animal, now extinct, that was a cross between a cat and a seal. The ancestor of dogs evolved in Europe. Rodents appeared.

Thirty million years ago modern types of mammals began to develop. Hoofed types of grazing animals appeared. Horses and rhinoceroses continued to evolve. A small hog-like creature developed which became the ancestor of swine, peccaries, and hippos. Camels, llamas, and ancient lemurs originated. A group of mammals took to the seas and became ancestors to whales, dolphins, seals and sea lions. Most modern bird types existed.

Twenty million years ago the Bering land bridge was above water. Deer, oxen, camels, bison and rhinoceroses migrated to North America from Asia. Fifty species of elephant overran the entire world except Australia. Giant pigs became extinct.

Fifteen million years ago enormous herds of horses roamed western North America. Primitive monkeys and gorillas evolved in Asia. Wolves and foxes came into existence; panthers and saber-tooth tigers represented the cat family.

Ten million years ago the last great world-wide animal migration began. Camels entered China; sloths, armadillos, antelopes and bears moved to North America. The giraffe evolved in Africa. Mastodons migrated into every continent except Australia. The ocean currents shifted and seasonal winds changed direction. Parts of Europe and North America rose up to 30,000 feet and more; the thick depths of snow that began to form on the highlands eventually became masses of solid creeping ice.

Two million years ago marks the beginning of the ice ages. Throughout the ice ages, glaciers advanced and retreated across the continents, carving the landscape as they went. Many animal species were destroyed and others were radically changed by the rigors of migration. In North America, the last glacier movement wiped out horses, tapirs, llamas, and saber-tooth tigers. The ice ages ended thirty-five thousand years ago.

62—THE DAWN RACES OF EARLY MAN

The great event of the ice age was the evolution of primitive man.

Several million years ago, North American lemurs migrated over the Bering land bridge and settled west of India. There, they united with other favorable strains from the central life implantation to produce a superior lemur type. When climatic and geologic factors isolated the region from the rest of world, the superior lemur strains were able to multiply without contamination from inferior stocks.

A little more than a million years ago, Mesopotamian dawn mammals *suddenly* arose from the lemurs. Dawn mammals were three feet tall, carnivorous, and had opposable thumbs and grasping big toes. They had the largest brain of any proportionately sized animal that existed to that date. The creatures experienced many emotions and instincts; the human tendency to harbor irrational fear dates from their time. Dawn mammals had a strong tribal spirit and did not hesitate to make war on their inferior neighbors. The species progressively improved by selective survival. For a thousand years they multiplied and spread throughout the Mesopotamian peninsula.

After seventy generations, twins far superior to their parents were born to a pair of the dawn mammals. These mid-mammals had larger brains and bodies, less hair, longer legs, and shorter arms than their parents. They grew to be a little over four feet in height and walked upright. The mid-mammal twins were soon recognized as leaders of the dawn-mammal tribe.

The twins instituted primitive forms of social organization and crude divisions of labor. They mated and produced twenty-one children, the nucleus of a new species. When the mid-mammals became numerous, war broke out, and dawn mammals were completely annihilated. The new species multiplied for fifteen thousand years.

Rudimentary human traits appeared in the mid-mammals. They collected stones for weapons, fought among themselves, hoarded food, and built homes in the treetops and underground. Six hundred generations after the first mid-mammals appeared, a superior couple produced twins that were the first primates, the direct ancestors of the human race. During the same era, another pair of mid-mammals gave birth to a set of twins who became the ancestors of modern simians.

The superior twins were more human and less animal than their predecessors. They had less hair on their bodies, had fully developed human-type hands and feet, and spoke to each other with signs and sounds. The twins grew to be over five feet tall. Even when very young, they insisted on walking upright. At fourteen years of age, the twins left home. Their descendants lived on the Mesopotamian peninsula where they were segregated from their less intelligent cousins.

After nine hundred generations—approximately 993,000 years ago—a mutation within this Primate stock gave origin to another set of twins, the first two true human beings. They had perfect human hands and feet; they walked and ran. The twins communicated verbally as well as through signs and symbols. These first two humans felt a range of emotions including curiosity, admiration, vanity, awe, reverence, humility, pity, shame, love, hate, revenge and jealousy.

When they were about nine years old, the twins pledged their lives to each other. Two years later, they decided to elope; they left their tribe to start a new life together. This conscious decision marked the moment when the mind-spirit of wisdom first began to function on earth. The twins were recognized as true human beings, and Urantia was officially registered as an inhabited world.

63—The First Human Family

Andon and Fonta, the first human beings, were in some respects the most remarkable pair of humans who ever lived on Urantia. They were in every way superior to their immediate descendants and radically different from all of their ancestors. Andon and Fonta's decision to flee from the primate tribes implied a high quality of mind. They knew they were more than mere animals; they possessed personality and the presence of indwelling Thought Adjusters.

Before they fled, Andon and Fonta prepared a treetop retreat half a day's journey away. They retained the primate fear of being on the ground after dark, but knowing that they were less likely to be pursued during the night, they set out on their own before nightfall.

On the northward journey, Andon and Fonta gathered a supply of flint stones for future uses. By accident Andon discovered their sparking quality. After many failed attempts they learned to create fire by using bird's nests as kindling. Andon and Fonta realized that their discovery would make it possible for them to defy climate and live away from the warm regions. Two years after they left home, Fonta gave birth to their first child, Sontad.

Andon and Fonta had nineteen children and lived to know almost fifty grandchildren and several great grandchildren. Their extended family lived in four rock shelters connected by hallways excavated with flint tools. They avoided separation, seeming to realize that they were an isolated and unique group. The family hunted in groups and never strayed far from home. Andon and Fonta lived to be forty-two years old; their family group held together for twenty generations.

Early Andonites resembled the present-day Eskimo. They were the first creatures to use animal skins to protect themselves from cold weather. They developed social groups and divisions of labor. They were less sensitive to pain than modern-day humans. They were very loyal to their families. Many of the most noble human traits were foreshadowed in these primitive people.

As time passed the Andonites grew in numbers. Tribal wars erupted. Serious losses were sustained among the best specimens of the more advanced groups; some of the most valuable human strains were forever lost to the world.

The Andonites spread northward until the third glacier advance stopped them. They established more than one thousand settlements along the rivers leading to the warm waters of the North Sea. Andonites were clever in disguising their homes and showed great skill in building stone sleeping chambers. They were fearless hunters, living almost exclusively on meat, wild berries, and fruits. They became skilled in fashioning flint tools. In some ways, the early Andonites showed a degree of intelligence that their retrogressing descendants did not attain again for half a million years.

Andonites developed a fear of the elements: thunder, lightning, rain, snow, hail and ice. Since they largely subsisted on animals, they evolved a form of animal worship. Andonite worship ceremonies eventually included the use of sacrifices.

After ten thousand years of Andonite retrogression, Onagar, a great mastermind and spiritual guide, assumed leadership of the tribes. Onagar established peace and led the tribesmen to worship the "Breath Giver." From his headquarters at a settlement near the present-day Caspian Sea, he sent out the world's first missionaries. The tribal government that Onagar instituted was extremely efficient. Although Andon, Fonta, and many of their immediate descendants had received Thought Adjusters, it was not until the time of Onagar that large numbers of Adjusters and guardian angels came to this planet.

64—THE EVOLUTIONARY RACES OF COLOR

To avoid co-mingling with the southern simian tribes, the early Andonites fled northward. Cold weather and frequent hunger in the northern lands stimulated action, resourcefulness, and invention.

One hundred thousand years after the time of Andon and Fonta the arts of the Andonites and the culture of Onagar were vanishing from the earth. Fewer and fewer of the primitive settlements maintained the worship of the Breath Giver. Culture, religion, and flint work were at a low point. The only groups who retained some of these high traditions were the Foxhall people of England and the Badonan tribes northwest of India.

The Foxhalls, being farthest west, maintained their racial purity and kept their primitive religious customs alive. They also succeeded in preserving knowledge of flint work, which they eventually passed on to their descendants, the Eskimos. Most of the settlements of these early people are now under water in the English Channel and the North Sea.

In the foothills of the Indian highlands among the tribes of Badonan, another struggling center of culture persisted. Fear of floods in the lowlands kept these tribes fairly isolated for many thousands of years. The mixed descendants of Badonan stock became the Neanderthals.

Neanderthals were excellent fighters, great hunters, and extensive travelers. They improved flint work so much that it approached the level of Andon's age. Neanderthals were superstitious—afraid of clouds, mists, darkness, and other natural forces. They used human sacrifices to coax the moon into shining. During the fourth and fifth glacial advances, the Neanderthal culture spread and dominated the world.

Five hundred thousand years ago, around the time of the Planetary Prince's arrival, the relatively pure Badonan tribes became involved in a great racial struggle. After more than one hundred years of warfare, only about one hundred families of Andon and Fonta's descendants were left alive.

Among these Badonites a man and woman began to produce a family of unusually intelligent children whose skins turned various colors in the sunlight. There were five red children, two each of orange, indigo, and green, and four each of yellow and blue. This was the Sangik family, ancestors of the six colored races on Urantia. For one hundred thousand years the Sangik peoples spread out among the Indian foothills and generally mingled together. India in that era became the most cosmopolitan place ever known on earth.

The red Sangiks were the first to leave their homeland. When they had built up sufficient numbers, they migrated northeast to occupy Asia. They were followed by the yellow tribes, who drove the red people out of Asia across the Bering land bridge into North America. The red man was accompanied to North America by three tribes of mixed ancestry, the largest being a combination of orange and blue. Leaving the purer reds behind in North America, these peoples journeyed together into Mexico and Central America, where they eventually were joined by a mixed group of reds and yellows. These travelers intermarried and founded a new race that was less warlike than the pure red race. Within five thousand years, these new people had divided themselves into three groups and established civilizations in Mexico, Central America, and South America.

Eighty-five thousand years ago the Bering land bridge sank, isolating the red men on the American continent. The red race was the first of the Sangik races to develop tribal government, but infighting and tribal wars nearly caused their extinction. Sixty-five thousand years ago, the leadership of Onamonalonton brought the red tribes temporary peace by reviving the worship of the Great Spirit. This great leader's teachings were eventually obscured but his descendants, the Blackfoot Indians, live on today.

The yellow race was the first to establish settled communities and base their home lives on agriculture. They were intellectually inferior to the red race, but socially and collectively they were superior to the other Sangik peoples. They lived together in relative peace. Their spiritual leader was Singlangton, who taught them to worship the One Truth.

In Asia, offspring of red and yellow races migrated to the eastern peninsulas and the islands of the sea; they are the present-day brown people.

The blue men traveled westward into Europe along the trails of the Andon tribes. There they came across Neanderthals, and the intermingling of these groups led to the immediate improvement of the Neanderthals. The blue man had the intelligence of the red race and the sentiment of the yellow race. He developed many of the arts of modern civilization; the tools, bones and art of the blue people are found throughout Europe by those who study the Old Stone Age. Orlandof was their great teacher. Their descendants, mixed with yellow, red, Nodite and Adamic stock, provide the biologic foundation for today's white races. The blue people who remained on the Arabian peninsula mated with other races, especially the yellow. This blend was upstepped by the later-appearing violet race and exists today as the modern Arabs.

The outstanding characteristic of the orange race was their urge to build anything and everything, even to the piling up of vast mounds of stone just to see who could build the highest mound. They were the first of the Sangiks to travel southward toward Africa. Before they were wiped out by the green race, they were uplifted by the leadership of Porshunta of Armageddon. The orange race was destroyed one hundred thousand years ago.

The green race was weakened by extensive migrations. Those who went north were enslaved and absorbed by the yellow and blue men; those who went east were absorbed mainly into the Indian people but survive in greatest numbers in Burma and Indo-China. Those who traveled south killed off and absorbed their orange brothers, and the resultant mix was subsequently integrated into the indigo people. While the darker races are generally shorter in stature, unexpected strains of giantism appeared in both the orange and the green man.

The indigo race was the last of the Sangiks to migrate from the Indian highlands. After incorporating the orange and green remnants, they took over the African continent. The purer indigo elements drifted southward. Alone in Africa, they made little progress until they were spiritually awakened by their leader, Orvonon, who believed in the God of Gods. They maintained a form of worship of the Unknown up to a few thousand years ago.

Although there were intense struggles between the various races, different races appear on evolutionary worlds to provide an opportunity for natural selection, healthy competition, the blending of superior characteristics, and the promotion of altruism.

65—OVERCONTROL OF EVOLUTION

Evolution is always purposeful, never accidental. Its course is directed by the combined teamwork of the Master Physical Controllers, who manage the mechanical, non-teachable types of life; the Adjutant Mind Spirits, who activate and regulate teachable life; and the Life Carriers, who plant life and oversee it until the appearance of human will.

Life Carriers perform on three levels: the physical, the quasi-morontial, and the semi-spiritual. When Life Carriers have chosen the sites for life implantation, they are modified to function on the physical level. Having started life, Life Carriers are returned to a morontial phase from which they can manipulate and maneuver evolving life. When will creatures appear, the Life Carriers cease their attempts to steer the course of organic evolution.

Life Carriers take advantage of environmental conditions to guide evolving life in favorable directions. Having selected southeast Asia as the best site for early man to evolve, and knowing that good prehuman stocks were developing in the central life group, the Life Carriers led man's North American lemur ancestors across the Bering land bridge and into that central region where the two superior stocks could continue to evolve.

The appearance of man during the ice ages was intentional. The rigors of a cold climate produce hardiness in humans. If man's ancestor strains had perished, evolution would have been retarded but not prevented; Life Carriers were simultaneously fostering over a thousand mutating strains of potential pre-human life. Even the loss of Andon and Fonta would only have delayed the eventual appearance of human beings.

Evidence that life was intelligently planned is demonstrated by the way an injured cell throws off chemical substances to alert neighboring cells to create replacement cells. This healing method was chosen by the Life Carriers after half a million laboratory experiments. The appearance of the Andonic will creatures prior to the evolution of the six Sangik races was a planned experiment. Another was the simultaneous appearance of the six colored races in one family.

A major advance in the evolution of higher mammals was the development of the ability of iron to double as oxygen carrier and carbon dioxide remover. The fact that evolution is still in progress is illustrated by the evolution of teeth in higher mammals—while man's remote ancestors had thirty-six teeth, humans are now gravitating toward twenty-eight.

Experiments in plant evolution include the development of chlorophyll-making ability and the evolution of the spore into a complex seed. A great disappointment for the Life Carriers on Urantia was the reversion of certain plant forms to parasitic bacteria, which later caused diseases in higher mammals.

66—THE PLANETARY PRINCE OF URANTIA

Most worlds receive a Planetary Prince when primitive man is able to choose eternal survival, which usually does not happen until the colored race emerges. The task of a Planetary Prince is to begin to transform primitive man from hunter to herder to farmer.

Urantia's Planetary Prince, Caligastia, was a Lanonandek Son of the secondary order. He had acceptably managed five successive assignments prior to his arrival on earth. Caligastia arrived nearly five hundred thousand years after the arrival of the first will creatures, concurrent with the appearance of the six Sangik races.

Caligastia was invisible to the mortals of the realm. He was assisted by Daligastia, a fellow secondary Lanonandek Son. The two were accompanied by a group of one hundred ascendant Jerusem citizens. To rematerialize these volunteers into human form, the Life Carriers transferred life plasm from one hundred Andonites into bodies created for the Jerusem citizens. The contributing Andonites were given access to the system circuits, which enabled them to live for centuries alongside the Prince's staff.

Caligastia's headquarters, Dalamatia, was established near what is now the Persian Gulf. Dalamatia was a simple, beautiful city surrounded by a forty-foot wall. The modest buildings were neat and clean. Agricultural land within the city walls was sufficient for the support of twenty thousand people. A temple to the unseen Father was built at the center of the city.

The Prince's staff gathered superior individuals from the surrounding tribes, trained them in Dalamatia, and then returned them to their tribes as teachers and leaders. The staff was divided into ten councils.

1. *The council on food and material welfare* was led by Ang. This corps taught well digging and irrigation. They introduced weaving, improved methods of creating clothing from animal skins, and advanced cooking and food storage.

2. *The board of animal domestication and utilization* was directed by Bon. This council helped select and breed animals for transport, food, and soil. They trained carrier pigeons to send messages and fandors as passenger birds. This corps introduced the wheel to the human races.

3. *The advisers regarding the conquest of predatory animals* taught protection from wild animals and hostile humans. Captained by Dan, this group built the wall around Dalamatia to prevent surprise attacks. They trained people outside the walls to improve their dwellings and to make better animal traps.

4. *The faculty on dissemination and conservation of knowledge* formulated the first alphabet. They introduced a system of writing using tree barks, clay tablets, stone slabs, and parchment. The Dalamatia library was named the House of Fad in honor of the leader of this group.

5. *The commission on industry and trade* was led by Nod. This council provided many new commodities and expanded trade. They introduced commercial credit, using tokens from a central exchange to substitute for objects of barter.

6. *The college of revealed religion* attempted to substitute Creator fear for ghost worship. Led by Hap, they established a form of religious ser-

vice, providing the Dalamatians with seven chants of worship and a daily praise-phrase.

7. *The guardians of health and life* were organized by Lut. This council introduced sanitation and promoted hygiene. They taught cooking as a means of avoiding sickness, persuaded people to bathe, and encouraged them to substitute handshaking for saliva exchange and blood drinking.

8. *The planetary council on art and science* elevated ideas of beauty and gave men instruction in rudimentary physics and chemistry. Under Mek's guidance this corps advanced pottery and metal work. Decorative and home arts were improved; the ideals of human beauty were enhanced.

9. *The governors of advanced tribal relations* were commissioned to bring human society up to the level of statehood. Tut was the chief of this group, which promoted intertribal marriage, social dances, and competitive games. They attempted to regulate warfare and worked to improve tribal governments.

10. *The supreme court of tribal co-ordination and racial co-operation* was directed by Van. This council served as the court of appeals for the other nine councils, and was entrusted with all matters that were not specifically assigned to the other groups.

The inhabitants of Dalamatia lived in family units. The staff served as parents to adopted children from the superior families of the surrounding tribes. Industrial schools were set up in which students learned by doing useful manual tasks.

The Dalamatia teachers wisely refrained from attempts to radically modify the human way of life. The backward races had spent ages acquiring their religion and morals, and these superhuman teachers knew that only confusion would result by teaching their students more than they could understand. The Prince's staff desired progression by evolution rather than by revolution or revelation.

67—THE PLANETARY REBELLION

Caligastia had been in charge of Urantia for three hundred thousand years when Satan, Lucifer's assistant, arrived for an inspection. During this visit, Satan discussed Lucifer's proposed Declaration of Liberty with Caligastia. Caligastia decided to betray his planet by casting his lot with Lucifer.

Shortly after Satan's visit, Daligastia called a special session of the ten councils. Caligastia announced that he was appointing himself absolute sovereign of Urantia, and demanded that all administrative groups resign their powers to Daligastia.

Van, chairman of the council of coordination, objected to Caligastia's announcement, and petitioned the councilors to abstain from any action until an appeal could be taken to Lucifer. The appeal was made. In reply, Lucifer designated Caligastia as supreme sovereign. Van formally accused Daligastia, Caligastia, and Lucifer of being in contempt of universe sovereignty, and appealed to the Most Highs of Edentia. By the time the second appeal was sent out, the system circuits had been severed, and Urantia was isolated from outside counsel.

The rebellion determined the fate of every superhuman personality on the planet. Debates continued until every personality concerned had made a final decision in the matter. Sixty members of the Prince's staff sided with Lucifer. The remaining forty relocated to an unwalled settlement a few miles east of Dalamatia guarded constantly by loyal midway creatures. Angels took control of the tree of life.

The sixty rebels chose Nod as their leader. They soon discovered that they had been degraded to mortal status. Daligastia, knowing that they would eventually die, ordered them to begin sexual reproduction. The disloyal staff migrated north and east; their descendants were long known as Nodites. We do not know the fate of the original sixty, although their Adjusters still tarry on Jerusem.

Caligastia's scheme for the reconstruction of human society proved a swift and complete failure. Liberty was quickly translated into license by the semi-savage population. One hundred and sixty-two years after the rebellion, a tidal wave washed over Dalamatia and the headquarters sank beneath the sea.

Van's followers moved to the highlands west of India where they planned for the rehabilitation of the world. Under the temporary leadership of the senior Life Carriers, Van divided his staff into ten councils of four along the lines of the Prince's staff. Van's people provided leadership until the days of Adam and Eve. Van remained on Urantia until the times of Adam and Eve.

68—THE DAWN OF CIVILIZATION

Civilization is a human acquirement; it is not biologically inherent. Its scientific, philosophic and religious qualities are transmitted from one generation to the next only by enlightened conservation.

Cooperation is not a natural human trait. It was first introduced by the Dalamatia teachers, who nurtured man in the idea of group activities for three hundred thousand years. Early men soon learned to appreciate the strength of union. They developed group associations primarily for survival reasons; civilization provided insurance against violent death. Hunger, sex, and fear were additional influences that prompted association between humans.

The family, the first successful group, satisfied the sex urge in males and maternal devotion in females. Women maintained settled homes where they could cultivate food. Men and women learned to adjust their antagonisms to ensure the survival of the species.

The greatest single factor in the evolution of human society was the ghost dream. Early people were afraid of dreams, and dread of the departed dead gave them special terror. Their senseless superstitions caused them to band tightly together for protection.

Urantia has had four stages of civilization. Early men sustained themselves by gleaning food from the land. The invention of tools made hunting for food possible; learning to cure meat was a forward step during the hunting era. Further liberation occurred during the pastoral stage, when the domestication of animals gave humans more time to devote to culture and progress. The highest type of material civilization was brought about through the cultivation of plants—horticulture.

69—PRIMITIVE HUMAN INSTITUTIONS

Long standing human social groups tend to culminate in institutionalization. Human institutions minister to social needs in three general classes. *Institutions of self-maintenance* grow out of hunger and self-preservation; they include industry, property, and war for gain. *Institutions of self-perpetuation* grow out of sex hunger, maternal instincts and the higher emotions, and comprise home-building, marriage customs, education, religion, and war for defense. *Institutions of self-gratification* grow out of vanity and pride; these embrace dress customs, war for glory, dancing, amusements, and games.

Poverty is man's natural estate; wealth springs from labor, knowledge, and organization. Primitive men disliked hard work, but the necessity of labor was early man's greatest blessing because it stimulated effort and industriousness. Primitive divisions of labor evolved based on sex, age, religion, and physical and mental endowments.

The first traders were women. The beginnings of trade and industry inspired innovations such as weights, units of barter, and the art of writing; the first human literature was a salt advertisement. New ideas were carried around the world by traders. Commerce, linked with adventure, led to exploration and discovery, improved methods of communication, the birth of transportation, and cultural cross-fertilization. People began to store food and other goods for future use. Military organization stemmed from the desire to protect and increase individual and group wealth.

Fire was a great civilizer of early humans. Fire made evening social intercourse more pleasant and enabled people to stay on the ground at night. It protected against cold and wild beasts, and was thought to protect against ghosts. People learned to be watchful and dependable by keeping watch over the family hearth. Fire led to cooking, opened the door to metal-working, and led to the eventual discovery of steam power and electricity. Andon did not worship fire, but many of his descendants regarded it as a fetish.

Humans learned to protect themselves from animals, then to domesticate them and put them to work. Men herded animals to insure a food supply. Animals that were easily tamed and that bred well in captivity were chosen for selective breeding. The first domesticated animal was the dog, which for ages was used for food, hunting, transportation, and companionship.

Slavery was an indispensable link in the chain of human civilization. Slavery temporarily created culture and social achievement. It enforced human industriousness and gave origin to the beginnings of government. Early slavery represented an advancement in mores from the times when prisoners were eaten, tortured, or sacrificed.

Primitive society was communal. The tribe owned all property, including women, tools and weapons. Among the first personal possessions were utensils, charms, sleeping spaces, and water holes. Communal life gave way to the concept of private property. The private ownership of property has been the nucleus of government, law, order, civil rights, peace, and happiness.

70—THE EVOLUTION OF HUMAN GOVERNMENT

Government evolves by trial and error. On an evolutionary world, peace is secured only by the development of a system to regulate social behavior. The natural antagonisms between tribes, clans, families, and individuals call for regulation and coordination. The development of industry demands law and order; private property requires government.

War, an animalistic reaction to misunderstandings and irritations, is the natural state of evolving man.

Though costly and dangerous, war contributes many benefits to society. It fosters discipline, cooperation, and courage, and accelerates social changes. But war, like slavery, must be abandoned as civilization advances. War will continue until people create adequate substitutes for the benefits that war provides.

Industrialism can triumph over militarism if we avoid the dangers of the worship of wealth, indolence, biologic deterioration, and industrial slavery. Peace will be promoted more efficiently by international trade organizations than by visionary planning. Trade relations improve through advances in language, communication, and transportation.

The first peaceful group was the family, then the clan, the tribe, and the nation. The first government was a council of distinguished elders. During wartime, the efficiency of having a single leader led to having one ruler of the tribe acting as chief executive. Councils of elders became the legislative and judicial branches of government. Effective state rule came when chiefs or kings were given full executive authority.

The inequality of human beings insures that social classes will appear. The only worlds without social strata are the most primitive and the most advanced. Flexible social classes are indispensable to an evolving civilization, but when class becomes caste, it curtails individual development. Classes will persist until people obliterate them through education, by eliminating inferior human strains, and through religious awareness of human brotherhood.

Nature conferred no rights on humans, only life and a world in which to live. So-called human rights are social concepts that change from age to age. During the European middle ages every man belonged to someone else; rights were favors granted to individuals by the church or state. The revolt from this error led to the equally erroneous belief that all men are born equal. The weak may insist that the state compel the strong to make up for their deficiencies, but this equality is not found in nature.

Justice as conceived by humans has been a matter of progressive evolution. Early administration of justice included trial by ordeal. Suicide was a common form of retaliation, because people believed that as a ghost they could return and visit wrath on their enemies.

Justice was first meted out by the family, then the clan, and later the tribe. True justice appears when revenge is taken from private hands and is administered by the state. When society fails to punish crimes, group resentment may assert itself through lynch law. The thoroughness and equity of the courts and the integrity of judges accurately determine the status of a civilization.

Law in advancing civilization becomes increasingly positive and directive. The ideal government for evolutionary people is a representative system where leadership is based on ability and where a proper balance of power is maintained between the executive, legislative, and judicial branches.

If people are to maintain their freedom, their government must prevent the following pitfalls: usurpation of unwarranted power by any one branch of government; machinations of ignorant agitators; retardation of scientific progress; the dominance of mediocrity; domination by vicious minorities; control by would-be dictators; taxation enslavement of the citizenry by the state; social and economic unfairness; union of church and state; and loss of personal liberty.

71—Development of the State

The state is not of divine origin, nor was it purposely produced by intelligent human action. It is an evolution of civilization that regulates social interaction and represents society's net gain after the devastation of war.

An enduring state needs to have common language, mores, and institutions. Strong states are held together by several factors, including private property, cities, agriculture, domestication of animals, patriarchal family units, a clearly defined territory, and strong rulers. Democracy is an ideal but has inherent dangers, one of which is the glorification of mediocrity. Democracy is a product of civilization rather than of evolution.

The ideal state is guided by the realization of human brotherhood, intelligent patriotism, and cosmic insight. It should provide for liberty, security, education, and social coordination. Society will not progress well if it permits idleness and poverty, but poverty will never be eliminated if degenerate stocks are freely supported and permitted to reproduce without restraint. A government must evolve if it is to survive.

An ideal society cannot be realized while the weak are allowed to take unfair advantage of idealists. People must live according to their ideals while maintaining adequate defense against those who may seek to exploit them. The test of the idealism of a government is the maintenance of military preparedness for defense but never for offense.

Profit motives are necessary to keep people at work, but profit motives must be augmented by service motives. In the ideal state, education continues throughout life. Philosophy, the search for wisdom, may become the chief pursuit of citizens. Control of education must be taken from lawyers and businessmen and entrusted to philosophers and scientists.

The only sacred feature of government is its division into executive, legislative and judicial domains; the universe is administered in accordance with such a plan. Apart from this divine concept, the form of government is not as important as the fact that its citizenry is ever progressing toward the goal of augmented self-control and increased social service.

The earmarks of ideal statehood are: the executive, legislative, and judicial branches; freedom of social, political, and religious activities; abolition of human bondage; citizen's control of taxation; universal lifelong education; proper adjustment between local and national government; fostering of science; conquest of disease; sexual equality; use of machines to reduce drudgery; universal language; end of war; and exaltation of the pursuit of wisdom.

72—Government on a Neighboring Planet

While it is most unusual for the system rulers to divulge information to one planet about the affairs of another, the revelators were granted permission to reveal something of the social, moral, and political life of a neighboring planet in the Satania system. This world, like Urantia, suffered from the disloyalty of the Lucifer rebellion and the default of its Material Son and Daughter.

On this neighboring planet, a superior civilization of one hundred and forty million people is evolving on an isolated continent about the size of Australia. The people are a mixture the blue, yellow, and violet races. Due to favorable climatic factors, natural resources, and advances in science, the society has become self-sustaining.

Cities are limited to one million inhabitants and are administered by the most advanced citizens. Their representative central government is divided into executive, judicial, and legislative branches. The central government oversees a federation of one hundred states. The federal chief executive is elected by the people and is advised by a team comprised of every living former chief executive.

This nation has two major court systems. Law courts decide cases on local, state and federal levels, while socioeconomic courts enforce laws affecting home, school, and economics. People regard the home as the basic institution of civilization. The smallest home site permitted is fifty thousand square feet. Families have an average of five children, and attendance of parents at parental schools is compulsory.

Instruction in sex and religion is done at home, although some moral instruction is provided by teachers at school. There are no churches. Religion is thought of as the striving to know God and to manifest love for one's fellows through service.

Children remain legally subject to their parents until they are fifteen. They can marry with parental consent and vote when they are twenty, and marry without parental consent at twenty-five. Permission to marry is granted after one year's notice and completion of training for the responsibilities of married life. All children must leave home by their thirtieth year.

Education is compulsory from ages five to eighteen. All students become assistant teachers, instructing those behind them. There are no classrooms; books are used only to find information to solve problems in the school shops and farms. The feeble-minded are trained only for agriculture and are segregated by sex to prevent parenthood. Students spend a quarter of the school day participating in competitive athletics. At the age of eighteen, each child graduates as a skilled artisan and self-supporting citizen; only then do they begin the study of books and pursuit of specialized knowledge. Special schools after compulsory education include those for statesmanship, philosophy, science, professions, and military training.

Industry operates on a thirty-hour week. Everyone takes vacation for one month of the ten-month year. The profit motive is being displaced by higher ideals; public service is becoming the chief goal of ambition. People must retire at sixty-five. Slavery has been abolished for over one hundred years, and the nation has turned its attention to reducing the number of degenerates.

The federal government cannot go into debt except in the case of war. Federal income is derived from five sources: import duties, royalties, inheritance taxes, leasing of military equipment, and natural resources. Every person over twenty years old has one vote. Those who have rendered great service to society and those who pay heavy taxes can have additional votes conferred upon them. Prisoners and government employees are not allowed to vote.

These people are passing from the negative to the positive era of law. Ordinary criminals and defectives are segregated by sex and placed in self-supporting agricultural colonies. Serious habitual offenders and the incurably insane are swiftly sentenced to death. Efforts to prevent breeding of criminals and defectives have been successful; there are no prisons or hospitals for the insane.

Courses pursued in the military schools include military training and professional mastery. During industrial slumps, unemployed people build military defenses; during periods of peace the mobile defense mechanisms are fully employed in trade, commerce, and recreation. This nation has not launched an offensive war in more than one hundred years, but has defended itself nine times in that period against the less advanced surrounding nations.

While in some ways this nation's society is superior to that of Urantia nations, it has not benefited by magisterial or bestowal missions of the Paradise Sons. Since Urantia has been blessed with the Spirit of Truth, it is better prepared for the more immediate realization of a planetary government.

73—THE GARDEN OF EDEN

The setbacks resulting from the Lucifer rebellion did not affect the biologic evolution of the human race, which approached its apex in 40,000

BC. The Life Carriers and Melchizedek receivers jointly petitioned the Most Highs for the immediate dispatch of biologic uplifters, and within a hundred years a Material Son and Daughter arrived on earth.

During this year, only the Nodites and the Amadonites retained traces of the Dalamatia culture. The rest of the world had reverted to the savagery of pre-Planetary Prince days. The most advanced and civilized races were settled near the Caspian Sea, Lake Van, and the eastern Mediterranean.

Van had been predicting the arrival of a Material Son and Daughter for nearly one hundred years. He dispatched a committee to find an optimal site for establishing a garden home for them. The site chosen for the garden of Eden was a peninsula—almost an island—projecting westward from the eastern shore of the Mediterranean Sea. The climate was ideal. A great river, fed by four tributaries, ran from the high lands and flowed east to the mainland.

Van and his associates spent two years transferring the world's cultural headquarters from the Indian highlands to the chosen peninsula. Three thousand volunteers began the construction of the garden homeland. Plans provided for homes and land for up to one million people. At the center of the Garden stood a temple of the Universal Father. To the north lay the administrative headquarters; to the south, the homes of the workers and their families; to the west, grounds for the proposed Adamic schools; and to the east, homes for Adam and Eve and their children. Drinking water was purified and all waste was scrupulously buried until a sewage-disposal system was established. Fruits, vegetables, and nuts were cultivated and improved. By the time Adam arrived, Eden had thousands of miles of irrigation ditches and over twenty-five thousand miles of paved roads.

Van planted the long-guarded tree of life in the center of the garden temple. Native to constellation headquarters spheres, the tree of life was a super-plant that stored certain space energies. Its fruit provided life-extension to the Prince's staff and their modified human associates, and Adam and Eve depended on it for their sustenance.

After the fall of Adam and Eve, the garden of Eden fell into the possession of Nodites. Eventually the temple and the tree were destroyed by fire. The Garden was occupied for four thousand years until geologic upheavals caused the peninsula to sink into the sea.

74—ADAM AND EVE

Adam and Eve had been employed in the physical laboratories of Jerusem for fifteen thousand years when they were selected for their mission to Urantia. The volunteer pool from which they were chosen included the entire senior corps of Material Sons and Daughters. Adam and Eve were thoroughly instructed concerning every danger and duty awaiting them on their strife-torn planet.

Leaving behind fifty sons and fifty daughters, Adam and Eve left Edentia for Earth almost thirty-eight thousand years ago. After being re-materialized in the Father's temple, they were greeted by Van, Amadon, and a large audience of supporters. Adam spoke to the Garden dwellers of his plans for the rehabilitation of the world. Concurrent with their formal installation as the new rulers of the world, the broadcast voice of Gabriel decreed that a new dispensation—the Age of Adam—had begun, and the sleeping survivors from the age of the Planetary Prince were resurrected on the mansion worlds.

Adam and Eve's second day on Urantia was spent learning details of the tragic history of the planet. On subsequent days they toured the garden, addressed the garden assembly, organized a temporary government, and inspected the various men and animals. On the seventh day they rested. The fable that our planet was created in six days was based on this period of time that Adam and Eve spent in surveying the Garden.

The Garden dwellers wholeheartedly accepted Adam and Eve as their rulers. After seven years, the Melchizedeks returned to Jerusem. Van and Amadon, who had been on Urantia for over four hundred and fifty thousand years, left with the Melchizedeks. The Material Son and Daughter were alone with their enormous task.

Eve bore sixty-three children who enjoyed a great appreciation for music, play, and humor. They attended school until they were sixteen, were betrothed at eighteen, and were allowed to marry at twenty.

The purpose of the schools of Eden was socialization. Younger children were taught by their siblings about healthcare, the golden rule, the relationship of individual rights to group rights, the history and cultures of the earth races, world trade, coordination of conflicting duties, play, humor, and competitive substitutes for fighting. Mornings were devoted to horticulture and agriculture, afternoons to competitive play, and evenings to developing social skills and friendships. Public worship was at noon, family worship at sunset.

For a while all went fairly well. Adam and Eve tried to teach sex equality and to improve worship by substituting offerings of fruit for animal sacrifice. They fostered trade relations and manufacturing, and began to establish laws and social organization. Yet whenever they tried to work outside the Garden, trouble arose. Caligastia, still present on earth, resisted all plans for the rehabilitation of society. Although Adam had a difficult task leading these mixed and mongrel savages in the better way, the more intelligent of the races looked forward to a future time when they would be permitted to intermarry with the children of the violet race.

75—The Default of Adam and Eve

Adam and Eve had labored in the Garden for over one hundred years with little progress, and their isolation weighed heavily on them. The situation Adam and Eve faced seemed so desperate that Adam wondered whether that the solution to their dilemma lay outside the ordained plan.

Caligastia was still titular Planetary Prince and was able to influence the minds of planetary inhabitants. He paid many visits to the Garden, but Adam and Eve resisted his suggestions for compromise and shortcuts. Caligastia soon gave up on Adam and began to focus on Eve.

Eve did not realize that Caligastia intended to exploit her friendship with a brilliant Nodite named Serapatatia, the leader of the most powerful and intelligent of the neighboring Nodite tribes. Serapatatia was deeply impressed with Adam's cause and announced his support for the Adamic program for world improvement. Adam and Eve were greatly cheered by his assistance; Serapatatia became one of the most efficient of Adam's lieutenants.

One day it occurred to Serapatatia that it would be helpful if something could be done immediately to advance world affairs while they waited for the violet race to increase. He reminded Eve that Adam was discouraged by the lack of progress in their mission. Serapatatia contended that a violet leader born to the Nodite race would constitute a powerful tie binding the Nodites to the Garden. After five years, Eve consented to meet secretly with Cano, a magnificent descendant of the Prince's staff, the most brilliant leader of a nearby colony of friendly Nodites.

Cano was wholly sympathetic to Adam and Eve's cause. Eve told Cano that she had been warned not to combine good and evil. Cano, not knowing the importance of such warnings, assured her that men and women with good motives could do no evil. Induced by flattery and personal persuasion, Eve mated with Cano.

The celestial life on the planet was astir; Adam recognized something was amiss. He confronted Eve and heard her plan for accelerating world improvement. It was then that Solonia, the "voice in the Garden," announced Eve's default. Eve's disillusionment was pathetic. Adam was heartbroken. He knew Eve had been reduced to mortal status. The thought of remaining on Urantia without her was unbearable; Adam chose to share her fate by mating with Laotta, a brilliant Nodite woman.

When the Garden inhabitants learned what had happened to Eve, they destroyed the nearby Nodite settlement, killing the entire tribe including Cano. Serapatatia, overcome with remorse, drowned himself. Adam wandered in solitude for thirty days, leaving his children to comfort their distraught mother.

Seventy days later, the Melchizedek receivers returned to the planet to resume jurisdiction. Adam and Eve knew their mission had failed.

When news of the annihilation of the Nodite settlement reached the home tribes of Serapatatia, an army assembled to march on the Garden. Adam sought advice from the Melchizedeks. They refused to intervene, promising only to cooperate with whatever path he chose. After an all-night conference with twelve hundred loyal followers, Adam elected to leave the Garden unopposed.

The next morning these sad pilgrims left Eden on a quest for a new home. On the third day their caravan was halted by the arrival of seraphic transports from Jerusem, who had come to take Adam and Eve's young children to Edentia. The grown children were given a choice to remain with their parents or go to Edentia. One third of the adults elected to remain with Adam and Eve; the rest, along with every child under the age of twenty, were transported to Edentia. Gabriel appeared to pronounce judgment on the Material Son and Daughter. Adam and Eve were officially in default and were reduced to mortal status.

Although Adam and Eve failed, there has been no "fall of man." On the contrary, the human race has profited enormously from the limited contribution made by Adam and Eve and their descendants.

76—The Second Garden

The Adamic caravan fled eastward to avoid the advancing hostile Nodites. Laden with seeds, cereals, bulbs, and herds, they set out on their journey. After a year the caravan reached one of the three sites originally proposed for the first Garden by Van and Amadon, a pleasant region between the Tigris and Euphrates rivers. During the journey Laotta died during childbirth; Eve delivered Cain, the offspring of her union with Cano.

In their new location Adam and his helpers built houses and established a new center of culture and religion. It was a difficult struggle, as the land had not been prepared for sowing. Adam, busy with building, defense, and agriculture, entrusted the organization of worship and education to the Nodite priests. In a short time the religious practices of the second Garden reverted to the standards and rulings of pre-Adamic times.

The first child of Adam and Eve to be born in the second Garden was Abel, who arrived two years after Cain. Cain chose agriculture as his vocation and Abel devoted himself to herding. The brothers often argued about whose occupation had more value, and when Abel was eighteen his repeated taunts infuriated Cain so much that Cain killed Abel.

Fear and remorse prompted Cain to seek help from Eve. In response to his honest appeal for divine guidance, Cain received a Thought Adjuster. Soon thereafter he departed for the land of Nod, where he married his distant cousin Remona. Cain matured to become a leader of his people, promoting peace between the Adamites and Nodites.

The violet race had blue eyes, fair complexions, and blonde, red, or brown hair. They did not suffer during childbirth until they became mixed with other races. The original Adamites' superior physical and spiritual senses enabled them to see midwayers, angels, and Mel-chize-deks. The Adamic children were usually Adjuster-indwelt. Their body cells, not being akin to the microscopic disease-producing organisms of the realm, were far more disease resistant than those of the indigenous peoples.

Adam spent most of his time teaching civil administration, educational methods, and religious devotions. The Garden dwellers developed an alphabet and maintained the arts of writing, metalworking, pottery making, weaving and architecture. Children were educated in agriculture, craftsmanship, and animal husbandry.

The line of civil rulers was drawn from Adam and Eve's sons. One son founded a secondary center of the violet race to the north, another became a great leader and administrator, and a third took over after Adam's death as head of the Adamic tribes. The religious rulers sprang from their son Seth and his descendants, who worked to improve the spiritual status of the Adamites and the surrounding tribes. Each Sethite was a physician and teacher as well as a priest.

After becoming established in Mesopotamia, Adam chose to leave behind as many children as possible to uplift the world's genetic stock. Eve selected nearly seventeen hundred women from the neighboring tribes to be impregnated. The resultant children, representing most of the races on earth, were born and raised in the tribes of their mothers.

Adam and Eve's mistake was an error in judgment, but it was not deliberate rebellion. Their human status coupled with sincere repentance enabled them to become Adjuster-indwelt, and this greatly comforted them. Eve lived on earth for 511 years; Adam died nineteen years later. After their deaths, Adam and Eve were repersonalized on the mansion worlds and quickly passed through the ascension worlds, attaining citizenship once again on Jerusem. They left their home in Jerusem as sons of God and returned as sons of man.

77—The Midway Creatures

Most inhabited worlds harbor groups of unique beings who fall into a category between humans and angels. These midway creatures are valuable helpers and are an essential order of planetary ministers. On Urantia there are two types: primary midwayers, whose origin dates back to early Dalamatia, and secondary midwayers, who came into existence during the days of Adam.

The physical members of the Prince's staff, though capable of sexual reproduction, had been ordered not to procreate. It came as a surprise to them when, as the result of a non-sexual liaison between a male and a female, the first of the primary midwayers appeared. Upon the discovery that such a creature could be of great service, permission was granted for each couple to produce a similar being. Eventually fifty thousand midway creatures were produced. These midwayers became Caligastia's intelligence corps, studying and observing the human races. They rendered invaluable service in the work of influencing human society.

The secondary midwayers also sprang partially from the Nodite race. The Life Carriers had projected that the flesh-and-blood staff members would sometime mate with the best of the Andonites. They planned that resultant offspring would mate with the first generation of Adam and Eve's children to produce a new order of teacher-rulers.

It was assumed that the Prince's staff, having bodies generated by the plasm of the Andonites, would have children resembling other Andonites. But when the rebel members of the Prince's staff resorted to sexual reproduction, their offspring proved to have superior mental, physical, and spiritual capacity. These children became the ancestors of the magnificent Nodite race, the "mighty men of old."

After the sinking of Dalamatia, the Nodites founded the city of Dilmun as their new racial and cultural headquarters. Gradually the pure-line Nodites intermingled with the evolutionary races and dispersed to form three great Nodite centers: The western, or Syrian Nodites, moved north and mated with the Andonites; the eastern, or Elamite Nodites, settled near Mesopotamia in "the land of Nod"; and the central Nodites eventually blended with Adamites to establish the Sumerian culture. A fourth strong Nodite center to the north was made up of the loyal followers of Van who had established their center of culture around the shores of Lake Van.

Among the children of Adam who elected to stay on earth after the default of his parents was Adamson, the first-born son. Adamson's wife and children had chosen to be transported to Edentia. When he was 120 years old, Adamson traveled north from the second Garden in search of the highland home of Van. Here he met a beautiful woman, Ratta, who claimed to be the last pure-line descendant of the fallen staff members. Within three months Ratta and Adamson were married.

Adamson and Ratta had sixty-seven children and founded a great line of world leaders. Sixteen of these children were of a unique order, often invisible. Ratta was perturbed by and even superstitious of these strange children, but Adamson well knew of the primary midwayers and concluded that these children were somewhat similar to the original midway creatures. He decided to mate male and female; their progeny constituted the origin of the secondary midwayers. The eight sets of male and female children of Ratta and Adamson lived and died as mortals, but produced 1,984 immortal secondary midway creatures. Adamson and Ratta had the benefit of these wonderful helpers throughout their long lives. Adamson lived for 396 years. The culture he and Ratta founded near the Caspian Sea lasted for almost seven thousand years.

After the death of Adamson, the secondary midwayers became disorganized. Over forty thousand primary midwayers and nine hundred secondary midwayers were influenced by the philosophy of Lucifer and fell into rebellion against the local universe government. These midwayers are now in custody, waiting for the final adjudication of the case against Lucifer.

The United Midwayers of Urantia currently function as a single corps numbering 10,992. Their motto is: "What the United Midwayers undertake, the United Midwayers do." They are able to follow human humor and worship, and enter into the spirit of mortal work, rest, and play. They do not sleep or procreate.

Primary midwayers are more like angels than humans. Secondary midwayers are nearer to humans than angels; they exist just outside the range of mortal vision. They can make contact with material things, and have power over the things of time and space. Many acts attributed to angels have been performed by secondary midwayers.

78—THE VIOLET RACE
AFTER THE DAYS OF ADAM

Apart from the Nodite centers, most of the world languished in savagery when the second Garden was established in Mesopotamia. For ten thousand years the Adamic people labored peacefully along the rivers, working on irrigation and flood-control, perfecting their defenses, and preserving the culture of Adam.

The major Adamic migrations began around 25,000 BC. The two largest populations of the violet race were the Adamites in Mesopotamia and the Adamsonites on the southern shores of the Caspian Sea. The purer Nodites, pre-Sumerians, were in Mesopotamia.

The Andonites maintained representative settlements to the north of the Adamsonites and in Turkestan. Isolated Andonite groups persisted throughout Eurasia, Iceland, and Greenland, but they had been driven out of Europe and Asia. The red man occupied the Americas, the yellow race was in control of Asia, and the blue man held Europe. A blended mixture of all six colored races, mainly green, orange, and indigo, settled in pre-Dravidian India; an indigo-black group carrying submerged strains of green and orange had their most progressive settlements in the Sahara desert. A highly blended race of Saharans, blue men, and Nodites occupied the Mediterranean basin.

The early pure-line Adamic migrants scattered in three directions. Some went west into the valley of the Nile. A few penetrated eastward into Asia. The largest contingent of the violet people moved northward around the Caspian Sea into Europe. As they moved into Eurasia, the Adamites absorbed the best of the Nodites and Andonites. By 15,000 BC, more descendants of Adam inhabited Eurasia that any other region on earth. The stage was set for the emergence of the Andites.

The Andite race took origin in the regions near Mesopotamia. They were a blend of pure-line violet and Nodites, mixed with the best strains of the yellow, blue, and green men. They were pre-Aryan and pre-white, neither Occidental nor Oriental. When the deteriorated Nodites added a belligerent strain to the Andite mix, migrations began to take the form of military conquests.

The Andite migrations occurred from 15,000 to 6,000 BC, mainly into Europe. By 12,000 BC three quarters of the Andites in the world were in northern and eastern Europe. Others had infiltrated China, India, Egypt, and both coasts of Africa. One hundred and thirty-two Andites traveled in boats from Japan to South America and founded the ancestry of the Incas. Others stopped permanently in the Pacific islands and mixed with the native groups there. As the Andites poured out of Mesopotamia, they strengthened the surrounding cultures, contributing art, music, manufacturing, agriculture, and the domestication of animals.

When the last three waves of Andites left Mesopotamia between 8000 and 6000 BC, the center of world civilization moved to the Nile and the Mediterranean. Five percent of the purer Andites remained in their Mesopotamian homeland and became the Sumerians—Nodite by culture and Andite by inheritance.

Barbarians of Turkestan and the Iranian peninsula, driven south by drought, invaded the Euphrates valley and assimilated the remainder of the Andites, taking over all except the Sumerian settlement. The resultant mix became the Babylonians, who adopted the arts of the valley tribes and much of the culture of the Sumerians. About 2500 BC, the Sumerians were conquered by invading northerners and subsequently were absorbed into the Semite race.

79—ANDITE EXPANSION IN THE ORIENT

Until 2000 BC, central Eurasia was predominantly Andite. The Andite centers of culture were located in the then-fertile Tarim River valleys and in the highlands of Tibet. Traders began to appear about 15,000 BC. Urban life, together with commerce in stone, metal, wood, and pottery, began to flourish. Adonia, located near the present-day city of Ashkhabad, became the Asian center of commerce.

Andites had been slowly filtering northward into Europe for many centuries, but by 8000 BC the aridity of the highlands began to drive them southward to the shores of the Nile, Euphrates, Indus, and Yellow rivers. Extensive migrations beginning in 15,000 BC brought Andites into India where all of the Urantia races, mainly the secondary Sangiks, had blended. An infusion of Andite blood resulted in a mixed people called the Dravidians, the most versatile civilization of their time.

The Dravidians were among the earliest people to build cities. They engaged in extensive trade by land and sea, and Dravidian commercial relationships greatly contributed to the further diversification of their culture. Much of their religious life stemmed from the teachings of Sethite priests who had entered India with the early Andite and later Aryan invasions.

Diminishing rainfall to the north drove the Andonites southward and forced the terminal exodus of Andites from their Turkestan homelands into the Eastern hemisphere. The final exodus of the Andites from Turkestan to India occurred around 2500 BC. These Aryan Andites greatly influenced culture and religion throughout India, but made little racial impression in India except in the north. The most characteristic feature of their society was an elaborate caste system, formed to preserve their racial identity. Brahmans of today are the cultural descendants of the Sethite teacher-priests.

China's story is primarily of two Sangik races, the red and the yellow, both of which largely avoided the Neanderthal race that had retarded the blue race of Europe. The red man moved around the highlands of

India into eastern Asia and ruled there for almost one hundred thousand years.

About three hundred thousand years ago, the yellow race entered China from the south and invaded the hunting grounds of the red men. For over two hundred thousand years these two races waged war. The yellow race assimilated much of the red stock, and eventually the united strength of the yellow race drove the red race—greatly weakened by a tendency to fight among themselves—out of China into North America across the Bering land bridge. The North American red men thereafter remained relatively isolated from the rest of the world.

In China, the expanding yellow race drove out the remaining Andonites. The strength of the yellow race was due to four factors: they had largely escaped mixture with inferior stocks; they valued peace among themselves; they had inherent spiritual tendencies; and they were protected geographically by mountains to the west and an ocean to the east.

Fifteen thousand years ago, the migrating Andites had begun to spread over the upper valleys of the Yellow River. The northern Chinese received enough of the Adamic strain to stimulate their minds, but not enough to cause the restless curiosity so characteristic of the white races. By 10,000 BC, the Chinese were beginning to build cities and engage in manufacture. Similarities between Chinese and Mesopotamian methods of time-reckoning, astronomy, and government administration sprang from their commercial relationships. The yellow race progressed in agriculture and horticulture, but the cumbersome nature of their writing system limited the numbers of their educated classes.

As time passed, the Chinese search for new truth became overshadowed by a tendency to venerate established ideas. The stability of Chinese family groups helped conserve wealth, property and experience, and promoted morality, ethics, and the efficient education of children.

80—ANDITE EXPANSION IN THE OCCIDENT

Thirty-five thousand years ago, the blue people of Europe were a highly blended race carrying strains of both yellow and red. The Adamites used a route around the Caspian Sea to enter Europe, where they united with the higher members of the blue race. The resultant mixture produced a dozen groups of superior blue men, including those whom we know today as Cro-Magnons.

The blue men were vigorous, honest, courageous, and monogamous. They were hunters, fishers, food gatherers, and boat builders; they made stone axes and cut trees to build log huts. The women were well versed in domestic arts and agriculture. Children were trained in the care of caves, art, and flint-making. The blue race had strong artistic tendencies, and the addition of Adamic blood accelerated their creativity.

Climatic changes fifteen thousand years ago altered the European landscape, turning the open grazing lands into Alpine forest. Hunters became herders, fishers, and farmers. By this time the pure Adamites worldwide had become thoroughly blended with the other races, particularly the Nodites, to produce the Andites.

The next twelve thousand years saw seven major Andite invasions into Europe from Mesopotamia and Turkestan. The Andites were aggressive militarists. The use of horses during the final three invasions increased Andite mobility enough to allow them to maintain coherent groups as they entered Europe, where they absorbed the best of the blue people and exterminated the worst of them. The racial mixing that resulted from these invasions produced the ancestors of the Nordic races: Scandinavians, Germans, and Anglo-Saxons.

For three thousand years, successive military campaigns were launched from Andite headquarters established in Denmark. The resultant early white men moved continuously southward, finally wiping out the last remnants of the Cro-Magnoid race in southern France. By 5000 BC, the evolving white race dominated northern Europe.

When the last exodus from the Euphrates occurred, many skilled Andite artisans moved to Egypt, which had received a steady stream of Mesopotamians for thousands of years. The Nodites introduced pottery, agriculture, metalwork, and domesticated animals to the Nile region. By 5000 BC, the cultural center of the world had shifted from Mesopotamia to the valley of the Nile. The Andites built the first stone structures and pyramids in Egypt. They developed an extensive theology and a burdensome priesthood.

About 12,000 BC, a brilliant tribe of Andites migrated to Crete. They were highly skilled in textiles, metals, pottery, plumbing, building with stone, writing, herding, and agriculture. Two thousand years later a group of tall, beautiful, intelligent descendants of Adamson journeyed from their highland home over the northern Aegean islands into Greece. A high civilization evolved. Presently Greece and the Aegean succeeded

Egypt as the center of world culture. The Greeks were great teachers, artists, traders, and colonizers. Advances earned by Greek civilization persisted in southern Europe even after the Greek culture itself declined under the weight of the rapidly multiplying descendants of imported slaves.

The Andonites had always inhabited the mountainous regions of central Europe and the Danube valley where they farmed and herded, made pottery, and tilled the land. They were often reinforced by Andonites from Asia Minor. By 3000 BC, the Asian Andonites, who had been pushed farther and farther to the north and into central Asia, were being driven by drought conditions back into Turkestan. Here they split and penetrated Europe through both the Balkans and the Ukraine, carrying with them the remaining Andites from Iran and Turkestan. By 2500 BC the Asian Andonites had overrun Mesopotamia, Asia Minor and the Danube basin, where they united with the older Andonites. It was during these great nomadic invasions that a great expansion of sea traffic and trade permeated the Mediterranean coast lands.

Three white races were in Europe at the close of the Andite migrations. The *northern* or Nordic race consisted of the blue and Andite races, with small amounts of red and yellow Sangik. The early Nordic people were tall, long-headed, and blond. The *central* group was predominantly Andonite with strains of blue, yellow, and Andite. Their descendants were broad-headed, swarthy, and stocky. The *southern* white race was largely Andite and blue with a considerable Saharan strain. It has been impossible to identify these distinctions for several thousand years.

81—DEVELOPMENT OF MODERN CIVILIZATION

The human race is made up of five basic racial stocks—Andonic, primary Sangik, secondary Sangik, Nodite, and Adamic—each of which could at one time be identified by distinct skeletal types. Extensive blending over the past twenty thousand years has resulted in mankind being divided into three basic groups: Caucasoid, Mongoloid, and Negroid.

Biologic evolution may advance in the absence of culture, but culture does not flourish without prior racial progression. The violet race improved human brain capacity and hastened natural evolution. The infusion of violet blood caused advances in civilization that exceeded the total biologic progress of the previous million years.

Early important events contributed greatly to the growth of human civilization. The taming of fire gave birth to modern science. The domestication of dogs, horses, sheep, goats, cows, camels, fowl, elephants, oxen, and yak lightened the human work load. Through agriculture, animal domestication, and improved architecture, mankind gradually began to seek higher standards of living.

About 12,000 BC, trade and manufacturing began to promote cross-fertilization of cultures. Two thousand years later, the era of independent cities dawned. Commerce quickly became the most effective influence in the spread of civilization. Military conquests, colonization, and missionary work also contributed to the exchange of ideas between people.

The socialization of human culture curtails personal liberty but enhances individual survival potential. Civilization protects group rights as well as those of individuals. The following essentials maintain and foster human civilizations:

Natural circumstances—Climate and geographic conditions contribute to cultural evolution.

Capital goods—Material prosperity and well-earned leisure time afford people the opportunity to think and plan for social progress.

Scientific knowledge—Science stabilizes philosophy, purifies religion, and trains people to think precisely.

Human resources—The number of intelligent people influences the progress of society.

Natural resources—Much depends on the wise utilization of natural resources, scientific knowledge, capital goods and human potentials.

Effectiveness of language—Common language facilitates peace; linguistic development facilitates the expression of evolving thought.

Effectiveness of mechanical devices—The progress of civilization is directly related to the development of tools, machines, and distribution channels.

Character of torchbearers—The home must be the basic institution of culture for education of young people. Social life and schools should be secondary.

Racial ideals—Intelligence controls civilization, wisdom directs it, and spiritual idealism uplifts it.

Coordination of specialists—Civilization is dependent on the effective coordination of social, artistic, and industrial specialists.

Place-finding devices—Not only must man be trained for work, but society must devise techniques for directing individuals to suitable employment. People lose morale when continually supported from public funds.

The willingness to cooperate—Nations tend to disintegrate without intelligent patriotism.

Effective and wise leadership—Teamwork depends on leadership.

Social changes—Changes must keep pace with scientific development, but great changes should not be attempted suddenly.

The prevention of transitional breakdown—Moving from established methods into new systems requires strong leadership.

82—The Evolution of Marriage

Marriage is the evolutionary social repercussion of mating, which is instinctive. Marriage is the basis of all social evolution and is certain of enduring in some form. It creates the home, the crowning glory of the human evolutionary struggle. Children learn most of what is essential about life from their family and neighbors. The family is a master civilizer.

Sexual experience was fairly simple for primitive people. There was little or no sex regulation; there was no marriage or prostitution. Intense modern sexual passions are mainly due to race mixtures, especially the Andite inheritance. Regulation of sex in relation to marriage indicates both the relative progress of civilization, and the amount of Andite stock in a society. Sex codes can be expressive of both the highest and the lowest of human physical and emotional natures. No human emotion when overindulged can cause as much harm as the sex urge.

There will always be two distinct realms of marriage: the law regulating the external aspects, and the personal relationship. Marriage balances self-maintenance and self-perpetuation. Marriage regulations serve to balance the conflicting interests of parents, children, relatives, and society.

Mating has progressed through a multitude of transitions. Brides have been purchased, kidnapped, and won as contest prizes. Husbands have been required to prove their skill in hunting and fighting. In ancient times there have been child marriages and marriages between dead people. Some tribes mated their young men to older women and older men to young women to ensure that children would have at least one good parent. There have been times when a widow was expected to commit suicide on her husband's grave, when wives took pride in their husbands' affairs, and when chastity in girls was frowned upon.

Marriage has been linked to property and religion. Property stabilizes marriage; religion moralizes it.

Modern sexual jealousy is a product of evolving mores. The chastity taboo had its origin in the idea that the wife was the property of the husband. As civilization advanced, adultery came to be recognized as a form of stealing. Chastity requirements were applied to wives but not to single women. When the idea of virginity before marriage took hold, it became the practice to imprison unwed girls to preserve their virginity.

The Adamites and the Nodites practiced mating among themselves, and this influenced later customs in Egypt, Syria, and Mesopotamia. Outside marriages eventually gained preference because they promoted peace, led to military alliances, and insured greater freedom from in-laws.

Hybridization of superior dissimilar stocks contributes to the creation of more vigorous strains. Race mixtures greatly increase creative potential. The prejudice against interracial mating arises because modern cross-breeding is often between inferior strains. Racial amalgamation is most successful when it takes place between the higher members of the races. There is jeopardy in the unrestrained multiplication of the degenerate strains within each race.

83—THE MARRIAGE INSTITUTION

Customs and rituals that surround modern-day wedding ceremonies stem from a number of sources. Magic and ritual surrounded the entire life of the ancients; marriage was no exception. Various ancient wedding rituals included eating together, the exchange of presents, consultation of astrologers, human sacrifice, lucky days, throwing grain, lighting candles, sprinkling holy water, and blessing the wedding bed. The bridal veil served to hide the bride from jealous ghosts. In some groups, wedding guests served as legal witnesses by observing the consummation of the marriage.

Group marriages preceded polygamy which preceded monogamy. Monogamy was unnatural to evolutionary man, but wholly natural to the purer Nodites and Adamites.

Monogamy has been of great cultural value to the advanced races. It is the idealistic goal of human sexual evolution and the measure of the advance of social civilization. Monogamy contributes to spiritual growth and to the refinement of moral character. It is the best arrangement for parental happiness, child welfare, and social efficiency.

Monogamy is good for those who attain it, but we are admonished to not disdain those unfortunate men and women who fail to achieve this ideal state. Large numbers of unmarried adults in a society indicate a temporary transition of mores. In modern times, the ideal of individual love in marriage has replaced the property motive; this has created temporary instability in the institution of marriage. Modern home life is also being challenged by the advancement of long-denied legal rights for women.

A successful marriage is a life-long partnership of self-effacement, dedication to child rearing, compromise, and devotion. Divorce will function as a social safety valve as long as society fails to provide premarital training, and as long as immature idealism is the arbiter of entrance into marriage.

Much spiritual development occurs from the sincere effort of a husband and wife to progress together, but marriage is not necessarily sacred. While it cannot be compared to the human relationship with the indwelling Adjuster, nor to fraternity with Jesus, the ideal mortal marriage may be considered humanly sacred.

84—MARRIAGE AND FAMILY LIFE

Before the connection between sex and pregnancy was understood, family units were maternal. Maternal love is an instinctive endowment of the adjutant mind-spirits, and is proportional to the length of infancy. Men were first attracted into marriage not by love but by hunger, because they knew that where women and children were sheltered, food could usually be found.

When herding gave control of the main source of food to men, the father-family came into being. Later, men became involved in agriculture, and women were able to devote more time to homemaking and child rearing. The shift from the mother-family to the father-family is one of the most radical adjustments that ever occurred in the human race. The mother-family is natural and biologic; the father-family is social, economic, and political.

Sexual equality is worthy of an expanding civilization, but it is not found in nature. When justice, peace and fairness prevail, women gradually emerge from slavery. The modern factory changed working conditions so that men and women compete more evenly in the work force. Evolution has succeeded in doing that which revelation failed to accomplish.

Civilization can never obliterate the differences of behavior between the sexes. Women cannot thrive on men's rights any more than men can thrive on women's; each sex will always remain supreme in its own domain. Men and women are two distinct varieties of the same species living in close association. Complete understanding between the sexes is not possible; differing male and female viewpoints persist throughout the superuniverse ascension. These differences are highly beneficial. A man and woman cooperating are vastly superior in most ways to either two men or two women.

Marriage is now passing out of the property stage and into the personal era. New mores are emerging to stabilize marriage and the home even as modern child rearing is becoming more difficult. Problems arise from the degree of racial mixtures, acceptance of superficial education, and parents' frequent absences from home. Advancing ideals will promote the idea that bringing a child into the world is the supreme responsibility of human existence.

Attempts to shift parental responsibility to the state or church are suicidal to civilization's advancement. Civilization depends on the willingness of one generation to invest in the welfare of the next. The family teaches the essentials of brotherhood: patience, altruism, tolerance, and forbearance. Families are best managed through family councils rather than through autocratic methods. A good family reveals the love of the Creator to parents and children alike.

85—THE ORIGINS OF WORSHIP

Humans have worshipped everything on earth, including themselves. The first object to be worshipped was a stone. Stone worship was followed by hill worship; humans believed that gods inhabited mountains. Plants were worshipped because they were a source of intoxicants—alcohol is still referred to as spirits. Sprouting grains were sources of awe, and many plants were venerated for their medicinal powers. Tree worship cults leave remnants of their beliefs in modern-day May poles, Christmas trees, and the superstition of knocking on wood.

The primitive races revered animals, earth, air, fire, water, springs, rivers, rainbows, wind, clouds, rain, hail, thunder, and lightning. Deification of the moon, stars and sun developed. Civilizations honored the sun by naming the first day of the week after it; sun veneration eventually led to Mithraism, the greatest of the mystery cults, which eventually wielded a potent influence on Christianity.

In some cultures people worshipped lunatics, epileptics, priests, kings, and prophets. When tribal chiefs died they were sometimes deified; later, distinguished people who died were sainted. The worship of man by men reached its peak when earthly rulers claimed to have descended from the gods.

The sixth adjutant mind-spirit has been at work throughout time, constantly stimulating the worship urge. When worship is directed by wisdom and meditation, it begins to develop into real religion. When wisdom prevails, worshippers turn from the adoration of nature to the adoration of the Creator of nature. Evolutionary religion creates gods in the likeness of mortal man, but revelatory religion seeks to transform mortal man into the image and likeness of God.

86—EARLY EVOLUTION OF RELIGION

Primitive people lived in constant danger. Their struggle for survival depended on factors over which they had no control. Chance played such a large role in early human life that people lived in continuous anxiety. Most people died violently; natural deaths were so unusual that people thought they were caused by spirits.

Helplessness against the forces of nature impelled early man to seek to understand supernatural phenomena. Belief in the afterlife began when people dreamt of deceased tribesmen. Belief in the soul started when men observed that breath was present in living creatures but not in the dead; they speculated that the breath lived on as a ghost after death. Disembodied ghosts were thought to be responsible for all inexplicable events.

Primitive people thought that the soul could escape the body during fainting, sleeping, comas, death, or sneezing. Dreams were thought to be adventures of the soul. People believed that disembodied souls could enter animals and inanimate objects. Shadows were feared and mirrors were regarded with superstition.

The religion of ghost fear led people to believe that a spirit world controlled human destiny and that they could appease the spirits by regulating personal conduct. Rituals helped to relieve people from their unrelenting fears by helping them believe that they had the power to influence their own fate.

The idea that specific actions could help one avoid angering wandering ghosts was the seed of the concept of right and wrong. From this humble beginning, human ethics were born. Mortal minds began to prepare for the bestowal of true spirit forces, the indwelling fragments of God who have labored ceaselessly to transform the fear of God into the love of God.

87—THE GHOST CULTS

Early men feared death because death meant the creation of a new ghost. Ghosts were thought to have supernatural powers, but not supernatural intelligence. Attempts to trick ghosts led to many strange behaviors, some of which continue in today's world. Some people still imagine that an outward pretense of piety can win the favor of God.

Primitive men believed that angry ghosts were sources of grief and misfortune. They avoided houses where death had occurred, and this ritual delayed early tribes from building permanent villages. People observed silence during mourning to encourage the ghost to leave. Wives were sometimes buried alive with their dead husbands, and slaves were buried with their masters.

Sometimes months were spent in the inactivity of mourning. Tools, weapons, and other property were destroyed for the use of the ghost. Ancient funerals wasted enormous amounts of resources, and it was a great advance when the notion of inheritance replaced burning and burying the dead person's property.

Divination, sooth-saying, astrology, magic, and many other strange practices developed from early people's attempts to trick ghosts. Children were kept inside after dark, people were afraid to yawn, and phallic cults appeared. Women were veiled. The advancement of art was stifled because beauty supposedly incited the envy of ghosts. Ghost cult rituals were designed to ward off bad luck. Later men attempted to court good luck by bribing ghosts; humans still tend to bargain with deity. Cursing and finger crossing are remnants of ancient ghost cult rituals.

Cults throughout history have had both positive and negative results for human civilization. Cults retard social progress but preserve ceremony; they can either stifle or enhance philosophy. Cults serve as skeletal structures around which the living body of personal spiritual experience grows.

88—Fetishes, Charms, and Magic

Fetishism is the belief that spirits can enter objects, animals, or persons. Primitive fetishes included volcanoes, comets, pebbles, fire, holy water, trees, plants, fruits, animals, days of the week, numbers, saliva, hair, nails, skulls, umbilical cords, handicapped people, lunatics, intoxicants, poisons, bones, fireplaces, altars, and temples.

Odd customs arose from fetishism. Friday was considered an unlucky day. Three and seven were lucky numbers, but thirteen was unlucky. When animals became fetishes, taboos evolved around eating them. When geniuses were considered fetishes, talented humans often resorted to fraud and trickery to wield power and authority over other men. The Israelites believed that the spirit of God literally lived in their stone altars. Skeletal remains of saints and heroes are regarded with superstitious awe even in modern times.

Magical properties were attributed to human flesh, tiger claws, crocodile teeth, snake venom, bones, bodily secretions, effigies, black cats, wands, drums, bells, and knots. Names were esteemed so highly that many ancients had two: a sacred name which they did not reveal, and a common name for everyday use. Moses tried to control the fetish worship of the Hebrews by forbidding them to create images. This lessened fetish worship but greatly retarded art and the enjoyment of beauty. Moses' mandate against fetishes became a fetish.

Words become fetishes, especially those words considered to be words of God. When doctrines become fetishes they can lead to bigotry, intolerance, and fanaticism. Holy books have become fetishes, and the practice of opening a book at random to seek advice is a form of fetishism.

Totemism was a combination of social and religious observance. Totems have largely been replaced by flags and other national symbols. Modern fetishes include the insignias of priests, the symbols of royalty, and public opinion.

In the past, medicine men, priests, and shamans practiced public magic for the good of the whole tribe. Witches, wizards, and sorcerers might use personal magic to bring evil to their enemies or good to themselves. Chants and incantations were thought to be magical; gestures, dances, and mimicry were even more so. Magic was thought to be a way to secure insight into the future. Magic gained a powerful influence over primitive people, who feared magic so much that their own fears sometimes killed them.

Ancient magic served the human race as the cocoon of modern science. Incantations became prayers, astrology became astronomy, and the study of magic numbers led to the science of mathematics. Such words as spellbound, possession, inspiration, ingenious, thunderstruck, entrancing, and astonished all have roots in the belief in magical spirits. Today, superstitions linger even in the minds of civilized people; mankind is slow to leave magic behind.

89—SIN, SACRIFICE, AND ATONEMENT

Primitive people believed that spirits enjoyed human misery, and that staying in favor with the gods depended on either doing or avoiding specific things. This belief led to the birth of taboos. Later, religion made taboos into sins; confession, renunciation, and sacrifices developed. People bargained for the favor of God by fasting, chastity, voluntary poverty, and self-torture.

Early sacrifices included plucking hair, knocking out teeth, cutting off fingers and other mutilations. People offered sacrifices to the gods as thanksgiving and for the redemption of debts. Later, the idea of sacrificial substitution evolved into the atonement concept—an insurance policy against the displeasure of deity.

Cannibalism at one time was nearly universal, serving social, economic, religious, and military purposes. The Sangik races were cannibalistic; the pure-line Andonites, Nodites and Adamites were not. The Dalamatia taboo against cannibalism spread throughout the world, and cannibalism fell greatly out of common practice once human sacrifice made human flesh the food of the gods. Human sacrifice endured various modifications, including animal sacrifice, enforced exile, temple prostitution, temple virgins, bloodletting, physical mutilation, circumcision, castration, piercing, tattooing, and scarring. Moses tried to put an end to human sacrifice among the Hebrews by inventing a system of ransoms to priests as a substitute.

The practices of ransom, redemption, and covenants have evolved into the modern-day sacraments. Early prayers were crude bartering agreements with the spirit world, but they demonstrated human progress in that people had evolved to the point that they dared to make deals with God.

90—SHAMANISM —MEDICINE MEN AND PRIESTS

As rituals became increasingly complex, people came to believe that only medicine men and shamans could communicate with the spirit world, and religion became a second-hand experience. Since abnormal human behavior was attributed to spirit possession, qualification for religious leadership included such things as epilepsy, hysteria, and paranoia. Some shamans were deliberate frauds, but many truly believed that they were possessed by spirits.

Shamans helped people control the hazards of their lives. They also specialized in rainmaking, healing, and crime detection. Shamans were great believers in chance as a revelatory tool. They frequently cast lots to arrive at decisions; evidence of this practice survives into modern times in children's rhymes. Other tools of a shaman's trade were astrology, interpretation of dreams, communicating with the dead, and fortune-telling.

Shamans were the original aristocracy, exempt from all tribal restrictions. They often functioned as doctors and surgeons. Injuries and illnesses that could not be attributed to obvious causes were thought to be caused by ghosts, magic, or a violation of the taboos. People greatly feared the sick, believing that ghosts had become displeased with the sufferer. Remedies for illness included chanting, howling, laying on of hands, breathing on the patient, massage, bloodletting, vapor baths, drumming, fasting, dieting, and purging.

Superstitious fears of the unknown and dread of the unseen were scaffolding for human concepts of God. Shamans eventually evolved into modern-day priests. Priests have done much to delay scientific development, but have also contributed to the stabilization of civilization and have sometimes been invaluable in pointing the way to higher realities.

91—THE EVOLUTION OF PRAYER

Early men often prayed for food, shelter, or rain. Praying for material blessings is a perversion of prayer, but it encouraged primitive people to seek these necessities by ethical means.

True prayer appears only in conjunction with the understanding that God is a personal being. Prayer contributes to the conservation of social, moral, and spiritual values. Prayer is a psychological procedure combined with a spiritual technique that promotes development of religious sentiment. It induces humans to look in two directions for help: to the subconscious mind for material aid, and to the superconscious mind for inspiration and guidance. Prayer must be a stimulus for action rather than a substitute for action. It often effects lasting change in the person who prays.

Prayer contributes to health, personal happiness, self-control, social harmony, and spiritual attainment. God does not solve man's difficulties, but he will provide wisdom and strength while man resolutely attacks his problems himself. Contact with the indwelling Adjuster is favored by meditation, but it is more frequently prompted through loving service to others.

Religious experience benefits the individual by bringing better physical health, more efficient mental function, socialization of religious experience, increased God-consciousness, and enhanced appreciation of truth, beauty and goodness. Genuine prayer is spontaneous God-consciousness. Words are irrelevant to prayer because God answers man's attitudes, not his words.

To attain effective prayer, one must consider the laws of prevailing petitions. Effective prayer requires the petitioner to: sincerely and courageously face problems that come up; exhaust the capacity to solve the problem by human means; surrender every wish of mind and every craving of soul to the transforming embrace of spiritual growth; make a wholehearted choice to follow the divine will; recognize the Father's will and translate it into action; pray for divine wisdom; and have living faith.

92—THE LATER EVOLUTION OF RELIGION

Religion has progressed from nature worship through ghost worship to fetishism. Throughout history fear has been the basic religious stimulus, but as civilization advances fear becomes modified by reverence and repentance.

Attempts to suddenly accelerate religious growth are unwise. Religion clings to mores; traditions become sacred; passing generations are afraid to discard what their ancestors deemed holy. Morality is not determined by evolutionary religion, rather, religious forms are dictated by morality. At some time in history, all that is now considered immoral was once accepted. Religion has handicapped social development in many ways, but without religion there would have been no enduring morality or worthwhile civilization. Religion has provided the discipline and self-control that makes wisdom possible.

Evolutionary religion, unlike science, does not provide for its own correction. The only two influences that can uplift religious dogma are the pressure of advancing mores, and periodic epochal revelations. Evolutionary religion must continue to be refined by revealed religion and genuine science, but revelation cannot be far removed from the thoughts of the era in which it is presented.

Evolutionary religion is a human reaction to the spiritual world; revelatory religion is the spirit realm's reaction to the human search for truth. Revelation is always limited by human capacity. There have been many events of religious revelation, but only five were of epochal significance: the Planetary Prince's arrival, the mission of Adam and Eve, Melchizedek's teachings, Jesus' teachings, and the Urantia Papers. The fifth epochal revelation differs from all previous revelations because it is the collaborative work of many persons instead of just one person.

There is an instinctive longing in the human heart for help from above. This impulse was designed to foster the work of the Planetary Prince and the Material Sons and Daughters. People have always venerated their leaders, sometimes even at the expense of his teachings. There have been hundreds upon hundreds of religious leaders on our planet who have served as the personality fulcrums on which the levers of revelation depend.

New religions cannot be invented; they either evolve or are suddenly revealed. Religions are good if they bring mortals to God and bring the realization of God to mortals. It is wise to study and assimilate the truths contained in every faith; it is arrogance for any group of religionists to think that they possess the only truth.

The quality of religion is indicated by loyalties, values, and the cosmic progress of the persons involved. Religion is devotion to the service of supreme values, a living experience of love, a technique of thinking, and the eternal foundation of all enduring civilizations. No revelation short of the attainment of the Universal Father can ever be complete—all other celestial ministrations are partial adaptations to local conditions in time and space.

93—MACHIVENTA MELCHIZEDEK

The Melchizedek Sons often function in emergencies and have been exceptionally active on our planet. Twelve Melchizedeks took authority here shortly after the Caligastia default. These same twelve stayed until Adam and Eve arrived and returned after Eve's default.

After the days of Adam and Eve, human beings slowly began to lose sight of the concept of God. To prevent the light of truth from going out, one of the twelve Melchizedeks, Machiventa, volunteered to personalize on earth in human form to bring a new revelation of truth to Urantia. Machiventa appeared in Palestine almost two thousand years before Jesus was born. His metamorphosis was achieved in cooperation with the Life Carriers and other celestial personalities. Machiventa was first seen on earth when he entered the tent of a herder and announced, "I am Melchizedek, priest of El Elyon, the Most High, the one and only God." Within a few years, Melchizedek had gathered a nucleus of disciples who formed the later community of Salem, now Jerusalem.

Machiventa resembled a man of the blended Nodite and Sumerian races. He spoke seven languages. Machiventa wore an emblem of three concentric circles on his clothing; this symbol became so sacred to his followers that they never dared use it. Few followers ever learned that the circles symbolized the infinity, eternity, and universality of the Paradise Trinity.

Melchizedek taught people that there was only one God, and that the favor of God depended on faith rather than sacrifices. Melchizedek substituted the sacrament of bread and wine for the older sacrifice of flesh and blood. He asked his followers to obey seven commandments and to spread the word of his teachings to all men. His ideas were too advanced for most people of those days; they simply could not grasp the idea of receiving divine favor through faith alone.

Because of the need to establish contact with a human family through whom Machiventa could work to promote the new teachings, the Melchizedeks for many generations had been watching the ancestors of Abraham. They were confident that within a certain generation, someone would appear who would be intelligent, wise, sincere, and capable of taking initiative. From this family, Melchizedek chose Abraham to study with him in Salem.

Abraham had kingly ambitions. In time, he was recognized as the civil ruler of Salem and seven other tribes. Melchizedek maintained peaceful relations with the neighboring tribes, but Abraham envisioned the military conquest of all Canaan. Only with difficulty did Melchizedek restrain Abraham from using warfare to force the neighboring tribes to more quickly learn the truths of Salem. Machiventa's disapproval of Abraham's schemes for military conquest caused a temporary severance of their relationship. As time passed, Abraham found himself well on the way to becoming the head of a powerful civil state in Palestine, but he was held back by two concerns; the lack of Melchizedek's sanction of his plan, and that he had no son to continue his reign.

Abraham arranged a conference with Melchizedek. Melchizedek persuaded Abraham to abandon his scheme of military leadership in favor of spiritual promotion of the kingdom of heaven. In exchange, Melchizedek promised Abraham that he would produce an heir and many descendants. Abraham's wife, Sarah, subsequently gave birth to Isaac.

Soon after the child was born, Abraham and Melchizedek made a formal covenant in which Abraham surrendered his personal ambitions on behalf of the greater good of fostering Melchizedeks' spiritual goals for humankind. The covenant between Melchizedek and Abraham represents the great agreement between divinity and humanity wherein God agrees to do everything, while man agrees simply to believe God's promises and to follow his instructions.

From their Salem headquarters, Melchizedek's missionaries traveled to Egypt, Mesopotamia, Asia Minor, the British Isles, Iceland, China, and Japan. His teachings reached the descendants of Adamson, still living around the shores of Lake Van. Machiventa continued to instruct his students for 94 years. When he had done all he could, he disappeared without fanfare, just as he had arrived.

Abraham's descendants lost much of the Salem teachings. Within five hundred years many people regarded the story of Melchizedek as a myth. The Melchizedek gospel was almost completely absorbed into the cults of the Great Mother, the Sun and other ancient beliefs. Hebrew scribes later edited out scriptural references to Melchizedek in an attempt to bolster their national ego by exalting the memory of Abraham.

After leaving Urantia, Machiventa Melchizedek resumed his career as one of the twelve receivers of Urantia. He continues to take great interest in the affairs of the descendants of those who had believed in him in the flesh. Machiventa has recently been named Vicegerent Planetary Prince of Urantia.

94—The Melchizedek Teachings in the Orient

The strength of the Brahman priests and their rituals prevented the people of ancient India from accepting the Melchizedek idea of salvation through faith alone. The Brahman priests had invested so much in being at the top of the caste system that they could not allow people to believe that faith was the only requirement for a relationship with God. The Rig-Veda, one of the oldest sacred books on earth, was written by the Brahmans in an attempt to combat the teachings of the Salem missionaries.

The rejection of the Melchizedek gospel was a major turning point in the civilization of India. As people rejected mortal ambitions and embraced reincarnation, they fell into a sense of spiritual hopelessness. Nevertheless, Brahmanism was a noble human effort into philosophy and metaphysics. It came close to the concept of an all-pervading Absolute, the IT IS rather than the I AM. Brahman teachings about universal overcontrol were very close to the truth about the Supreme Being. The idea of karma bears some similarity to truth about inevitable repercussions of one's actions. The teaching of the soul being the indwelling of the Brahman approaches the concept of the Thought Adjuster, even including the point that the soul returns to Brahman as the Adjuster returns to the Father. The Hindu religion today is a composite of the Brahman teachings, ancient Vedic rituals, Buddhism, and Jainism. Hinduism is the most tolerant religion on earth and has survived as part of the social fabric of India.

In China, the Salem teachings led to an early form of Taoism, a very different religion from that which exists today. Early Taoism encompassed the monotheistic teachings of Singlangton, a version of the Melchizedek teachings, and the Brahman concepts. In Japan, this version of Taoism was known as Shinto. In both Japan and China, Taoism eventually became mixed with ancestor worship.

In the sixth century before Jesus' bestowal, an unusual coordination of spiritual agencies influenced a great number of religious teachers throughout the world. Lao-tse taught about One First Cause, the Tao, man's destiny of being united with Tao, the Trinity as the source of all reality, and returning good for evil. Lao-tse's teachings about nonresistance later became perverted into the erroneous belief of seeing, doing, and thinking nothing. Today's Taoism has little in common with the teachings of Lao-tse.

Confucius' chief work was a compilation of the wise sayings of ancient philosophers. His writings were not widely known or accepted during his lifetime, but became a great influence ever afterward in both China and Japan. Confucius put morality in the place of magic, and taught about the Way of Heaven, the patterns of the cosmos.

In India, Guatama Siddhartha formed the beginnings of Buddhism. He fought against the growing caste system by teaching a gospel of universal salvation, and freedom from sacrifice, rituals, torture, and priests. He taught that divine nature resided in all men, and that all could attain the realization of this divinity. His ideas were surprisingly similar to the Salem gospel.

Modern Buddhism is no more the teachings of Siddhartha than modern Christianity is the teachings of Jesus. The farther Buddhism spread from India, the more it was mixed with other religions; it was affected by Taoism, Shinto, and Christianity. Buddhism today is a growing religion because it conserves high moral values, promotes calmness and self-control, and augments serenity and happiness.

95—Melchizedek Teachings in the Levant

In Mesopotamia, Salem missionaries failed to bring a permanent realization of monotheism. Mesopotamians believed in multiple gods and were especially fond of Ishtar and the sex worship that accompanied her devotions. When the Salem teachers tried to abolish temple harlotry Mesopotamians resisted; they subsequently rejected all of the spiritual and philosophic teachings of the Salemites.

In Egypt a strong moral code was already in place, and the Salem religion flourished. One of the few great Egyptian prophets was Amenemope. He taught that riches were a gift from God, that every moment should be lived in the realization of the presence of God, and that all things earthly were fleeting. Amenemope wrote the Book of Wisdom, much of which is preserved as passages in the book of Proverbs, and also the first Psalm. His writings were translated into Greek and Hebrew.

Ikhnaton, Pharaoh of Egypt, had been taught monotheism by his mother. Ikhnaton kept the doctrine of One God alive in Egypt. He had the clearest grasp of the religion of Salem of any person outside of Melchizedek's time. In his determination to swing the nation from polytheism to monotheism, Ikhnaton broke with the past, changed his name, abandoned his capital, built a new city, and created new art and literature for his people. Ikhnaton taught that God made not only Egypt, but all the lands and all the people in the world. This teaching was too much for the nationalistic priests, who sprang back into power after Ikhnaton's death. Although his teachings did not remain in force after he died, the concept of monotheism never again entirely died out in Egypt.

Ikhnaton wrote 137 hymns, twelve of which are recorded in the book of Psalms.

In Iran, Melchizedek's doctrines advanced for five hundred years until a change of rulers led to the persecution of monotheistic teachers. Monotheism had become practically extinct in Iran when Zoroaster, the great prophet of Persia, appeared to revive the Salem gospel. He used the flame as a symbol of the wise Spirit of universal dominance. Zoroastrianism is the only religion on earth that retained the concepts of the Seven Master Spirits, which Zoroaster learned about in Ur. Jewish beliefs in heaven, hell, and devils all derived from Zoroastrianism.

The Salem teachers failed most completely in Arabia, so near to Salem itself. This desert region continued as it had for thousands of years, with each tribe worshipping its ancient fetish and many families praying to their own household gods. Long did the struggle continue between the Babylonian Ishtar, the Hebrew Yahweh, the Iranian Ahura, and the Christian Father of Jesus. Never was one concept able fully to displace the others; the people of Arabia did not universally embrace monotheism until the times of Islam.

96—YAHWEH—GOD OF THE HEBREWS

The early Semites had varying ideas of God, even during the same period. They worshipped Yahweh, El Elyon, El Shaddai, El, and Elohim; they believed in nature gods and other subordinate spirits.

Moses initiated the Hebrew belief in monotheism. Moses' mother was a member of the Egyptian royal family, and his father was a Semite liaison between the Egyptian government and the Hebrew slaves. Moses tried to negotiate for Hebrew freedom, but the agreement was later repudiated by the Pharaoh. A year later, while the Egyptian armies were busy elsewhere, Moses led his followers out of Egypt in a spectacular escape.

Moses comprehended Egyptian philosophy. He had been educated as a child about El Shaddai, and through his father-in-law he learned of El Elyon. The slaves he led knew little about such things but had retained a vague memory of Yahweh, the god of Mount Horeb (Sinai). During their extended encampment at the base of Mount Horeb, Moses wisely adjusted his teachings of the One God, attributing all the qualities of the Creator to Yahweh, the familiar god of his ignorant people.

It is unlikely that Moses' advanced monotheistic teachings would have held the attention of the ex-captives if it had not been for the fortuitous eruption of the Horeb volcano during the third week they camped there. Moses used the occurrence to convince his people that their God was mighty and all-powerful, above all other gods, who had singled out the Hebrews as his chosen people. The Hebrew concept of a jealous God first sprang from this event.

Moses was the most important spiritual teacher between Mel-chize-dek and Jesus. He was an extraordinary combination of military leader, social organizer, and religious teacher. After his death, progress in the understanding of Yahweh rapidly deteriorated among the Hebrews. Leaders of Israel continued to believe, but the common people drifted backward in their beliefs, becoming contaminated with the less advanced Canaanite religious practices.

The Book of Psalms records various concepts of God from the times of Amenemope to Isaiah, from the crude idea of tribal deity to the expanded ideal of a loving and merciful Father. The Book of Job is derived from over twenty Mesopotamians who lived over a period of three hundred years. The idea of God during those centuries was best preserved near Ur in Chaldea. In Palestine, the wisdom of God was understood, but his love and mercy were not. Only those from Ur continued to preach about the mercy of God and salvation by faith.

97—EVOLUTION OF THE GOD CONCEPT AMONG THE HEBREWS

The Hebrews accomplished the greatest feat in the evolution of religion when they transformed Yahweh, the savage, jealous god of Sinai, into the loving creator of all things, the merciful Father of all mankind.

After the times of Moses, the Hebrew people regressed in their religious practices. When Hebrew leaders combined their tribes to stave off hostile neighbors in Palestine, Samuel, a teacher from a long line of Salem teachers, used the new central government to turn Israel away from the worship of Baal and back to the worship of Yahweh. His great contribution was the pronouncement that Yahweh was changeless, perfect, and divine. Samuel taught that the favor of Yahweh was not shown through material prosperity. Samuel progressed in his understanding of God throughout his lifetime, eventually knowing him as a merciful judge. Samuel's successors continued his legacy, preaching a god of divine power.

One thousand years before Christ, the Hebrews split into two nations. Spiritual decadence set in. Elijah worked diligently to restore the northern kingdom to a God concept similar to the days of Samuel by devoting himself to demolishing the altars of Baal and other idols.

There was a long-standing controversy between followers of Yahweh and followers of Baal (Baal means owner). The southern tribes believed in one God. They thought that land belonged to Yahweh; it could not be bought and sold. The northern tribes, Canaanites and Baalites, believed in many Baals, and in the right to buy and sell land. Elijah succeeded in his work by shifting the Yahweh-Baal controversy from the issue of land ownership to the issue of monotheism vs. polytheism.

Amos discovered new concepts of Deity. From Amos, the Hebrews heard for the first time that God would no more tolerate their sins than he would tolerate the sins of other nations. This direct attack on the chosen people doctrine was resented by many Hebrews. Amos proclaimed that Yahweh was the God of all nations, and that ritual could not replace righteousness. Hosea followed Amos with a doctrine of forgiveness through repentance rather than sacrifice; his gospel was one of divine mercy and loving kindness.

The first Isaiah preached the eternal nature of God, his infinite wisdom and reliability. He was followed by Micah and Obadiah, who denounced priestly rituals and attacked the systems of sacrifice. Jeremiah declared that Yahweh was God of all the earth, of all nations and all peoples, and that God did not defend Hebrews in their military struggles against other nations. He was cast into a dungeon for this accurate statement.

The Hebrew nation fell before the armies of Babylon. While in captivity in Mesopotamia, Hebrew priests prepared a textbook to bolster the courage of their people. Although they had no intention of writing a sacred book, their textbook later became scripture. In their fervor, these priests destroyed every known record of Hebrew history to make way for their newly written glorification of the Hebrew race.

The priests were greatly hindered in their influence over the captives by Isaiah the Second, a true believer in the God of justice, love and mercy. His theories of the nature of God were so compelling that he made converts equally among the Jews and their captors. The writings of the second Isaiah are preserved in the Book of Isaiah, chapters forty through fifty-five. Isaiah taught eloquently about God as universal creator and upholder. His writings are among the truest presentations of God's character before the time of Jesus.

The Jewish religion of the Old Testament was born in Babylon during the captivity. The Hebrews concluded that if they were to prevail, they must convert the gentiles; they had to become the chosen servants of God. The leaders preached that the Jews would be a chosen people, not due to special indulgences from God, but because they would perform the special service of carrying the truth of one God to all people. But when the Babylonian captivity ended, the Jewish people returned to their rituals. Without losing the concept of the Universal Father, the Hebrews fell into spiritual retrogression. Jewish theology refused to expand. Judaism persists today by virtue of its strong institutions and deep love of justice, wisdom, truth, and righteousness.

98—THE MELCHIZEDEK TEACHINGS IN THE OCCIDENT

In Palestine, religious dogma stifled rational thinking; in Greece, human thought became so abstract that the concept of God faded. The Salem missionaries failed to build a great religious structure in Greece. Their rigid interpretation of Melchizedek's admonition not to function as priests prevented any priesthood of influence from arising in Greece. The Greeks rejected monotheism because they believed that fate controlled even the gods. Eventually, Greek ethics and philosophy advanced beyond the boundaries of their spirituality.

Intelligent Greeks steeped themselves in philosophy and metaphysics, disdaining all forms of worship. They held loosely to the idea of a Great Source. Socrates, Plato, and Aristotle forged Hellenic intellectual advancement. The common people who could not understand deep philosophy rejected both the philosophers and the Salem teachers in favor of the mystery cults.

The Roman state religion, greatly influenced by the Greeks, had a full range of gods and goddesses. Many cults flourished in Rome until the time of Augustus Caesar, who reorganized the state religion and appointed himself supreme god. A small cult of Cynics were the last of the believers in Melchizedek's teachings. The majority of Greco-Romans turned to the spectacular and emotional mystery cults, which offered promises of salvation after death. The most popular mystery cults were the Phrygian cult of Cybele and her son Attis, the Egyptian cult of Osiris and his mother Isis, and the Iranian cult of Mithras, redeemer of all mankind.

Mithraism eventually overshadowed every other cult. By the time it entered Rome, the Mithraic cult had been upstepped by the teachings of Zoroaster. Legends and rituals of this cult included a flood from which one man escaped in a special boat, a last supper after which Mithras ascended into the heavens, and an annual festival on the twenty-fifth of December. Mithraics believed that the unbaptized would be annihilated, the wicked would be destroyed by fire, and the righteous would rule with Mithras forever.

During the third century after Jesus, Mithraic and Christian churches were very similar. Most churches were underground and contained altars depicting the suffering of the savior. Mithraic worshippers dipped their fingers in holy water upon entering the temple. Both religions baptized believers and used the sacrament of bread and wine. The two religions differed in that Mithraism encouraged militarism while Christianity was pacifist. The deciding factor in the struggle between the two faiths was that Christianity allowed full fellowship for women.

The Christian religion is a complex combination of the Melchizedek teachings; Hebrew morality, ethics, and theology; the Zoroastrian concept of the struggle between good and evil; the mystery cults, particularly Mithraism; the teachings of Jesus of Nazareth; the personal beliefs of Paul of Tarsus; and Hellenistic philosophy. Christianity valiantly portrays a beautiful religion about Jesus but has long ceased to be the religion of Jesus. It glorifies Jesus as Christ, but has largely forgotten his personal gospel—the Fatherhood of God and the universal brotherhood of all people.

99—THE SOCIAL PROBLEMS OF RELIGION

In the modern age, we are faced with rapid adjustments of civilization. Society is becoming more mechanical, more complex, and more interdependent; it will not be settled for a thousand years. The function of religion during this transition period will be to stabilize human ideals. In the midst of the confusions of a rapidly changing environment, humans need the sustenance of a cosmic perspective.

Religionists should function individually rather than as groups. Individual religionists are certainly sympathetic to social suffering, civil injustice, economic thinking, and political tyranny, but as a group, they should confine their efforts to the furtherance of purely religious causes. Religion directly influences social reconstruction by increasing the spirituality of individuals. Religion creates insight into human fellowships, puts new meaning into group associations, imparts new value to play, and exalts true humor. It grows when it is disciplined by constructive criticism, amplified by philosophy, purified by science, and nourished by loyal fellowship. True religion is a meaningful way of living everyday life.

Religion inspires us to live courageously and joyfully, joining patience with passion, insight with zeal, sympathy with power, and ideals with energy. Religious experience unfailingly yields the fruits of the spirit. Religionists express their religion through wholehearted service to the brotherhood of man. Knowing God as a Father is a personal religious experience. The corollary of this experience—knowing others as brothers—leads to the group aspect of religious life.

Group religious activities enhance the service of unselfish fellowship, glorify the potentials of family life, promote religious education, provide spiritual guidance, encourage group worship and friendship, conserve morality, and facilitate the spread of the gospel. The dangers of formalized religion include crystallization of beliefs, diversion of religion from the service of God to the service of the church, the inclination of leaders to become administrators instead of ministers, the tendency to form sects and competitive divisions, the establishment of oppressive ecclesiastical authority, the creation of a "chosen people" attitude, exaggerated ideas of sacredness, a tendency to venerate the past, and failure to hold the interest of youth.

100—RELIGION IN HUMAN EXPERIENCE

Spiritual growth is stimulated by intimate association with other religionists; love is the soil for religious growth. A person cannot cause growth, but he can supply favorable conditions. Religious growth is inhibited by prejudice and ignorance. Habits which contribute to religious growth include meditation, sensitivity to divine values, worshipful problem solving, sharing the spiritual life, and avoidance of selfishness. Religious growth requires self-realization, the coordination of natural talents, curiosity, a sense of adventure, awareness, and humility.

Initial awareness of God—spiritual birth—may occur either suddenly or gradually. A spirit-born individual becomes so remotivated in life that he can calmly stand by while his fondest ambitions perish, knowing that the experience will lead to a more noble and enduring universe reality. Genuine religion takes nothing away from life, but adds new meaning, enthusiasm, and courage. A religious outlook elevates the drudgery of daily living.

Spiritual growth yields lasting joy. One of the earmarks of religious living is a peace which passes all human understanding, that peace which Paul spoke of when he said, "I am persuaded that neither death, nor life, nor angels, nor principalities, nor powers, nor things present, nor things to come, nor height, nor depth, nor anything else shall be able to separate us from the love of God."

Ideals worth striving for are those that are divine, spiritual, and eternal. The struggle for cosmic ideals is characterized by increasing patience, forbearance, fortitude, and tolerance. Spiritual development depends on maintaining a connection with spiritual forces and in ministering to others. Relationships between religionists stimulate spiritual growth. Understanding others leads us to tolerance, which leads to friendship, which leads ultimately to love. If one could only fathom the motives of others, he would eventually learn to love them.

Jesus was the perfectly unified human personality. Jesus was sincere, reasonable, approachable, unafraid, considerate, and cheerful. He taught the truth, he lived the truth, he *was* the truth. Jesus continues to unify mortal experience and transform the human mind. He unifies life, ennobles character, and simplifies experience.

101—The Real Nature of Religion

Religion is the true experience of eternal realities in time. Religious experiences result from the combined operations of the Thought Adjuster and the Spirit of Truth as they work with human ideas, ideals, insights, and spiritual strivings. Religion lives and prospers by faith and insight, eventually resulting in the consciousness of God and assurance of survival.

Revelation compensates for the absence of the morontia viewpoint by providing a technique for comprehension of the relationships of matter and spirit through the mediation of mind. Personal revelation is continuous; epochal revelation is periodic. Revelation enlarges ethics and expands morals; it is validated only by human experience.

True religion cannot be observed or understood from the outside. The assurance of a personal God depends wholly on spiritual insight. For people who are assured of spiritual realities, no argument about the reality of God is necessary; but for those who do not know God, no possible argument could be convincing.

Spiritual intuition is the endowment of the cosmic mind in association with the divine Adjuster. Spiritual reason is the endowment of the Holy Spirit, and spiritual philosophy is the endowment of the Spirit of Truth. The coordination of these spirit endowments creates a potential spirit personality within the mortal host. It is this embryonic spirit personality that is the part of a person that survives after death.

A soul reveals itself by the manner in which it reacts to difficult intellectual and social situations. Genuine spiritual faith engenders moral progress, sublime trust in God, profound courage, inexplicable poise, and unswerving faith—in spite of adversity, calamity, disappointment, suffering, injustice, and defeat. The teachings of Jesus provide temporal tranquility, intellectual certainty, moral enlightenment, philosophic stability, ethical sensitivity, God-consciousness, and the assurance of personal survival.

A personal religious philosophy is derived from both inner and outer experiences. Social status, economic conditions, education, moral trends, politics, racial tendencies, religious teachings, temperament, intellect, vocation, marriage, and kin all influence personal standards of life. There are four levels in the evolution of personal religious philosophy:

1. Submission to tradition and authority

2. Small spiritual attainments that stabilize daily life

3. Dependence on logic, which may stagnate into cultural or scientific bondage

4. Freedom from tradition and convention—to think, act, and live honestly, loyally, and fearlessly

Belief becomes faith when it motivates life and shapes behavior. Living religious faith is more than a set of noble beliefs; it is a living experience concerned with spiritual meanings, divine ideals, and supreme values. Faith is God-knowing and man-serving. Living faith never fosters bigotry, persecution, or intolerance.

In the spiritual sense, mortals are the children of God. Man discovers divinity through the avenue of religious experience and by the exercise of faith. Faith provides the escape from material limitations and the hope of safe conduct between the material and the spiritual realms. Religion cures spiritual loneliness and allows each child of God to feel at home as a citizen of the universe.

102—The Foundations of Religious Faith

Faith stimulates the realization that values can be translated from the material to the spiritual, from the human to the divine, from time into eternity. The certainties of science proceed from the intellect; but the certainties of religion spring from the entire personality. The indwelling Adjuster promotes a hunger for perfection that can be satisfied only by communion with God.

Religious experience requires spiritual growth, intellectual expansion, factual enlargement, and social service. No real religious growth can be accomplished without a highly active personality. Lazy people may seek to escape the rigors of religious activities by retreating to the false shelter of religious dogmas; poorly disciplined souls may use religion as an escape from the demands of living; but the true mission of religion is to prepare religionists to bravely face the vicissitudes of life. True religion must act.

The pursuit of knowledge constitutes science; the search for wisdom is philosophy; the love of God is religion; the hunger for truth is revelation. Revelation unifies history and coordinates science. Religion is to morality as love is to duty, sonship is to servitude, essence is to substance. The relation between an individual and his Creator is a living experience. To isolate religion as one part of life is a disintegration of life and a distortion of religion.

The Universal Father is self-existent and self-explanatory; he lives within every rational mortal being. God is the only self-caused fact in the universe. He is the order, plan, and purpose of creation. Certainty about God is possible because he is the most inescapable of all presences, the most real of all facts, the most living of all truths, and the most loving of all friends.

Human things must be known in order to be loved, but divine things must be loved in order to be known.

Prayer is part of religious experience, but it has been wrongly emphasized by modern religions to the neglect of the more essential communion of worship. The reflective powers of the mind are deepened and broadened by worship. Prayer enriches life, but worship illuminates destiny.

103—The Reality of Religious Experience

Although religious awakening is a gradual process, some spiritual births are accompanied by crisis and anguish while others are a natural growth of the recognition of spiritual values. Because personalities are unique, no two individuals interpret divine leadings the same way. People tend to agree more easily on religious goals than on beliefs or creeds.

Every human being experiences conflict between self-seeking and altruistic impulses. An unselfish choice in the face of a desire to be selfish constitutes a primitive religious experience. God-consciousness is sometimes attained as the result of seeking for help in the resolution of such moral conflicts.

In the absence of wrong teaching, the minds of normal children move toward moral righteousness and social ministry. The first emergence of a child's moral nature is a response to justice, fairness, or kindness. Unselfish interest in the welfare of others springs from the divine within; animals cannot make such a choice.

Only a fairly well unified personality can arbitrate the conflicts between ego and social consciousness. When there is failure of personality unification, altruistic tendencies may become overdeveloped and injurious to the welfare of the self. The rights of the self and the rights of one's neighbors must be balanced, although this dilemma cannot always be resolved in time and space.

Man's ideals tend to grow by geometric progression, while his ability to live up to his ideals grows only arithmetically. Rather than hoping to live up to his highest ideals, he can try to seek God and become more like him. The pursuit of the ideal—striving to be Godlike—is a continuous effort before and after death. The good accomplished in mortal life carries over to the enhancement of life after death and directly contributes to the first stages of immortal survival experience. Man is truly the architect of his own eternal destiny.

Neither science nor religion can hope to provide a complete understanding of universal truths. An analytical study of the cosmos will reveal to the mind and the physical senses that the universe is mechanical and material. A view of the universe from the perspective of the inner life makes all of creation appear to be spiritual. Failure to coordinate these two viewpoints is due to ignorance of the domain between the spiritual and material worlds—the morontia phase of reality.

Man's highest philosophy should be based on the reason of science, the faith of religion, and the insight of revelation. Science and religion are each incomplete and are predicated on assumptions. In the mortal state, nothing can be proven absolutely; revelation must compensate for the frailties of evolving philosophy. Genuine religion is not merely thinking, but is also feeling, acting, and living. The earmarks of true religion are faith in a supreme Deity, hope of eternal survival, and love—especially love of one's fellows.

104—Growth of the Trinity Concept

The first revelation of the Trinity on earth was made by the Planetary Prince's staff five hundred thousand years ago. Subsequent revelations were presented by Adam and Eve, Melchizedek, and Jesus. It has been difficult for cultures emerging into monotheism from polytheism to accept the concept of the Trinity. People of the Hebrew and Islamic faiths find it difficult to differentiate between worshipping multiple gods (polytheism) and the worship of one Deity in a triune manifestation.

The Paradise Trinity is an entity. The Trinity is not a personality, but is a true and absolute reality eventuating from the conjoining of the Father, the Son, and the Spirit. Recognition of the Trinity concept leads to understanding the interrelationship of love and law and to the investigation of other triune associations of the First Source and Center in which the Infinite functions in various capacities of force, energy, power, causation, reaction, potentiality, actuality, gravity, tension, pattern, principle, and unity.

The completeness of infinity must be reconciled with the incompleteness of the evolving universe. Total reality—infinity—is presented as existing in the seven Absolutes:

The Universal Father

The Eternal Son

The Infinite Spirit

The Isle of Paradise

The Deity Absolute

The Universal Absolute

The Unqualified Absolute

The Paradise Trinity is not a triunity. It is an undivided and indivisible Deity, but the three Deities also function as the first triunity. The common factor between trinity and triunity is that they each result in functions other than what is discernible from the sum of the attributes of component members.

The Universal Father exercises control of the functions of infinity as the primal member of many triunities. He reveals himself as love to the creatures of the evolving cosmos through the personal purposive triunity of the Father, Son, and Spirit. God patterns the universes and organized energy through the power pattern-triunity of the Father-Son, the Paradise Isle, and the Conjoint Actor. All spirit finds reality expression in the spirit-evolutional triunity of the Father, the Son-Spirit, and the Deity Absolute. Altogether there are fifteen triune associations of the First Source and Center in his various functions, and these associations make the sub-infinite manifestations of God's reality possible.

Other triune relationships—triodities— do not involve the Father, but they result as a consequence of the existence of the triunities. Triodities are directly concerned in the experiential Deities—the Supreme, Ultimate and Absolute.

105—DEITY AND REALITY

Infinity is only partially comprehensible, even to high orders of universe intelligence. To the finite mind, it seems there must be a beginning, but there never was a beginning to reality. There is much about Deity which cannot be grasped by universe creatures. Mortals can know God as a Father, but the Father aspect of God is only one phase of the I AM. The enormous magnitude of the visible universes is only a partial revelation of the Infinite.

By internal metamorphoses, the I AM establishes a sevenfold self-relationship. The seven-phase nature of I AM includes: the Universal Father, the Universal Controller, the Universal Creator, the Infinite Upholder, the Infinite Potential, the Infinite Capacity, and the Universal One of Infinity—I AM as I AM. These seven realities are coordinately eternal, even though in time-space they are described as though they originated sequentially. Explanations of the relationships of absolutes in eternity involve paradoxes when they are presented in the language of time and the patterns of space.

Through these seven phases, the I AM encompasses all personal relationships, all impersonal relationships, the creative cycle, all actual and potential reality, and absolute coherence of energy and spirit. The primacy of the First Source and Center covers everything in the universe, which is how it can truly be said of all creatures, from the lowest mortals to the citizens of Paradise, that "in him we all live and move and have our being."

The seven phases of the infinite I AM eternalize as the Seven Absolutes of Infinity. The seven Absolutes had no beginning. They are eternal and constitute the beginning of reality. The Seven Absolutes are:

1. The First Source and Center—God

2. The Second Source and Center—the Eternal Son

3. The Paradise Source and Center—the foundation of universe gravity

4. The Third Source and Center—the Conjoint Actor

5. The Deity Absolute—the total of potential Deity reality

6. The Unqualified Absolute—the total of potential non-deified reality

7. The Universal Absolute—the unifier of the deified and non-deified

Duality becomes existent by the association of the Seven Absolutes of Infinity with the seven phases of the I AM. The I AM is unity. Unity begets duality, duality begets triunity, and triunity is the eternal ancestor of all things. The dualities eternalize reality foundations; the triunities eventuate universal function.

The diversification of the I AM is attributed to his inherent volition. Only the infinity of the Father's will could qualify absolute existence so as to create finite realities. With the appearance of qualified reality, there came into being the growth cycle that marks the beginning of universe history and the existence of time.

Many repercussions occurred when the infinite created the finite. The deity response to the creation of the finite eventuated in the evolution of supremacy. The superuniverse reaction concerned the architectural plans of space. The creature repercussions resulted in the appearance of perfect beings in Havona, and of evolutionary ascenders in the seven superuniverses. The divinity response produced the time lag of evolution that makes creature participation in divine creation possible.

To finite creatures, the beginning of the finite seems to be the beginning of reality.

There are two phases of finite creation: the Havona type, which is created in perfection, and the superuniverse type, which is created to become perfect. Mortals can attain perfection because they evolve; they grow. Humans measure growth in time, and because of this growth, they appear to be incomplete in time. Mortal incompleteness seems to differentiate evolving beings from those finite beings of Havona who are created in perfection, but differences between the two types of creatures are nonexistent in eternity.

That mortals attain perfection implies something other than perfection as a point of departure. At this point, imperfection arises and the potential for evil seeps into the universe. Disharmony and conflict are inherent where evolutionary growth is allowed.

Transcendental realities are both sub-infinite and super-finite. From various viewpoints they seem to be a consequence of the finite, an anticipation of the finite, or even a "pre-echo" of the finite. As the Supreme is associated with finites, so the Ultimate is identified with transcendentals; the Ultimate is an eventuation of new Deity realities. The universes of time and space exist on finite, transcendental, and absolute levels.

106—UNIVERSE LEVELS OF REALITY

The evolving master universe contains multiple phases of existential and experiential reality. Although there are many ways of looking at reality, human perception is constrained by language, mind capacity, human inability to grasp even a partial view of eternity, and the limited development of the seven superuniverses.

God the Sevenfold provides the superuniverse time lag that makes creature participation in evolutionary growth possible. Mortals are truly partners with the Creator in their own evolution. As God the Sevenfold coordinates finite evolution, the Supreme Being synthesizes destiny attainment. The Supreme Being embraces everything evolving in time and space and invests all with spirit personality. God the Supreme is both experiential and experiencible.

It is conjectured that when the Supreme Being emerges at the end of the present universe age, the first experiential Trinity will eventuate. The functioning of this Ultimate Trinity may result in the emergence of the apex of transcendental reality—God the Ultimate. This theoretical occurrence leads to anticipation of the second experiential Trinity, the Absolute Trinity, which would come into existence only at the completion of the entire master universe, from Havona to the fourth space level. If at some future time there exists the original existential Paradise Trinity and two experiential Trinities, we come to the possibility that, at some far distant moment, a Trinity of Trinities may emerge.

It is difficult to develop concepts of infinite reality. All such concepts must embrace the finality of universal development, the experiential realization of all that could ever be. Mortals, spirits, even the universes themselves have potential final destinies, but it is doubtful that any being will ever completely attain all aspects of this destiny. No matter how much a creature grows in Father comprehension, he will always be staggered by the unrevealed infinity of the Father-I AM. The infinity of the I AM is the assurance that throughout the endless future, ascending beings will enjoy continuing possibilities of personality development which even eternity will never exhaust. The inconceivably distant future moment when the entire master universe is completed may signal the beginning of even greater and more enthralling metamorphoses.

When human beings try to understand the unification of the finite and the infinite, they face inherent intellectual limitations. Time, space, and experience are barriers to understanding these concepts, yet without time humans could not discern sequence, without space perception they could not fathom simultaneity, and without experience they could not even exist. Time, space, and experience simultaneously aid and create obstacles to human perceptions of reality. The space-time phenomenon does not take place on Paradise; potentials on Paradise are perceived as actuals.

The unification of all realities must involve both existential and experiential realities. The concept of the existential, solitary, pre-Trinity nonattainable I AM, and the postulate of the experiential post-Trinity of Trinities and the attainable I AM, are one and the same. The I AM exists before all existentials and after all experientials.

Mortals will grapple with the never-ending paradoxes of infinity and eternity throughout their eternal careers. The final quest of eternity is the endless exploration of infinity—the never-ending voyage of discovery into the absoluteness of the First Source and Center. Creature growth is proportional to Father identification, and living the will of God is the eternal passport to the endless possibility of infinity itself.

107—ORIGIN AND NATURE
OF THOUGHT ADJUSTERS

Although the Universal Father resides on Paradise, he is also present in the minds of his countless children in the worlds of space. The fragment of God that indwells mortals, the Thought Adjuster, creates an incessant longing to be like God and to attain Paradise. The Adjuster is an infallible cosmic compass which unerringly guides human beings to Paradise.

A Thought Adjuster has one of three destinies: attainment of personality by fusion with a mortal, attainment of personality by fiat of the Universal Father, or liberation from known assignments. Fusion between a person and the Adjuster provides personality to the Adjuster and eternal life to the human being.

Thought Adjusters are of the essence of original Deity. They are fragments of the presence of God and proceed directly from the Universal

Father. Adjusters are of God and are like God; they reveal his supernal love and spiritual ministry. Thought Adjusters have minds; they can plan, work, and love. Their valor and wisdom suggest that they have undergone a training of tremendous scope and range. Adjusters truly love us; they long for our divinity attainment and for the time when they will be delivered from the limitations of our material bodies.

Thought Adjusters are pure spirits, presumably absolute spirits. Adjusters do not require energy intake because they *are* divine energy. They can use the material-gravity circuits but are not subject to gravity as we are; they are fragments of the ancestor of gravity. Thought Adjusters are not personalities—they are the divine presence.

Adjusters volunteer to indwell humans. They can adapt and modify according to circumstances, and they act in accordance with human choice. Adjusters have genuine volition, but, being prepersonal, are subservient to the mortal will of their indwelling. Throughout the cosmos, that which is prepersonal, nonpersonal, or subpersonal is ever responsive to the will of personality.

Through Thought Adjusters, the Father has direct communication with every material creature throughout his infinite realms. The full possibilities inherent in this partnership between man and God are yet to be disclosed.

108—MISSION AND MINISTRY OF THOUGHT ADJUSTERS

When Thought Adjusters are sent out from Divinington to indwell mortals, they are identical in divinity endowment but may vary in experience. An Adjuster volunteers for assignments after reviewing data concerning the mortal candidate's heredity, intellect, and spiritual capacity.

Adjusters volunteer for service as soon as personality forecasts are received, but are not dispatched until the first time a mortal subject makes a moral decision—usually just prior to the sixth birthday on our world. Mortal minds are not ready for Adjuster bestowal until they have been prepared by the ministry of the adjutant mind-spirits and the Holy Spirit. On Urantia, Adjusters have been universally bestowed on all normal minds since the day of Pentecost.

It is not fully understood how the Adjusters live and work within the human mind. They appear to come and go independently of other spiritual presences, yet they function in perfect coordination with all spirit ministries, including adjutant mind-spirits, the Holy Spirit, and the Spirit of Truth. Adjusters never lose anything entrusted to their care; they are absolutely dependable. They are chiefly concerned with a mortal's future life rather than life on earth. Thought Adjusters are not interested in making life easier; a reasonably difficult life creates many decision-making opportunities, and growth is stimulated by daily choices and decisions. It is the business of Thought Adjusters to ensure human survival and to prepare humans for the eternal adventure.

Adjusters truly become "the kingdom of Heaven" within us; they are wellsprings of spiritual attainment and the hope of divine character. Because they exist within our minds, they are distressed when subjected to sordid thoughts, selfishness, or irreverence for that which is beautiful and good. Human fears and anxieties delay their work. An Adjuster is the divine parent, as we are the mortal parent, of our own evolving immortal souls.

109—RELATION OF ADJUSTERS TO UNIVERSE CREATURES

Life experience has no cosmic substitute. In common with all living beings in the superuniverse, Thought Adjusters must acquire experience. Thought Adjusters acquire skill and ability through contact with the material races, and are classified according to their experience.

Virgin Adjusters are on their first assignment. They are usually sent to worlds during early epochs when people are so primitive that few will attain higher levels of spirituality. Others are on loan to individuals on worlds whose mortals are destined to attain eternal life through Spirit fusion. On these worlds, Adjusters can give more help to their human subjects than is normal on earth.

Advanced Adjusters have served on one or more worlds where the mortals are destined for Spirit-fusion.

Supreme Adjusters are those which previously indwelt mortals who failed to choose survival, and have subsequently been reassigned to another mortal. Adjusters are seldom given two indwelling experiences on the same planet—there are no Adjusters on Urantia now who have been here previously. It is believed that nearly all Adjusters living in mortals of survival capacity on Urantia are advanced or supreme Adjusters.

Self-acting Adjusters are the most versatile group. They are capable of carrying out extraordinary missions. Their subjects are often mustered into the reserve corps of destiny; fusion is regarded as a fact. Supreme and self-acting Adjusters are able to leave the human body at will, although they rarely do so.

An Adjuster's work is hindered by preconceived opinions, settled ideas, long-standing prejudices, and shifting mental attitudes. Sometimes they are able to arrest the mental flow and divert ideas to effect deep spiritual transformations in the superconscious mind. Intelligent communication between humans is facilitated by Adjusters, and Adjuster type has much to do with potential human personality expression.

Adjusters never fail. Nothing worthwhile is ever lost; every meaningful value in every will creature is certain of survival. Even if a mortal creature rejects survival, his Adjuster will carry his life experiences to some other world and some other survival candidate.

110—Relation of Adjusters to Individual Mortals

The Adjuster is not an organic part of the human body. It would be more accurate to think of Adjusters as indwelling the human mind rather than indwelling the human brain. Adjusters are chiefly concerned with the spiritual preparation for upcoming stages of existence, but are also interested in the temporal welfare of their human host.

Adjusters begin to work with a predetermined plan for development, but humans are not required to accept this plan. Adjusters are subservient to human will and will never force us to follow their guidance. They are dedicated to improving, modifying, and adjusting mortal thought processes. Adjusters do not try to control our thinking, but attempt rather to spiritualize it. The more we attune ourselves with our divine Adjusters, the more we approach the morontia order of existence. Morontia mind is the sum of our material and spiritual natures—dual mind dominated by one will.

The success of our Adjusters depends not on our beliefs, but on our decisions, determinations, and steadfast faith. Our eternal survival depends on our desire to be Godlike and on our willingness to do and to be anything that is essential to the final attainment of that desire. The ideal life is one of loving service, but many humans spend so much time on the trifles of living that they overlook the essential task of developing a working relationship with the indwelling divine gift. Adjuster harmony can be consciously augmented by choosing to respond to divine leading, loving God and desiring to be like him, loving man and sincerely desiring to serve him, and joyfully accepting cosmic citizenship.

The Adjuster's influence is not "conscience." Conscience admonishes us to *do* right, while the Adjuster endeavors to show us what *is* right.

There exists a large gulf between the human and the divine. Mortals are so electrically and chemically controlled that it is difficult for Adjusters to guide them. Few people are true thinkers—they do not develop themselves physically, mentally, and spiritually enough for the divine spark within to lead them easily. Confusion and discouragement do not necessarily signify resistance to the leading of the Adjuster.

Certain abrupt thoughts and mental pictures may be the work of the Adjuster, but more often they are simply the emergence of ideas which have been grouping themselves together in the subconscious mind. Many a new religion and strange "ism" has arisen from misunderstood communications from Thought Adjusters.

During sleep, Adjusters attempt to communicate within the higher levels of the human mind. Some grotesque dreams indicate failure to make efficient contact. Speculation about the Adjuster content of dreams is dangerous; it is better to risk rejecting an Adjuster's suggestion than to mistake something originating in the human mind as a communication from the indwelling fragment of God.

Adjuster attunement is related to the attainment of the seven psychic circles of mortal potential. The seventh circle marks the beginning of human personality function, and the first circle represents relative maturity. Moving through the circles demands the harmonious function of the entire personality—material, intellectual, and spiritual. Every decision we make either impedes or facilitates the Adjuster's function; likewise do these decisions determine our advancement in the circles.

The seven levels of human personality growth are variable in each person and seem to be determined by the growth capacity of each individual. It is to the mind of perfect poise, housed in a body of clean habits, stabilized neural energies, and balanced chemical function that a maximum of light and truth can be imparted with a minimum of temporal risk.

We literally become more real as we ascend from the seventh to the first psychic circle.

Faith gives us the experience of being a child of God, but action is essential to consciousness of kinship with the evolving Supreme Being. In the finite realm, potential becomes actual through our choices, but in the spiritual realm, potentials are transmuted into actuals through faith.

Immortality is attained through Adjuster fusion. Many people have attained their circles, but fusion depends on a final and complete attunement of the mortal will with the will of God. Subsequent to mortal fusion, the Adjuster shares our destiny and experience—mortal and Adjuster become a single entity. While for most humans the emerging soul is liberated from the body through death, it is possible for a person to fuse with the Adjuster without passing through material death.

111—THE ADJUSTER AND THE SOUL

The soul is neither the human mind nor the divine spirit that dwells within the mind. Material mind is the arena in which we live, make decisions, choose or forsake God, and survive or destroy ourselves. Material evolution provides us with a body and the Father endows us with spirit reality, but it is by mind that we live or die. The mortal mind is merely a temporary system lent to us for use during our material lives. Our evolving souls will faithfully portray the decisions made with the minds we have been given.

The human soul has three antecedents: the human mind, the divine spirit, and the relationship between these two. The relationship between mind and spirit produces the soul, an entirely new and unique universe value. The human soul is an embryonic form of the future vehicle of personality. If this evolving soul becomes permeated by truth, beauty, and goodness—if it becomes God-conscious—it becomes indestructible. The soul exists as morontia reality midway between the material and spiritual worlds.

An Adjuster's work is spiritual, but is accomplished in the intellectual realm. The mind is the ship, the Adjuster is the pilot, and human will is the captain. With mortal consent, the faithful pilot will safely carry his captain across the barriers of time and the handicaps of space to the source of divine mind, even to the Paradise Father.

The mortal career is an education. It is not so much what we comprehend, as what we desire to comprehend that insures our survival. It is not what our minds are like, as what our minds are striving to be like that constitutes spirit identification. What we are today is not as important as what we are becoming.

Doing the will of God is the willingness to share the inner life with God. Peace in this life, survival in death, perfection in the next life, and service in eternity are all achieved when the human will chooses to become subject to the Father's will. Such choice is not a surrender of will, but is the consecration and perfecting of will—the Father's will *becomes* the mortal's will.

Many human problems come from our two-fold natures: we are part of nature, yet we are able to transcend nature; we are finite, but we are indwelt by a spark in infinity. Religious confidence—living faith—can sustain us amid conflicts born of this dual nature. The indwelling Adjuster cannot stop or even materially alter the career struggle of time; the Adjuster cannot lessen the hardships of life on this world. But humans would be comforted and inspired if they would allow the Adjuster to reveal the eternal purpose of the difficult struggle of the material world.

Uncertainty with security is the essence of the Paradise adventure. God lives in us and trusts himself to us, and we live in him and learn to trust ourselves to him. We may not be certain of the details of the coming events of our lives, but we are always secure in the infinite love and compassion of our Father.

112—PERSONALITY SURVIVAL

While we cannot adequately define personality, it is helpful to know that personality is bestowed by God, is relatively creative, unifies the identity of living energy systems, is changeless, discriminates between levels of conduct, is unique, and is capable of responding to other personalities. The Adjuster and the personality are both changeless, but the relationship between them is nothing *but* change.

Life is a process that takes place between an organism and its environment. Personality impacts life by imparting values and meanings into the life process. In humans, personality unifies all activity and confers identity and creativity. Humans are spiritual beings; the unity of self and the self-consciousness of personality are endowments of the supermaterial world. The purpose of cosmic evolution is to achieve unity of personality through increasing spirit dominance and increasing response to the indwelling fragment of God.

The material self is dependent during the physical life on the continuing function of the material life vehicle. Mortals transcend death by transferring the seat of their personality identities from the material body to the more enduring morontia soul. This transfer is effected by sincerity, persistence, and steadfastness of God-seeking decisions.

There are three kinds of death. Spiritual death happens when a person rejects survival. Mind death takes place when the body continues to function after the essential mind circuits have been destroyed. Physical death occurs when both body and mind cease to function.

After physical death, two nonmaterial pieces of a surviving personality persist: memory transcripts and the immortal soul. The Thought Adjuster carries the mortal's memory transcripts to Divinington, while the soul is remanded to the care of the seraphim. Temporarily after death, the Thought Adjuster loses personality and the mortal loses identity until they can be reunited in a new manifestation on the mansion worlds. A mortal is repersonalized on the mansion worlds either at the end of a dispensation or within three "periods." Reassembly of the parts of a onetime material being involves the fabrication of a suitable form, the return of the Adjuster, and the bestowal of the soul into the awaiting morontia form by the seraphic custodian.

Selfhood persists in spite of a continuous change in all of the factors of self. In physical life, changes are gradual. At death and depersonalization, the change is sudden. Human life is endless change unified by the stability of the unchanging personality.

The universe government always manifests patience, tolerance, and mercy. If there is ever any doubt as to the advisability of allowing a mortal to advance, the universe government invariably rules in the favor of the individual. Will creatures must be given one true opportunity to make their final choice about the eternal life; the soul of each person is allowed to fully reveal its true intent and purpose.

There is much about our mortal lives that we will not remember in the future. Our Adjusters will retain only those memories and experiences which are essential to the universe career. Much of material experience will pass away, but personality and relationships between personalities will persist. We will always remember, and be remembered by, the people known in this life. On the mansion worlds, personalities are revealed for the first time apart from material flesh. In physical life, one may be outwardly beautiful while inwardly ugly, but in the morontia form and higher levels, outward appearance varies in accordance with the inner nature.

Mortals pass through a relatively short and intense testing period. On the evolutionary worlds, survival decisions are formed; in the morontia state, survival decisions are confirmed; at the spiritual level, survival decisions have been made. Fusion with the indwelling Adjuster usually happens within the local system when there has been a final and irrevocable choice for the eternal career. After fusion, there is never any doubt as to the eternal career of such a personality.

After passing through the local universe, ascenders meet the local universe sovereign who grants credentials for the quest for the Universal Father. Fused mortals become a member of a unique order of ascending personalities who are ever serviceable, faithful, and efficient; never ceasing to ascend until they stand in the presence of the Father on Paradise.

Mortals have every opportunity to determine their own destiny. The cosmos is an infinitely integrated aggregation of units, all of which are subject to the destiny of the whole. Those units that are personal are endowed with the choice of destiny acceptance or rejection. Personality will attain Deity destiny, but humans must choose whether or not to be present at the attainment of such destiny.

113—SERAPHIC GUARDIANS OF DESTINY

Guardian angels are seraphim who serve mortals in the quest for spiritual advancement. One thousand humans of seventh circle attainment share one pair of seraphim and a company of cherubim. Five hundred sixth circlers share a pair of seraphim and a company of cherubim. By the fourth circle, mortals are supervised in groups of ten. Once the third circle is attained, a personal seraphic pair is exclusively devoted to a single person; such seraphim are known as guardians of destiny.

Only experienced volunteers are assigned as seraphic guardians of destiny. Like cherubim, seraphim occasionally work singly but usually work in pairs. They develop a deep affection for humans. Seraphim share most human emotions and experience additional ones. The emotions that they find hardest to understand are fear, dread, and anxiety.

One of the most important things angelic guardians do for us is to coordinate the spirit influences which indwell and surround us. Because they are children of the Creative Spirit, they are able to correlate the influence of the Infinite Spirit with the Thought Adjuster and the Spirit of Truth. They interpret morontia reality to mind and manipulate the physical environment through liaison with the master physical controllers and midway creatures.

Our seraphic friends continually seek to promote circle-making decisions. Guardian angels are most active when the Adjuster is least active, but the ministry of the two is correlated. The urge to pray is often the result of seraphic influence.

Seraphim work through our social, ethical, and moral environments. Angels labor independently of human appeals; they perform their tasks as they are directed by their superiors, regardless of the changing whims of their mortal charges. The seraphic mission is to guard rather than to influence. Human beings chart their own courses, and the seraphim act to make the best possible use of the chosen course.

In this life we are rarely aware of our seraphic guardians, but we will become conscious of them on the next world. Our angels will remain with us through the mansion worlds, through fusion with the Adjuster, on through Jerusem and Edentia, and beyond Salvington through the minor and major sectors of the superuniverse. Our association with our guardians will never be forgotten or completely severed. In the eternal ages, humans and angels will forever cooperate in divine service.

114—Seraphic Planetary Government

The Most Highs rule in the kingdoms of men chiefly through the ministry of seraphim, who carry out much of the detail of superhuman planetary government. Urantia's planetary government is unique in Nebadon due to several unusual circumstances, including earth's life modification status, the Lucifer rebellion, and the Adamic default. Urantia is also unique in being a bestowal planet and the location of an archangel circuit.

Urantia's Planetary Prince is Michael of Nebadon, who has made no action to personally administrate our world other than to establish a commission of twenty-four counselors to supervise the affairs of the planet. Machiventa Melchizedek has recently been given vicegerent authority to act as Planetary Prince. He has continued the established routine of having one of the twenty-four counselors serve as resident governor general. Urantia will continue to have twenty-four counselors in charge of affairs until Machiventa returns, but the timing of his return is a matter of some speculation.

The resident governor general, as the representative of the twenty-four counselors, passes down scores of rulings each day. Twelve corps of special seraphim perform diverse tasks under the immediate direction of the governor general.

Epochal angels oversee the affairs of each generation.

Progress angels initiate the evolutionary progress of successive social ages.

Religious guardians endeavor to maintain ideals and values from one generation to another.

Angels of nation life direct the political performance of national affairs on Urantia.

Angels of the races work for the conservation of the evolutionary races.

Angels of the future forecast the events of a future age and plan for the realization of more advanced dispensations.

Angels of enlightenment foster mental and moral training.

Angels of health assist mortal agencies dedicated to the promotion of health and prevention of disease.

Home seraphim advance the home, the basic institution of human civilization.

Angels of industry foster industrial development and improved economic conditions.

Angels of diversion promote uplifting play, humor, and rest.

Angels of superhuman ministry minister to all other superhuman life on the planet—these are the angels of the angels.

None of these groups of seraphim directly control their assigned domains, but they can manipulate planetary conditions to favorably influence the human activity with which they are concerned. Aside from these specific tasks, seraphim mobilize, train, and maintain the reserve corps of destiny. The reserve corps are living men and women in the service of the superhuman administration of world affairs. Reservist service is possible only when the mortal displays a special capacity for being secretly rehearsed for emergency missions, wholehearted dedication to some special cause, willingness to serve without human recognition, and the possession of an extraordinarily versatile Thought Adjuster. On Urantia, there is one corps of destiny for each of the seraphic groups. Although these people are seldom noted in the pages of human history, it is to a certain extent through this group that the Most Highs are able to rule in the kingdoms of men.

No one seems to know when the unsettled status of Urantia's planetary administration will terminate. There has been no precedent for Urantia's situation in the history of the local universe. Even so, mortals on earth are watched as faithfully and cherished as lovingly as if the sphere had never been betrayed.

115—The Supreme Being

To become part of the Supreme Being, one must *do* something as well as *be* something.

All minds must develop a framework in which to think rationally and, although such frames are indispensable, they are, *without exception,* erroneous. Finite creatures in an infinite cosmos must live with distorted conceptions of limitless, never-beginning, never-ending existence. Infinity is beyond the human ability to comprehend, but contemplating infinity can help expand current universe frames.

There is a unity in infinity which is expressed as the I AM—the premier postulate of the human mind. Our distance from infinity causes us to inaccurately express this concept with a single word. Infinity on one hand is unity, but on the other hand it is diversity without end or limit. Infinity, from the human point of view, is the maximum paradox of philosophy.

To help us comprehend the universe, it is reasonable to describe the levels of universe reality as finite, absonite, and absolute. Only the absolute level of reality is eternal without qualification. Absonites and finites are modified attenuations of original, absolute reality. One way to consider the absolute level of reality is to imagine three phases:

1. *The Original*—the I AM from which all reality takes origin—that which is.

2. *The Actual*—the union of the Eternal Son, the Infinite Spirit, and Paradise—that which was and is. Together the Son, Spirit, and Paradise constitute the actual revelation of the I AM.

3. *The Potential*—including the Deity, Unqualified, and the Universal Absolutes—that which is becoming and will be, which together constitute the full potential revelation of the I AM.

From the eternal viewpoint, these qualities are not separately distinguished. In eternity, all already IS, but all has not yet been revealed in time and space. The interassociation of the Original, the Actual, and the Potential results in the possibility for all growth in the universes. All decisions, even human decisions, open up a new capacity for potential growth. From a limited viewpoint, activities have endings, but from an expanded view, endings are merely transitions from one phase of development to another.

The dynamics of the cosmos ensure the continuous transfer of reality from potentiality to actuality. This metamorphosis will never end, since Potential and Actual are both included in the Original I AM. As potentials become actualized, they, by becoming actual, open up new potentials that were previously nonexistent.

The evolution of the Supreme involves the transformation of potentials to actuals on the finite level of existence. The Supreme is a spirit person who originated in the Paradise Trinity, but the Supreme is also a Deity of evolutionary growth, growth which comes from the constant tension between actuals and potentials. The motion of the Supreme is twofold: inward toward Paradise and outward toward the limitless Absolutes of potential. In the present age, this dual motion is revealed in the descending and ascending personalities of the grand universe.

Through the creation of the Supreme, the Father I AM has achieved nearly complete liberation from the limitations inherent in his infinity status, eternal being, and absolute nature. In achieving liberation from eternity, the Almighty encounters the barriers of time; the Supreme experiences growth only as a consequence of the incompleteness of his nature.

God the Father's plan predicates finite progress upon effort, creature achievement upon perseverance, and personality development upon faith. God the Supreme is the personification of the finite shadow cast on the universe by the infinite unity of the Paradise Father, the First Source and Center, the I AM. As the Supreme Being encompasses the sum of evolutionary experience, he connects the finite with the absonite.

116—The Almighty Supreme

The Almighty overcontrol of the grand universe is physical, intellectual, and spiritual. God the Supreme derives his spirit and personality from the Paradise Trinity, but the source of his growing power as sovereign of the seven superuniverses lies in the collective acts of the Creator Sons, the Ancients of Days, and the Master Spirits.

The experience of every evolving creature is a phase of the experience of the Almighty Supreme.

Unqualified Deity is incomprehensible to evolving creatures. Paradise Deity originated God the Sevenfold—attenuations of deity that carry the light of life from Paradise to the evolutionary worlds. Mortals encounter the successive levels of God the Sevenfold in this order:

1. The Creator Sons and Creative Spirits

2. The Ancients of Days

3. The Seven Master Spirits

4. The Supreme Being

5. The Conjoint Actor

6. The Eternal Son

7. The Universal Father

The first three categories are Supreme Creators, the final three are the Paradise Trinity. God the Supreme links the existential Paradise Trinity with the experiential Supreme Creators. The Almighty Supreme actualizes in time and space through the activities of the Supreme Creators, just as the Conjoint Actor sprang into existence through the will of the Father and the Son.

The local universes are laboratories in which the Supreme is achieving deity evolution through the experiences and progressions of the creatures within them. The local universes are birthplaces for the personalities farthest from God, those who are destined to experience the greatest degree of spiritual ascent in the universe. These same local universes provide depth of experience for descending personalities as well.

The universes are not perfect, and the struggle for perfection pertains to the physical level as well as the intellectual and spiritual levels. The Supreme is evolving as the overcontroller of the physical power of the grand universe. In the present universe age, this potential of physical power appears to be centered in the Seven Supreme Power Directors. The power directors are devoted to bringing about the material control of the universes. Established circuits of physical creation are constantly jeopardized by the appearance of new energy and mass, and because of this growth, the time-space universe is unsettled. No part of the whole will find stability until the material creation is complete.

The goal of the evolutionary universes is the subjugation of energy-matter by mind and coordination of mind with spirit, by virtue of the creative unifying presence of personality. In relation to personality, physical systems become subordinate, mind systems become coordinate, and spirit systems become directive. On absolute levels, energy and spirit are one. But as energy and spirit move outward from Paradise, the gulf between them widens until they are no longer identical. As evidenced by the work of the power directors, both energy and mass are responsive to mind; mind intervenes to interrelate mass and energy. The potential unity of all finite creation is disclosed in the fact that spirit in volitional personality can strive through mind for mastery of energy-matter.

There is an interdependence of all forces and personalities throughout the universes. The wide gulf between energy and spirit in time-space creates experiential potential for mind to unify physical patterns with spiritual purpose. Evolutionary experience on finite levels is shared by all, from mortal man to the Supreme Being. All personally strive in superuniverse achievement, as all will personally participate in universe destiny.

The grand universe is not only a material creation, it is also a responsive living organism. The physical universe is permeated by energy lanes that activate material creation, even as the human body is nourished by the circulatory system. Much as mortals look to solar energy for the maintenance of life, so does the grand universe depend on the unfailing energies emanating from nether Paradise.

Man's urge for God-attainment creates a genuine divinity tension in the cosmos that can only be resolved by the evolution of an immortal soul. When all creatures and all Creators in the universe strive for God-attainment, a profound cosmic tension builds which can find resolution only in the evolving God of all creatures, the Supreme Being.

117—GOD THE SUPREME

The potential of the Supreme increases in actuality as each creature learns to do the will of God. The individuals of the grand universe evolve as a reflection of the total evolution of the Supreme, while the Supreme is the cumulative total of all grand universe evolution. The Supreme is the oversoul of the grand universe, the personification of Creator-creature experience. The Supreme is God-in-time. Through him, human spiritual growth is possible, and through his creatures, the Supreme's growth is possible. The incompleteness of the Supreme makes the evolution of the present universes possible.

In some way, human evolution resembles the growth of the Supreme. Mortals consciously grow from the material toward the spiritual by the power of their own decisions, while the Supreme grows through the acts of the Creator personalities. Humans have liaison with an indwelling fragment of the Universal Father; God the Supreme has liaison with the Paradise Trinity. As mortals strive for self-expression, the Supreme strives for deity expression.

The personality of any individual mortal is insignificant compared to the total of Supremacy, but the personality of each individual represents an irreplaceable value. Personality, once expressed, never again finds identical expression unless in the continuing existence of that person. The relationship of humans to the Supreme is the foundation for cosmic morality—universal sensitivity to duty. Morality is directly predicated on the creature's appreciation of his obligation to experiential Deity. When mortals consecrate their will to doing the Father's will, when they give God all that they have, then does God make them more than they are.

The evolving Supreme will eventually compensate finite creatures for their inability to achieve more experience with the universes. We are incapable of understanding the infinite Father, but all of our experiences are part of the Supreme. When the Supreme becomes fully completed, our contact with him will inherently connect us with total experience.

All true love flows from God, and we receive divine affection as we bestow love on each other. Love is dynamic, it is alive. The Father's love becomes real to us only when we allow it to pass through us as we love each other; and this fraternal affection is the essence of the love of the Supreme. God the Father can be found by any individual who has attained the divine level of Godliness, but God the Supreme will never be personally discovered by any one creature until all creatures simultaneously find him at the completion of light and life.

118—SUPREME AND ULTIMATE —TIME AND SPACE

In the evolutionary universes, eternity is the everlasting NOW. We become eternal by identifying with the indwelling spirit. We identify with the indwelling spirit by choosing to do the will of the Father. Complete consecration of will is the guarantee that no future event will change our intention to serve God.

There is a direct relationship between maturity and the mortal unit of time consciousness. Experience, wisdom, and judgment help to lengthen a person's reckoning of time; the older one gets, the less dependent they are on making judgments based on the present moment. Past experiences and future possibilities illuminate the true meaning of daily life. On the absolute and eternal level, potential reality is as meaningful as actual reality; only time-bound creatures perceive a vast difference between potential and actual.

Truth is radiantly alive. When truth becomes linked with fact, time and space condition its meaning. Such truth-facts become relative reality. The absolute truth of the Creator linked with the factual experience of the finite creature eventuates new values in the Supreme.

Space comes nearest of all nonabsolute things to being absolute. Material bodies exist in space, but space also exists in material bodies. On material levels, patterns occupy space, but spirit patterns do not occupy, displace, or contain space. Ideas do not contain space, but it is not safe to postulate that the immaterial is always nonspatial.

Difficulties arise when subordinate Divinity and Deity are assigned infinite attributes. It is true that there is a First Cause, but there are also a host of coordinate, subordinate, associate, and secondary causes. Causation has three functions: to activate static potential, to eventuate universe capacities, and to create and evolve universe actualities.

The omnipotence of Deity does not imply the power to do the undoable; God cannot create square circles or produce evil that is inherently good. God cannot do an ungodlike thing. Also, God is not omnificent—he does not personally do all that is done.

Only the Father-I AM possesses finality of volition; there is but one uncaused Cause in the universe. This fact does not deny the free will of the myriads of children of God scattered throughout the universe. Mortal volition is not absolute, but it is relatively final concerning the destiny of the individual concerned. Volition on any level below God himself includes inherent limitations; for example, a human cannot choose to be something other than human. The entire range of human will is limited to the finite except when we choose to find God and to be like him.

There are no limitations for partnerships between God and man. That God has foreknowledge—makes full allowance for all finite choice—does not in any way abrogate human free will. A mature human may accurately forecast a decision of a younger person, but this foreknowledge takes nothing away from the genuineness of the younger person's decision.

Sin occurs when immature creatures accept the freedom of volition while failing to perceive the obligations and duties of cosmic citizenship. If a person has the prerogative to choose his very existence, and if this is a true and free choice, then that evolving person must also have the possible choice of destroying himself. The possibility of cosmic self-destruction cannot be avoided if the person is to be truly free to exercise his finite will.

We are rooted in the physical world. Human beings are machines—living mechanisms. But we are also much more than machines. We are endowed with mind and indwelt by spirit. During the material life, mortals cannot escape the chemical and electrical mechanisms of existence, but we can increasingly learn how to subordinate our physical mechanism by consecrating our minds to the spiritual urging of the indwelling Adjuster.

Biologic evolution makes it impossible for primitive people to appear with any large endowment of self-restraint. External restraints such as time, space, hunger, and fear effectively limit the range of choices for early humans. As we gain experiential wisdom, internal restraints begin to balance diminishing external restraints. Systems settled in light and life are allowed liberties that would prove destructive to men of earlier eras.

Basic universe mechanisms exist in response to the will of the First Source and Center. Time and space are a conjoined mechanism whereby finite creatures are enabled to coexist in the cosmos with the Infinite. The grand universe is a living mechanism activated by Supreme Mind and coordinated by Supreme Spirit. Even the human body is a mechanism, one which can never be perfectly controlled by man himself since it is the product of supermortal creation.

There is providence in the universe, and it can be discovered only if a mortal has attained capacity to perceive the purpose of the universes. Most of what a mortal would call providence is not; much of what we call good luck may really be bad luck. Fortune that bestows unearned leisure and undeserved wealth may be the greatest of human afflictions. Similarly, seemingly cruel tribulation may be the method by which an immature person develops real character.

It is true that the love of the Father operates directly in the heart of each individual, but the impersonal presence of Deity is concerned for the whole of creation rather than its parts. Providence in the overcontrol of the Supreme becomes increasingly apparent as each part of the universe progresses. Providence becomes increasingly discernible as ascenders reach upward from the material to the spiritual. Although much that happens on an evolving world is hard to understand, the human viewpoint can be modified by understanding, vision, increased control of physical surroundings, and harmony with the Paradise Trinity and the Supreme Being.

119—THE BESTOWALS OF CHRIST MICHAEL

The ability for bestowal is an inherent gift of the Creator Sons. Divine Sons learn to become sympathetic, merciful, and understanding sovereigns by incarnating as lower beings. It is so important that a Creator Son understand the perspective of even the lowest of his creatures, that he must actually *become* a being of his realm seven times. Creator Sons are never certified as sovereigns of their local universes by the Ancients of Days until they have acquired creature viewpoint through actual experience.

Michael of Nebadon, our local universe sovereign, is the 611,121st of his order to achieve approval of the Ancients of Days for local universe sovereignty. Michael made his first bestowal nearly one billion years ago and embarked on a new bestowal mission every 1,500,000 years. Michael's seven incarnations in Nebadon were as:

1. Melchizedek Son.

2. Lanonandek Son.

3. Material Son.

4. Seraphim.

5. Ascendant mortal of spirit status.

6. Morontia mortal.

7. Joshua ben Joseph, an infant on Urantia.

PART IV

THE LIFE AND TEACHINGS OF JESUS

PART IV
THE LIFE AND TEACHINGS OF JESUS

120—THE BESTOWAL OF MICHAEL

A Creator Son can, at any time, rule his local universe in his own right, but he can rule as a representative of the Paradise Trinity only after completing seven creature bestowals. The seventh and final bestowal of Michael, the Creator Son of Nebadon, took place on Urantia when he incarnated as Jesus of Nazareth. Prior to his bestowal, Michael's brother Immanuel advised him to:

1. Maintain unbroken communion with his Paradise Father.

2. Terminate the Lucifer rebellion.

3. Attend first to men's spiritual needs, then their intellect, and lastly their physical health.

4. Lead a life that would educate and inspire the entire universe of Nebadon.

5. Refrain from using the superhuman powers associated with being a creator son.

6. Give precedence to the established customs and practices of the family life in which he appeared.

7. Confine his efforts to spiritual regeneration, avoiding economic and political commitments.

8. Avoid the formation of an organized cult.

9. Leave no writings behind.

10. Leave no human offspring.

Jesus was not God in association with man, but God incarnate in man. Jesus did not progressively become God; God did not at some moment become man. Jesus was God and man, always. The supreme spiritual purpose of Michael's bestowal on Urantia was to enhance the revelation of God. Through Jesus, the Father chose to manifest himself as he always does—in a usual, normal, dependable way.

121—THE TIMES OF MICHAEL'S BESTOWAL

Michael chose a unique time to visit Urantia. European civilization unified under three influences: Roman political systems, Greek language and culture, and Jewish religious and moral teachings. Palestine was the crossroads of three continents. More than half of the caravan traffic arriving from the Orient passed through or near Galilee. Travel and trade were more vibrant during this period than during any previous era.

The Jewish people were fairly self-governing. At the time of Jesus' birth, the king of Judea was Herod the Idumean. Friendly relations between Herod and the Roman rulers made travel safe for Jews and opened the way for increased Jewish penetration into distant areas of the Roman empire.

Mediterranean society included five classes: The upper class, the business class, a tiny middle class, the free proletariat, and the slaves. Slaves comprised half of the total population. The early Christian church was largely composed of the lower classes and slaves.

Four philosophies dominated the gentile world. Epicureans were dedicated to the pursuit of happiness. Stoics believed in a controlling Reason-fate and taught that the soul of man was divine. Cynics drew from the remnants of the teaching of Melchizedek, preaching simplicity and virtue. Skeptics espoused a negative view; they believed that knowledge was never certain.

Religions in the Occident included the pagan cults, emperor worship, astrology, and the mystery religions. The embrace of the mystery religions caused the birth of numerous personal cults. Mystery cults were generally interracial brotherhoods, characterized by elaborate ceremonies and a belief in a mythical legend about some god's life, death, and return to life. These cults invariably promised salvation, deliverance from evil, and survival after death. Although they failed to truly satisfy people's longings for personal religion and salvation, mystery cults paved the way for the acceptance of the teachings of Jesus.

Three languages were spoken in Palestine: Aramaic, Hebrew, and Greek. The eventual translation of the Hebrew scriptures into Greek later influenced the movement of Paul's Christian cult toward the West instead of the East. Philo of Alexandria harmonized Greek philosophy and Hebrew theology, and Paul used this synthesis as a foundation for Christianity. Paul's Christianity eventually became a blend of the gospel of Jesus, Greek philosophy, the mystery cult teachings, and Jewish morality.

Jerusalem was the center of Jewish culture and religion. Jews held the gentiles in contempt; they thought gentiles were heathens and sought to separate themselves from the gentile world. The Jewish people were held in subjugation to the letter of the law and also to the demand of traditions. The scribes, the Pharisees, and the priests held the Jews in a bondage far more restrictive than that of their Roman rulers.

The writing of the gospels was greatly delayed because the apostles observed that Jesus had avoided leaving written records. Many decades passed before some disciples began to preserve the stories of Jesus' life in writing. Of the records that survived into our times, the gospel of Mark is the earliest; John Mark wrote this record soon after Peter's death in AD 68, after being encouraged to do so by Peter. The gospel of Matthew was written by one of his disciples, Isador. This record was written to influence Jewish Christians, and it tends to show Jesus' life in such a way as to fulfill the words of earlier scriptures. The gospel of Luke was written in AD 82-90 by Luke, a gentile physician who began to follow Paul in AD 47. In some ways, this record was the gospel according to Paul. The gospel of John was written by Nathan, an associate of John Zebedee, in the year 101; only the epistle known as First John was written by John himself.

These records, imperfect as they were, were powerful enough to change the course of history for two thousand years.

The Urantia Book's account of the life and teachings of Jesus is derived from several sources including writings of the apostle Andrew; the gospels of Matthew, Mark, Luke and John; and the records of a host of celestial beings who were on earth during Michael's bestowal. New revelation has been used only when human records and concepts failed to supply adequate thought patterns.

122—BIRTH AND INFANCY OF JESUS

Based on a report by the Melchizedeks, Michael chose Urantia as the planet of his final bestowal. Subsequently, Gabriel visited Urantia to study the spiritual, intellectual, racial, and geographic features of the world and its people. He selected the Hebrews as the bestowal race. A commission appointed by Gabriel was sent to investigate Jewish family life, after which Gabriel personally judged Joseph and Mary to be best suited to become the earthly parents of the local universe Creator Son.

Jesus' lifework was begun by his distant cousin, John the Baptist. John was born to Zacharias and Elizabeth in March of 7 BC. Gabriel appeared to Elizabeth before John's birth to reveal John's mission as forerunner of a divine teacher who would soon be born to Elizabeth's kinswoman, Mary. Gabriel appeared to Mary in November, 8 BC, to tell her that she had conceived a son who would inaugurate the kingdom of heaven on earth. Joseph had doubts about the Gabriel visitation but was reconciled to it after he had an impressive dream. Joseph and Mary eventually came to believe that they were to become the parents of the Messiah.

Joseph was mild-mannered, conscientious, gentle, sympathetic, meditative and worshipful. Mary was cheerful, composed, courageous, optimistic, and a gifted teacher. They were both well educated for their time. Joseph leaned toward the Eastern, Babylonian view of the Jewish religion, while Mary leaned toward more liberal, Hellenistic interpretations.

In 7 BC, a census for the Roman empire was taken in the Palestinian kingdom of Herod. Joseph was required to travel from Nazareth to Bethlehem to enroll in the census. Mary, fearful of being left alone while so near delivery, insisted on accompanying him. Bethlehem was so crowded when they arrived that Joseph and Mary settled into a grain storage room in front of a stable for the night.

At noon the next day, August 21, 7 BC, Mary gave birth. The following day Joseph and Mary were offered a room at the local inn where they stayed for nearly three weeks. Three priests from the city of Ur came to visit after a religious teacher had a dream that the light of life was to appear on earth as a baby.

When Jesus was eight days old, he was circumcised and given the name Joshua. Zacharias confided to a singer, Simeon, and a poet, Anna, that the baby was to be the deliverer of the Jewish people. During Jesus' ceremony at the temple, Simeon sang a poem that Anna had written describing the mission of this child of promise who was to bring salvation from the enemies of the Jewish people.

Herod's spies reported that the priests of Ur had visited Bethlehem. Herod questioned the priests, but they gave him no satisfactory answers. After informers brought Herod information about Simeon's song, Herod decided to destroy the potential "king of the Jews" by having all male babies in Bethlehem killed. One of Herod's court attachés came to warn Zacharias the night before the massacre. Zacharias warned Joseph and Mary, who fled to Egypt for two years. They did not return to Bethlehem until after the death of Herod.

123—THE EARLY CHILDHOOD OF JESUS

When Jesus was just over three years old, Joseph and Mary returned to their Nazareth home. Joseph built a workshop close to the village spring. He made yokes and plows and worked with leather, rope, and canvas. Jesus' brother James was born in April, 3 BC. His sister Miriam was born in July, 2 BC.

Jesus' Thought Adjuster, which had previously served with Machiventa Melchizedek, arrived when Jesus was four and a half years old. When Jesus turned five, Joseph assumed responsibility for his son's education and started teaching Jesus from a Greek copy of the Hebrew scriptures.

In the summer of 1 BC, Zacharias and Elizabeth brought John to visit Nazareth. Meeting his cousin prompted Jesus to become interested in the history of Israel and the Jewish rites and feasts. About this time Joseph began his career as a builder, working in Cana, Bethlehem, Magdala, Nain, Sepphoris, Capernaum, Endor and Nazareth. Jesus often accompanied Joseph in his work.

During this year, Joseph and Mary started to have concerns about how Jesus said his prayers. Jesus insisted on talking to his heavenly Father in the same way that he talked to Joseph. Since Jesus knew that this departure from reverent prayer was disconcerting to Mary, the boy would first say his prayers as he was taught, and then have "a little talk" with his Father. He learned to adjust his feelings and impulses to the demands of home and family. Joseph explained the reasons for curtailment of personal desires in deference to the welfare of the family, and when Jesus understood the situation he always willingly cooperated.

Jesus was a normal but inquisitive child. He liked to look at flowers and plants and stars. Jesus enjoyed playing with other children with wooden blocks and wood shavings in the carpentry shop. He administered a charity fund from the proceeds of a dovecote that Mary kept. Jesus was not immune from accidents. When he was seven, his fall from an outdoor staircase during a sandstorm caused Mary great anxiety.

His brother Joseph was born in March, 1 AD. In August Jesus entered formal school where he spent the next six years learning to read, write, and speak Hebrew. It was customary for a child to choose a birthday text at the onset of the school career. The passage Jesus chose was from Isaiah: "The spirit of the Lord God is upon me, for the Lord has anointed me; he has sent me to bring good news to the meek, to bind up the brokenhearted, to proclaim liberty to the captives, and to set the spiritual prisoners free."

Joseph and Jesus enjoyed going for walks on Sabbath afternoons. When he was eight, Jesus learned to milk the cow, make cheese, and operate a loom. He enjoyed playing with clay at the potter's shop with his friend Jacob. Jesus did his school work so well that he was given a week off every month, which he usually spent either at an uncle's farm or on the shores of the Sea of Galilee. He developed a keen sense of numbers, distances, and proportions. Jesus liked music, and arranged to trade dairy products for lessons on the harp. In school he asked many questions, particularly about geography and astronomy.

A third brother, Simon, was born in April of 2 AD.

Nahor, a rabbi from Jerusalem, advised Joseph and Mary to send Jesus to Jerusalem for his education. Mary supported the plan, but Joseph hesitated. When Jesus was asked his opinion of the matter, he told Nahor that he felt he should remain at home with his parents because they loved him and could guide him more safely than strangers.

124—THE LATER CHILDHOOD OF JESUS

Jesus delighted in drawing landscapes and modeling in clay, but these activities were forbidden by Jewish law. One day when Jesus was nine years old he drew a charcoal likeness of his teacher. The elders of the community, after viewing his drawing, sent a committee to demand that Joseph suppress this behavior in his son.

Jesus listened to the discussion between his father and the elders. Resentful that they blamed Joseph for this misdeed, Jesus insisted on being heard by the committee. He defended his viewpoint courageously, then announced that he would abide by the decision of his father. Jesus never again drew or modeled in clay as long as he lived in Joseph's house; giving up this favorite pastime was one of the trials of his youth.

Jesus' sister Martha was born in 3 AD. This year Joseph built an addition onto the house, a combined workshop and bedroom. Jesus had his own workbench and tools, and eventually became proficient at making yokes. His trips away from home during his breaks from school did much to help him understand his own family, and his parents began to learn from him as well as teach him.

When Jesus was ten, he began to become aware of the nature of his life mission. His parents listened to his comments, but neither one volunteered information about what they knew. At school, he was constantly asking questions. His most unusual trait was his unwillingness to fight for himself, and his friend Jacob saw that no one took advantage of Jesus' aversion to fighting. This year he also began to show a preference for the company of older people, delighting in discussing culture, education, economics, politics, and religion. Jesus spent a lot of time at the caravan supply shop, conversing with travelers from around the world. He was a born leader, even when engaged in play. Joseph began to teach Jesus about the various ways of making a living.

When Jesus was eleven his brother Jude was born. Complications from the birth made Mary so ill that Joseph remained at home for several weeks. Jesus became occupied with many duties caused by his mother's illness, and was compelled to assume the responsibilities of first-born son two years earlier than was normally the custom.

In May, 5 AD, Jesus and Joseph traveled to the Greek city Scythopolis on business. It was time for the annual competitive athletic games, and Jesus insisted that his father take him to the amphitheater to watch. Joseph was shocked to see his son's enthusiasm for these games; it was the only time in his life that Joseph was visibly angry with Jesus. Jesus remained unconvinced of the evil of such games, but never again discussed his opinion of athletics while Joseph lived.

Jesus taught home school for his sisters and brothers. He began to notice the difference between Joseph's and Mary's views about the nature of his life's mission. He was inclined to favor his father's viewpoint, that his was a spiritual mission. As time went on, Jesus did much to modify the family's practice of prayer and other religious customs. He also struggled to alleviate his personal conflict between loyalty to his convictions and duty to his family.

A new brother, Amos, was born in 7 AD. This was also the year that Jesus graduated from the Nazareth synagogue school, which gave him the right to participate in the Passover celebrations in Jerusalem. On the day before the Passover Sabbath, a messenger from Salvington appeared to Jesus, declaring, "The hour has come. It is time that you began to be about your Father's business." Jesus was not yet thirteen years old.

125—JESUS AT JERUSALEM

Jesus was thrilled that he would be allowed to participate in the Passover rituals as a full-fledged son of Israel. From the time the group left Nazareth for Jerusalem, he looked forward to the experience with great anticipation. Although women seldom attended the Passover in Jerusalem, Jesus insisted that his mother accompany him and was shocked that Mary and the other women separated from the men when they reached Jerusalem. Mary was not allowed to watch her son's consecration ceremonies.

Jesus was further disappointed by the perfunctory nature of the rituals. While he found some Jewish rituals beautiful, he could not accept those which required belief in the wrath of God. When Joseph became mildly insistent that Jesus accept the orthodox beliefs, Jesus responded, "I refuse to believe that my Father in heaven loves me less than does my father on earth."

Jesus was also upset by the irreverence of people in the temple, and by the moneychangers, animal vendors, and courtesans in the court of the gentiles. He was especially sickened by the killing of animals in the priests' court. Jesus was sure that God was not pleased with these sacrificial offerings. As time passed he became increasingly determined to establish a bloodless Passover.

Often during this Passover week Jesus sat off by himself, thinking. Joseph and Mary were perplexed, and looked forward to the time when they could bring their son home.

At the end of the week the Nazareth company gathered to travel home. It was customary for the men to travel separately from the women and children. Jesus, now a consecrated son of Israel, could have traveled home with the men, even though he had accompanied the women and children on the journey into Jerusalem.

As he waited for the group to assemble, Jesus became absorbed in the temple discussions. Joseph and Mary, each thinking that their son was with the other, left for Nazareth without him. Neither realized that Jesus was missing until they stopped for the night in Jericho. The next morning Joseph and Mary returned to Jerusalem to find him.

Jesus spent his time in the temple, asking many questions of the teachers. He showed such hunger for knowledge that most of the temple teachers humored him, even when his questions seemed critical. The teachers were impressed at Jesus' familiarity with the scriptures in Hebrew and Greek. Some of Jesus' questions were:

1. What exists in the holy of holies?

2. Why are mothers segregated during worship?

3. Why would the slaughter of animals gain divine favor?

4. Why is secular barter allowed in a temple dedicated to the worship of God?

5. Is the Messiah to be a temporal prince or a spiritual leader?

Meanwhile, Joseph and Mary continued their anxious search for the boy, never thinking to find him in the temple. On the fourth day, they looked for Zacharias, hoping that he would know Jesus' whereabouts. As they walked through the temple, they were surprised to recognize the voice of their missing son, who was giving his views on prayer and worship. Mary ran up and chastised Jesus in front of the assembly, bringing his instruction at the temple to a halt.

Jesus said to Mary, "Why is it that you have so long sought me? Would you not expect to find me in my Father's house since the time has come when I should be about my Father's business?" The crowd was astonished at his words.

Jesus said little during the three-day journey back to Nazareth. Upon reaching home, Jesus told them that although he must do the will of the heavenly Father, he would also be obedient to his father on earth. Jesus became adept in adjusting his spiritual duty to his family obligations. Joseph was puzzled by his son's words and behavior, but Mary was more convinced than ever that her son was to be Israel's deliverer. From then on she worked to prepare Jesus for his place on the throne of David.

126—The Two Crucial Years

The story of Jesus' experience in the temple at Jerusalem gratified the people of Nazareth, especially his former teachers. By now Jesus had become adept at yoke making and leather work. He was learning carpentry and cabinet making. The family finances were improving; Jesus was permitted to resume his music lessons. During this year Joseph and Mary began to entertain doubts about Jesus' destiny—he was so difficult to understand, and nothing miraculous had happened.

In September, 8 AD, Joseph was killed at work by a falling derrick. Mary and the children were overcome with sadness. Jesus, just fourteen years old, became the sole support and guardian of his father's family. The youngest of the children, Ruth, was born the following April, and Jesus took his father's place in the delivery and care of the child.

Family responsibility removed all thought in Jesus' mind of immediate plans to be about his Father's business. He understood that the welfare of his earthly family took priority over all other duties; the support of his family became his first obligation.

During his fifteenth year, Jesus became convinced that he was not to be the Jewish Messiah. He was impressed by the phrase "Son of Man" in the book of Enoch, and decided to adopt it as his title when he began his public work.

The greatest confusion of his youth arose when he tried to understand the Scriptural reference to the coming Messiah. Would he recognize this messiah? What would his relationship be to him? Jesus thought through these and many other problems as he worked at the carpenter's bench. Mary was alarmed at his strange ideas and his frequent trips to the hilltops for meditation and prayer.

Jesus worked long hours, faithfully fulfilling the responsibilities of his immediate situation. Each passing month necessitated the practice of greater frugality. Jesus donated his copy of the Greek scriptures to the Nazareth synagogue rather than risk its confiscation by tax collectors.

He rented a piece of land where the other children each planted a vegetable garden. Jesus gave serious thought to purchasing a small farm, but when their claim for Joseph's back pay was denied, the family's dream of a life in the country ended.

127— THE ADOLESCENT YEARS

Jesus attained full physical growth when he was sixteen. He had a healthy body, a keen mind, a kind disposition, and a strong personality. His siblings were becoming confused about his mission. Mary intimated that Jesus was to be the deliverer of the Jewish people, but Jesus denied it.

James took over the schooling of their three sisters, which freed Jesus to devote himself to earning a living for them at his workbench. Jesus gradually spoke less about his thoughts concerning his life's mission. Although there was much Mary could not understand about her son, she appreciated his diligence in providing for their family.

When Jesus was seventeen, there was growing political discontent in Judea. The Zealots wanted to revolt against Roman rule. Mary pressured Jesus to enlist in the Zealots, but he refused. A moneylender named Isaac offered to support the family if Jesus would enlist, but still he refused. After consulting with his chazan, Jesus announced that his family needed not just those things that money could buy, but also a father's care. Jesus began working in the old family repair shop, where he was cheered by daily contact with people from all over the country.

Over time, Jesus persuaded Mary to accept his method of child rearing—encouraging the positive instead of forbidding the negative. This theme carried on into Jesus' public teachings. He always emphasized what should be done rather than what should be avoided.

Rebecca, daughter of Erza, fell in love with Jesus and asked him to marry her. Jesus thanked her for her offer, but refused, saying that he was not free to consider marriage until his family was raised, and even then, he would have to wait until his destiny became clear. Rebecca was heartbroken, but remained in such a state of admiration for Jesus that she followed him throughout his public work.

By the end of his teenage years, Jesus had learned to take responsibility well, to carry on in the face of disappointment, to bear up bravely when his plans were thwarted, to be fair when faced with injustice, to adjust spiritual living to the demands of existence, and to depend solely on the guidance of his Father in Heaven.

128—JESUS' EARLY MANHOOD

By the time Jesus was twenty-one, he had learned to blend his two natures, the divine and the human. He studied, gained experience, and developed wisdom just as other people do. Not until after his baptism did Jesus tap into his divine powers; he wanted to live life as a normal mortal.

When Simon graduated from school, the family members agreed to diversify their trades. Simon began work as a stone mason with Jacob. James worked at the caravan repair shop, and Joseph did carpentry at the work bench at home. Jesus spent some time working in a metal shop in Sepphoris, where he had the chance to study the gentile way of life.

By patient planning, Jesus made his withdrawal from active participation in family affairs. He made James the acting head of the family before he left for Sepphoris. Jesus returned to Nazareth after six months, but he never again assumed leadership of the family.

In 17 AD, Simon came of age and Jesus took him to Jerusalem for the Passover. Later that year, Jesus spent four months in Damascus as the guest of a merchant he had met in Philadephia. This merchant was interested in establishing a school of religious philosophy and wanted Jesus to tour the educational institutions of the world as preparation for becoming the head teacher of this new school. Another offer was extended by a company of Jews in Alexandria, who wanted Jesus to begin as assistant chazan in their main synagogue. He refused both positions.

In 18 AD, James and Miriam each approached Jesus about the possibility of their future marriages. It was decided that in two years time, if Joseph was ready to assume the leadership of the family and Martha could assume responsibilities of eldest daughter, that James could marry Esta, from Nazareth, and Miriam would wed Jacob, the stone mason.

The next year Jesus took Jude to Jerusalem for the Passover. There they witnessed a Roman guard making improper comments to a passing Jewish girl, and Jude expressed his resentment so directly that he was arrested and taken to prison. Jesus accompanied him. After two days in prison they were brought before a magistrate, and Jesus spoke on his brother's behalf. Hearing the circumstances of the arrest, the judge released Jude with a warning.

For years James had trouble with Jude, who didn't like to work and was not dependable in providing his share of the family's expenses. Jude was so prone to patriotic outbursts against the Romans that James and Joseph were inclined to cast him from the family. Jesus counseled patience, advising that Jude would learn a better way from observing their own wise behavior.

In 20 AD Miriam married Jacob and James married Esta. Jesus confided in James that he was preparing to leave home. The brothers signed a secret contract in which James accepted title to the repair shop in exchange for relieving Jesus from all future obligations for the finances of the family. Even so, Jesus continued to send home funds until his public ministry began.

129—LATER ADULT LIFE OF JESUS

Jesus left home when he was twenty-six years old. After visiting several cities on the Sea of Galilee, he accepted a job in Capernaum building boats with Zebedee, a friend of his father. Jesus worked in Capernaum for more than a year, creating a new style of boat that was so superior that the shop had more work than it could handle for several years.

Five evenings a week Jesus studied at the Capernaum synagogue. One night each week he spent with young people, and one with the elderly. Jesus endeared himself to both age groups because he was always interested in what people were doing. He seldom offered advice unless asked. He made a habit of conducting question-and-answer sessions each evening before going out to study, discussing such topics as politics, science, philosophy and religion.

In March, 22 AD, Jesus left for Jerusalem. Salome, Zebedee's wife, wrote a letter for Jesus introducing him to her relative, Annas, who was once a high priest in Jerusalem. Through this connection, Jesus visited the Jerusalem schools; he also spent much of his time listening to the temple discussions.

Near the end of Passover week, Jesus met two travelers from India, Gonod and his son Ganid. The travelers hired Jesus as an interpreter and tutor to accompany them on a business trip around the Mediterranean.

The experiences of this Mediterranean tour gave Jesus the opportunity to grow close to people of many colors, education levels, cultural backgrounds, social strata, and religious persuasions.

130—ON THE WAY TO ROME AND
131—THE WORLD'S RELIGIONS

Jesus, Gonod, and Ganid left Jerusalem on April 26, 22 AD to embark on a tour of the Mediterranean that included Alexandria, Crete, Carthage, Naples, Rome, Corinth, Athens, Ephesus, Cyprus, Syria, Damascus, Mesopotamia, Babylon, and Ur. Jesus spent half of each day teaching Ganid and acting as interpreter for Gonod's business contacts, and the other half getting to know people. Ganid learned much from Jesus during their association.

While in Joppa, Jesus met Gadiah, a Philistine interpreter. One day as Jesus and Gadiah were walking by the sea, Gadiah pointed out the place that was reputed to be the site from which Jonah had begun his ill-fated voyage. Gadiah asked Jesus whether he thought Jonah really had been swallowed by a big fish.

Jesus perceived that Gadiah, through the story of Jonah, had been impressed against the folly of running away from duty. Jesus answered, "My friend, we are all Jonahs with lives to live in accordance with the will of God, and at all times when we seek to escape the present duty of living by running away to far-off enticements, we thereby put ourselves in the immediate control of those influences which are not directed by the powers of truth and the forces of righteousness. The flight from duty is the sacrifice of truth. The escape from the service of light and life can only result in those distressing conflicts with the difficult whales of selfishness which lead eventually to darkness and death unless such God-forsaking Jonahs shall turn their hearts, even when in the very depths of despair, to seek after God and his goodness. And when such disheartened souls sincerely seek for God—hunger for truth and thirst for righteousness—there is nothing that can hold them in further captivity."

Sometime later Gadiah asked why God, who is infinitely good, permits the existence of evil. Jesus replied, "My brother, God is love; therefore he must be good, and his goodness is so great and real that it cannot contain the small and unreal things of evil. God is so positively good that there is absolutely no place in him for negative evil. Your Father in heaven, by endowing you with the power to choose between truth and error, created the potential negative of the positive way of light and life; but such errors of evil are really nonexistent until such a time as an intelligent creature wills their existence by mischoosing the way of life."

In Caesarea, Jesus and his friends were delayed because one of the boats on which they intended to travel was being repaired. There was a shortage of skilled woodworkers, and Jesus volunteered to assist in the repair. Anaxand, one of the men who worked on the boat with Jesus, became interested when Jesus spoke of the Father in heaven being interested in the welfare of his children on earth. The young man asked, "If the Gods are interested in me, then why do they not remove the cruel and unjust foreman of this workshop?"

Jesus answered, "Since you know the ways of kindness and value justice, perhaps the Gods have brought this erring man near that you may lead him into this better way. Maybe you are the salt which is to make this brother more agreeable to all other men; that is, if you have not lost your savor. As it is, this man is your master in that his evil ways unfavorably influence you. Why not assert your mastery of evil by virtue of the power of goodness and thus become the master of all relations between the two of you? I predict that the good in you could overcome the evil in him if you gave it a fair and living chance."

When the boat was ready, the company left for Alexandria. While Gonod attended to his business affairs, Jesus and Ganid explored the museums and library. From Alexandria, the travelers journeyed to Crete to relax.

One day in the mountains, Jesus met a distressed young man. Jesus asked the youth for directions to a certain place, and the young man marked out the trails on the ground and explained the route in detail. Jesus soon turned the conversation to the young man's disconsolation. "My friend, arise! Stand up like a man! You may be surrounded with small enemies and be retarded by many obstacles, but the big things and the real things of this world and the universe are on your side. The sun rises every morning to salute you just as it does the most powerful and prosperous man on earth."

After further discourse, Jesus continued, "This day, my son, you are to be reborn, re-established as a man of faith, courage, and devoted service to man, for God's sake. And when you become so readjusted to life within yourself, you become likewise readjusted to the universe; you have been born again—born of the spirit—and henceforth will your whole life become one of victorious accomplishment. Trouble will invigorate you; disappointment will spur you on; difficulties will challenge you; and obstacles will stimulate you. Arise, young man! Say farewell to the life of cringing fear and fleeing cowardice. Hasten back to duty and live your life in the flesh as a son of God, a mortal dedicated to the ennobling service of man on earth and destined to the superb and eternal service of God in eternity."

This young man later became the leader of Christians in Crete.

From Crete the sojourners traveled to Carthage, Malta, Syracuse, Messina, Naples, and Rome.

132—THE SOJOURN AT ROME

In Rome, Jesus had six months to become acquainted with the city and its people. Jesus' work during this period was entirely personal. He made valuable contact in Rome with leaders of the Stoics, Cynics, and mystery cults. Thirty of this group of thirty-two religionists later became proponents of Christianity. Jesus' contact with these leaders was one of three acts that most effected the rapid growth of Christianity in the first century; the other two were the choice of Peter as an apostle, and Jesus' talk with Stephen, whose death led to the conversion of Paul.

Some of the highlights of Jesus' various talks with the religious leaders in Rome were:

"In every age scientists and religionists must recognize that they are on trial before the bar of human need. They must eschew all warfare between themselves while they strive valiantly to justify their continued survival by enhanced devotion to the service of human progress."

"If you are ethically lazy and socially indifferent, you can take as your standard of good the current social usages."

"The spiritually blind individual who logically follows scientific dictation, social usage, and religious dogma stands in grave danger of sacrificing his moral freedom and losing his spiritual liberty."

"Actual evil is not necessary as a personal experience. Potential evil acts equally well as a decision stimulus in the realms of moral progress on the lower levels of spiritual development."

"Revealed truth, personally discovered truth, is the supreme delight of the human soul; it is the joint creation of the material mind and the indwelling spirit."

"Human life continues—survives—because it has a universe function, the task of finding God."

Jesus spent a great deal of time preparing religious leaders for the future. He also enjoyed learning about how people felt about life, and giving them the message of the Father's love and mercy. While he usually started conversations with people by asking questions, frequently he would end up answering questions. He taught the most to people to whom he said the least. Jesus was very fond of doing things for people.

One Roman senator, after talking with Jesus, spent the rest of his life trying to change state policy from having the government support the people to having people support the government. A slaveholder released over one hundred slaves the day after he had a long talk with Jesus. Jesus counseled a rich man who wondered what he should do with his money. Jesus advised the man to first investigate where the money came from, after which he could decide how to disburse it wisely.

One day Jesus and Ganid spent several hours bringing a lost child home to his mother. During this adventure, Jesus said, "...most human beings are like the lost child. They spend much of their time crying in fear and suffering in sorrow when, in very truth, they are but a short distance from safety and security...."

Jesus also talked about how we cannot reveal God to those who do not seek him. He said that people become hungry for truth either as a result of the experiences of living, or as the result of contact with the lives of those who know God. If we know God, our real business on earth is to live so as to permit the Father to reveal himself in our lives.

133—THE RETURN FROM ROME

Jesus, Ganid, and Gonod walked across Italy on the great Appian Way. During a discussion about India's caste system, Jesus said, "There are only two groups of mortals in the eyes of God: those who desire to do his will and those who do not."

The trio saw a child being attacked by a bully. Jesus assisted the child by restraining the bully until the boy made his escape. As soon as Jesus released the offender, Ganid began to beat him. Jesus promptly restrained Ganid. Ganid couldn't understand why Jesus didn't let him punish the bully. Jesus explained, "Mercy ministry is always the work of the individual, but justice punishment is the function of the social, governmental, or universe administrative groups." Jesus said that mercy may be lavish, but justice must be precise. They talked about this subject for days.

In Corinth, Jesus and Ganid were approached by two prostitutes. Ganid, assuming that Jesus would be offended, shooed them away rudely. Jesus' response astonished both Ganid and the women: "You mean well, but you should not presume thus to speak to the children of God, even though they chance to be his erring children. Who are we to sit in judgment on these women?" Jesus eventually led the women to the house of his friend Justus, a local merchant. There the women were presented to the merchant's wife, Martha, for nourishment and counsel. Martha did everything for the strangers that Jesus had hoped. The elder woman soon died, but the younger went to work for Justus, eventually joining the first Christian church in Corinth.

Jesus had many other interesting conversations with people in Corinth. He tailored his saving message to each person—the Mithraic leader, an Epicurean, a builder, a Chinese merchant, a British traveler, a condemned criminal. To a miller, he described how to grind truth in the mill of living experience to make it suitable for other people's capacity of receptivity. Jesus advised the mistress of an inn to minister her hospitality as one who entertains the children of the Most High. He told a runaway that there are two things people cannot run away from—God and themselves.

After two months, the party sailed to Athens, where Ganid and Gonod enjoyed a discussion Jesus carried on with a Greek philosopher. Jesus discussed the limits of logic and mathematics as they apply to life. Jesus said that a group of human beings working in harmony creates a force far greater than the sum of the personalities involved. He said that there is unity in the universe, and that the universe is friendly to every child of God.

Later in Cyprus, Ganid asked Jesus to explain how people experience a higher form of self-conscious than animals. Jesus emphasized that self-consciousness is a reality. The attainment of self-consciousness warrants the bestowal of the spirit of the Father in heaven, which is the absolute focal point for the human personality. Humans differ not only in heredity and environmental influences, but also in the degree of unification with the indwelling spirit of God. Unification of mind depends on being wholly dedicated to doing the will of the Father in heaven.

The travelers made their way to Salamis, Antioch, and the ancient city of Ur. In Ur Jesus left his Indian friends, never to see them again in the flesh. Later in life, Ganid heard of the so-called Son of Man who lost his life on a cross in Palestine, but he never knew that this was his beloved tutor.

134—The Transition Years

After spending a few months visiting with his family in Nazareth, Jesus worked for a year as a driver on a caravan traveling to the Caspian Sea. During this trip he visited an amphitheater in Urmia that was used as a temple of the philosophy of religions. Teachers at this temple represented over thirty religions and religious cults, all of which believed in a supreme Deity.

On Jesus' journey home from the Caspian Sea, he gave a series of lectures in Urmia about the kingdom of God and the kingdoms of men. Jesus taught that the kingdom of heaven is neither material nor intellectual, but rather a spiritual relationship between man and God. Religious peace—brotherhood—will not exist until all religions surrender ecclesiastical authority and accept God alone as spiritual sovereign.

He discussed how political sovereignty arrives from the surrender of self-determinism; first by the individual to the family, then the family to the clan, and then to the tribe and the state. Patriotism makes the evolution of a government of all mankind difficult.

Jesus said that confederations of nations may reduce conflicts, but war will continue until the world government is created. War is not a disease, but a symptom of the disease of national sovereignty. The problem of war cannot be solved by armaments or disarmaments; men will continue fighting with fists and stones as long as they cling to the delusion of the right of national sovereignty.

He taught that mortals cannot live together in peace without becoming subservient to laws that grant each person a degree of freedom while safeguarding an equal amount of freedom for others. The political sovereignty of a representative government of humankind will bring lasting peace on earth, and spiritual brotherhood will forever insure good will among people. This is the only way that peace on earth and good will among men can be realized.

The following year, Jesus' family moved to Capernaum. After visiting their new home, Jesus traveled much of the year through Palestine and Syria. He spent six weeks on Mount Hermon, communing with the Father and consecrating himself to the remainder of his life's work. During this period of isolation Jesus became absolutely assured of the ascendancy of his divine nature.

Near the end of this time on the mountain Jesus requested a conference with the rebels of Satania. Satan and Calagastia, emissaries of Lucifer, suggested many compromises and proposals. Jesus responded by saying that they had already spurned his mercy; he committed them to the judgment of the Ancients of Days. The Lucifer rebellion was settled.

When Jesus came down from Mount Hermon he met with his family again in Capernaum, and then traveled to Jerusalem with John Zebedee for three weeks. After this holiday he returned to Zebedee's workshop, saying, "It behooves me to keep busy while I wait for my hour to come." Jesus worked until January with his brother John, building boats.

135—JOHN THE BAPTIST

John the Baptist grew up in a small town west of Jerusalem. He took the vows of a Nazarite when he was fourteen years old. At twenty, he left home to tend sheep in a colony of Nazarites headed by Abner. As time passed, John became convinced that he was to become the herald of the coming kingdom of heaven. At the age of thirty-two he embarked on his short, brilliant career as a public preacher.

John's message, "Repent, for the kingdom of heaven is at hand!" can best be understood within the context of his time. For almost one hundred years, Israel had been suffering under the continuous control of gentiles. The Jewish people could not understand why God's chosen people should be thus humiliated. Most Jews were confident that the kingdom of heaven was coming and that God would rule the nations of earth during their generation. The vast majority of Jews believed that God would accomplish his plan by sending a Messiah.

John began his public preaching tour in March, 25 AD. He added a new twist to an old custom when he baptized to symbolize the remission of sins; in the past only gentile proselytes had submitted to baptism. John baptized more than one hundred thousand believers in fifteen months of active preaching. James and John, sons of Zebedee, were baptized.

Jesus' brothers, James and Jude, considered being baptized as well. When they asked for Jesus' advice, the three brothers made their way together to the Jordan valley. Jesus and his brothers were baptized in the Jordan river at noon on Monday, January 14, 26 AD. An apparition appeared over Jesus' head, and a voice was heard to say, "This is my beloved Son in who I am well pleased." After his baptism, Jesus took his leave, going into the hills for forty days.

When Jesus returned in mid-February, John knew that the responsibility for the coming kingdom no longer rested with him. His preaching changed into an expression of mercy toward the common people and a denouncement of corrupt political and religious rulers. In June, Herod Antipas had John arrested.

John was imprisoned for a year and a half. He was lonely and sometimes bitter. A group of his disciples who came to visit expressed wonderment that Jesus didn't try to save John. In response to their concerns John said, "This man can do nothing unless it has been given him by his Father in heaven. You well remember that I said, 'I am not the Messiah, but I am one sent on before to prepare the way for him.' And that I did. He who has the bride is the bridegroom, but the friend of the bridegroom who stands nearby and hears him rejoices greatly because of the bridegroom's voice. This, my joy, therefore is fulfilled. He must increase but I must decrease. I am of this earth and have declared my message. Jesus of Nazareth comes down to the earth from heaven and is above us all. The Son of Man has descended from God, and the words of God he will declare to you." John was amazed because he understood that he had spoken a prophecy. Never again did he doubt the divinity of Jesus.

Jesus loved John. He knew that John's life's work was finished, and that great things were in store for John once he departed this world. Jesus restrained himself from interfering in the course of the great preacher's end.

John remained in prison because Herod feared releasing John almost as much as he feared putting him to death. But Herod's unlawful wife, Herodias, hated John. One night, during a feast for Herod's birthday, Herodias's daughter danced for Herod. He was so enchanted with her that he promised her anything she asked. After seeking counsel from her mother, the daughter asked for John's head on a platter. John's life on earth ended that night.

136—BAPTISM AND THE FORTY DAYS

Following his baptism, Jesus went into seclusion for forty days. He was now fully aware of his relationship to the universe, and recalled Immanuel's instructions concerning the bestowal mission. While Jesus was in seclusion, Gabriel appeared to him to discuss the welfare of the local universe. He was accompanied by the Constellation Father of Edentia who informed Jesus that he was now at liberty to terminate his incarnation.

After Jesus' celestial visitors left he planned for his remaining days on earth. Jesus decided not to teach until John's work was finished. He reviewed Immanuel's instructions and pondered the methods of ministry open to him. Jesus realized that situations might arise in his public career in which his concern for the planet could conflict with his Father's desire for an illustration of the ideal mortal life. He decided that if he had to choose between these two, he would subordinate his own wishes to the will of his Father.

Three days after Jesus secluded himself in the hills, he was given a vision of the assembled hosts of seraphim and other celestial beings who had been sent to serve him. Twelve legions of seraphim, nearly six million angels, awaited his command. Jesus decided that he would not use them unless it was evident that it was his Father's will.

Jesus made a conscious decision not to transcend natural law to obtain personal necessities or to prevent his own untimely death. Neither would he use superhuman power to win favor for his saving message. Jesus decided that he would not allow his followers to think of him as the Messiah, and that he would remain completely subject to the Father's will in all matters.

Jesus did not intend to use miracles or wonders to win people to his message. He knew the Jewish people were expecting a Messiah who could perform miracles, but Jesus refused to prostitute his divine powers. Miracle-working might have gratified the Jews, but would not have been a revelation of the heavenly Father. Jesus chose to establish the kingdom of heaven by the natural, ordinary, and difficult methods that all humans must use in their work of expanding the kingdom.

137—Tarrying Time in Galilee

In February, 26 AD, Jesus chose Andrew as his first apostle. At Andrew's suggestion, Simon Peter became the second apostle. Jesus welcomed Simon, saying, "I admonish you to become more thoughtful in your speech. I would change your name to Peter."

Meanwhile James and John, sons of Zebedee, returned from a futile search for the Master in the hills of Pella. When they heard Jesus had chosen his first associates in their absence they were upset. Jesus admonished them, "You should learn to search for the secret of the new kingdom in your hearts and not in the hills." He asked them to be of good cheer and to prepare to accompany the other men into Galilee.

The next morning, this small band of men started on their journey. On the road to Galilee they met Philip of Bethsaida and his friend Nathaniel. Peter consulted with Philip, urging him to offer his services to Jesus. Philip, having been on his way to visit John the Baptist, was unsure of what to do. He decided to let Jesus decide the matter. "Teacher, shall I go down to John or shall I join my friends who follow you?" And Jesus answered, "Follow me." Philip then presented Nathaniel to Jesus, and Nathaniel was likewise welcomed into apostleship.

The group crossed the Jordan river and reached Nazareth late that evening. The next day, the apostles went to Cana to prepare for a wedding feast, while Jesus visited his family and the Zebedees in Capernaum.

His mother and friends suspected that Jesus would soon announce that he was the Messiah. In spite of Jesus' warnings to tell no one about him, they quietly spread the news that something was about to happen. As a result, more than four times the number of invited guests showed up in Cana for the wedding of Naomi and Johab.

Jesus became aware that the people at the wedding were expecting something of him, and he was especially concerned that his family and apostles seemed to be waiting for a sign. Early in the afternoon, Mary and James frankly asked Jesus to tell them how he was going to demonstrate his power to the wedding guests. Jesus, disappointed and indignant, replied, "If you love me, then be willing to tarry with me while I wait upon the will of my Father who is in heaven." He gathered his apostles and told them, "Think not that I have come to this place to work some wonder for the gratification of the curious."

Later that evening, the mother of the bridegroom confided to Mary that the wine supply for the wedding feast was running short. Mary asked Jesus to help, but Jesus said, "What have I to do with that?" Mary told him that she had promised to get him to help. When Jesus replied that she shouldn't have promised such a thing, Mary began to cry.

Jesus, trying to comfort Mary, said, "Grieve not. Most gladly would I do what you ask of me if it were a part of the Father's will— ." Jesus stopped, suddenly realizing that something had happened. The moment Jesus desired to fulfill his mother's request, his wish was implemented by the unseen celestial personalities accompanying him. Wine appeared in the water jugs.

Jesus was more surprised than anyone by the appearance of wine at the wedding feast. Throughout his subsequent career, he tried to keep his guard up against such events, but many similar wonders happened during his life on earth.

Jesus and his apostles left early the next morning for Capernaum. On the way, Jesus tried to describe the nature of his mission on earth. He told his men not to talk about how he had turned water into wine. As Jesus tried to explain his mission, he began to realize that their idea of a Jewish Messiah was so set that he would not be able to dissuade them from it. He decided to leave this problem to the Father.

Jesus and his six apostles stayed in Capernaum for four months, working during the day and spending three hours each evening preparing for their future work. This time of waiting tested the apostles' patience; absolutely nothing miraculous happened. As Jesus instructed them night after night, they began to know each other well.

In June Jesus preached at the synagogue in Capernaum. He told the crowd that when he finished his work on earth, the Spirit of Truth would come to all people, both Jew and gentile. Jesus explained that his kingdom was not of this world, and that his followers needed to have the faith of children to gain admission. He announced, "And whatever it shall cost you in the things of the world, no matter what price you may pay to enter the kingdom of heaven, you shall receive manyfold more of joy and spiritual progress in this world, and in the age to come eternal life."

All who heard him speak that day were astonished. One third believed him even though they could not completely comprehend, one third rejected his spiritual concept of the kingdom, and one third thought he was mentally unbalanced.

138—TRAINING THE KINGDOM'S MESSENGERS

In June, 26 AD, Jesus sent the apostles out for two weeks. Each apostle was asked to invite one other man to join the group and to speak personally with people about the kingdom. The apostles began to sense the spiritual hunger in people and learn the value of personal contact. Meanwhile, Jesus visited with his family in Nazareth.

When they returned, each man proposed his candidate for the group. Andrew selected Matthew Levi, Philip chose Thomas Didymus, James Zebedee invited James Alpheus, John Zebedee chose Judas Alpheus, Peter chose Simon Zelotes, and Nathaniel invited Judas Iscariot. Jesus personally called the new apostles to their work.

Arrangements were made for the apostles to live in the Zebedees' house in Capernaum while they spent a week in training. By day, the six new apostles learned from the original six, and each evening all learned together from Jesus. For the next five months, the apostles went out in pairs, alternating personal ministry with fishing. Jesus divided his time among the six pairs of apostles. In January, 27 AD, Jesus formally ordained the twelve as preachers and ambassadors of the kingdom.

This was a period of quiet ministry and growth. The apostles had trouble understanding much that Jesus taught because they insisted on trying to fit his teachings into their old religious beliefs. They were shocked by his treatment of women as equals in spiritual matters. Judas Iscariot was unsatisfied with Jesus' lack of action in the imprisonment of John the Baptist. The six original apostles complained when they heard that the newer six would be granted equal status. All questioned Jesus about how he was going to establish the kingdom, and what positions each of them would have.

Jesus instructed the apostles to portray the revelation of the Father's love without being sidetracked into preaching about him. He asked them to seek sinners and to comfort the downhearted. Jesus tried to convince the apostles that his kingdom was a spiritual one, rather than a rule of power and glory on earth.

Jesus taught the apostles about forgiveness of sin through faith, without penance or sacrifice. Jesus wanted them to have the personal experience and assurance of God's indwelling love and grace. The apostles learned that Jesus had a profound respect for every human being he met;

nothing was so important to him as the individual person who happened to be in his presence. They did not comprehend Jesus' teachings completely, but they truly believed in him.

The common people marveled at the teachings of Jesus and his apostles. They had been told by rabbis that ignorant people could not be pious or righteous, but Jesus' apostles disproved this.

139—THE TWELVE APOSTLES

Andrew, the first chosen apostle, was chairman of the group. He was thirty three years old when Jesus called him, the oldest of all the apostles. Andrew was a good administrator, efficient at personal ministry but never an effective preacher. He got along well with his brother Simon Peter, but was quite unlike him in temperament. Of all the apostles, Andrew was the best judge of people. He had a knack for discovering hidden talents. He was even-tempered, stable, and logical. Andrew died by crucifixion after bringing many thousands in Armenia, Asia Minor, and Macedonia into the kingdom.

Peter was married with three children when he joined the group. He was an impulsive optimist, and often caused trouble by speaking thoughtlessly. He was a natural speaker—fluent, eloquent and dramatic. Peter asked more questions of Jesus than all the other apostles put together. He is described as "one of the most inexplicable combinations of courage and cowardice that ever lived on earth." Peter was a loyal friend, but he feared ridicule. He did more than any of the other apostles to establish the kingdom after Jesus' death; he was a saving light to thousands of people. Peter's wife became a member of the women's corps and was thrown to the beasts in the arena the same day that Peter was crucified in Rome.

James Zebedee was married and had four children when Jesus chose him. He, John, and Peter were assigned to be the personal companions of Jesus. James was an exceptional public speaker and of all the apostles came the closest to grasping the importance of Jesus' teaching. James was a well-balanced thinker. He was modest, undramatic and unpretentious. The first apostle to be put to death, he was killed by Herod Agrippa. When death came, James bore himself with such grace that Herod's informer against James was inspired to join Jesus' disciples.

John Zebedee, the youngest of the twelve, was twenty four when he joined. John was dependable and faithful. His gospel reveals how the concept of love became dominant in his life. John was conceited but usually concealed this trait. He was somewhat bigoted and intolerant of people he considered beneath himself. John had courage unmatched by the other apostles—he followed Jesus throughout the night of his arrest. He was the first apostle to believe in the resurrection, and the first to recognize Jesus in his morontia form. John married his brother James' widow. He was imprisoned several times, and wrote the book of Revelation while in exile on the isle of Patmos. John died a natural death at Ephesus when he was 101 years old.

Philip was married when he joined the apostles. He was methodical, tenacious, and thorough; he was appointed the steward of the group. Philip's weakest trait was his lack of imagination. His effectiveness lay in his habit of showing people what he meant; he always said, "Come and I will show you" rather than, "Go and see." Philip's wife was a fearless member of the women's corps; as Philip was dying, she stood at the foot of his cross encouraging him, and when his strength failed she continued to preach until irate Jews stoned her to death.

When Nathaniel joined the apostles he was twenty-five and unmarried. Honest and sincere, Nathaniel moved easily between philosophy and humor. He was the best storyteller of the apostles. In spite of a tendency toward prejudice, Nathaniel got along well with everyone except Judas Iscariot. His apostolic duty was to care for the families of the twelve and he saw to it that the needs of each family were well met. Nathaniel died in India.

Matthew was a married customs collector with four children. He was a good business man and got along well with a variety of people. Matthew was in charge of fundraising for the apostles. He was wholeheartedly devoted to the cause of the kingdom. He made extensive notes on Jesus' talks, and these notes later became the basis of the narrative known as the gospel according to Matthew. The fact that he was a publican caused some consternation among the other apostles, but it was a comfort to many downhearted souls who had previously regarded themselves as unworthy of religious consolation. After Jesus died, Matthew traveled north, preaching and baptizing until he was put to death in Thrace.

Thomas was twenty-nine and married, with four children. Thomas was logical, somewhat skeptical, and courageously loyal. He possessed the one truly analytical mind of the twelve. He was pessimistic and somewhat quarrelsome, tending toward suspicion. He was also honest and unflinchingly loyal. Thomas' task was to manage the itinerary, and he did this well. He was cautious, but if his conservative vote was overruled, he fearlessly supported the decision of the group. After Jesus' death, Thomas traveled to Cyprus, Crete, and North Africa, and was put to death in Malta.

James and Judas Alpheus were twenty-six-year-old twin fishermen when they were called. They were almost identical physically, mentally, and spiritually. James and Judas understood little of the discussions of the apostles, but they rejoiced to be among such a group of men. They were the chief ushers during the preaching tours and helped Philip and Nathaniel with their work. The acceptance of these two men into the corps was a great encouragement to the common people of the time. James and Judas could not comprehend Jesus' teachings but they did experience his spiritual nature. The twins were good-natured, simple-minded, and well loved by the other apostles. After Jesus died they returned to their families and their fishing nets.

Twenty-eight year old Simon Zelotes was a fiery agitator who often spoke without thinking. His great strength was his loyalty; material-mindedness was his weakness. Simon was an excellent debater. Growing from a Jewish nationalist into a spiritually-minded internationalist was a difficult challenge for Simon. He despaired after the Jewish dispersion, but rallied himself and eventually proclaimed the gospel throughout Alexandria, the Nile River valley, and into the heart of Africa.

Judas Iscariot was unmarried and unemployed when he came to the apostles. He was the most well educated of the twelve, and the only Judean. Judas was appointed treasurer, a duty that he fulfilled efficiently and honestly. He was a good business man, discharging his duties with tact and patience. Judas was often critical of Jesus and the other apostles in his own mind. He was never able to rise above his prejudice against Galileans. Judas had exaggerated ideas of self-importance; he was a poor loser.

For Jesus, Judas was a "faith adventure." By accepting Judas as his associate, Jesus demonstrated to mortals of all worlds that when doubt exists about the sincerity of a creature's devotion to God, the universe practice is to give the person every benefit of the doubt. To the very end, Jesus tried to transform Judas' weak spirituality, to prevent him from going the wrong way. Judas brooded over imagined slights and personal disappointments and became steeped in suspicion and malice. After Judas betrayed Jesus, he experienced a moment of regret before committing suicide.

140—The Ordination of the Twelve

Having selected his apostolic corps, Jesus called the apostles together in the highlands north of Capernaum to formally present them to God as messengers of his kingdom. What is known today as the "Sermon on the Mount" is a fragmented recollection of Jesus' ordination speech to the twelve that day. Jesus advised his apostles that all things essential to their eternal survival would be secure if they first found the kingdom of God. Jesus told them that whosoever wished to become great in the kingdom should serve his brothers, and that men would know them not by the words they spoke but by the lives they lived. He asked them to think of themselves not as men among men, but as enlightened citizens of a heavenly country among the ignorant creatures of a dark world.

During the following week the apostles prepared for their pending public ministry, teaching by day and holding private conferences by night. Jesus constantly repeated the two great motives of the upcoming mission: to reveal God to people, and to lead people to realize that they are the children of God.

Toward the end of the week Jesus gave special instruction to Peter, James, and John. He taught that to trust in the overcare of the Father was not the same as passive fatalism. He quoted the scriptures, saying, "He who will not work shall not eat." He told them to abandon anxiety and worry, but not prudence and forethought. He said that while individuals should not resist evil, civil government must sometimes employ force in the interest of social order. He made it clear that his instructions applied only to individuals and not to the state or society.

Jesus taught his followers to feed the poor, but admonished them that indiscriminate kindness is the cause of many social evils. He exalted family life as the highest human duty but counseled that family should not interfere with religious obligations. Jesus did not concentrate on relieving social, political, or economic problems. He worked to perfect men's spiritual life to enable them to more competently solve their own human problems. Jesus taught that morality rises not from human nature, but from the relationship between man and God. He asked his followers to show fatherly love rather than brotherly love.

141—Beginning the Public Work

In January, AD 27, Jesus and the apostles left Bethsaida to set out on their public ministry. A crowd arrived to see them off and wish them well. Just as the apostles prepared to leave, they noticed that Jesus was missing, and Andrew set off in search of him. He found Jesus alone on the beach, weeping. Andrew asked, "Which of us has offended you?" Jesus replied, "I am saddened only because none of my father Joseph's family have remembered to come over to bid us Godspeed."

Over one hundred believers desired to accompany the group but, knowing that Herod would soon take notice of them, Jesus asked them not to. Jesus and his men traveled to Pella, where they spent two weeks, preaching by day and conferring each evening.

The apostles spent the next three weeks at Amathus. Andrew organized a system by which ten apostles worked each day while two rested. The apostles taught twice daily and Jesus preached on Sabbath afternoons. Peter, James and John did most of the preaching. Philip, Nathaniel, Thomas, and Simon did personal work and conducted smaller classes. Andrew, Matthew and Judas did general management as well as religious work. During this first year the apostles spent much time working with followers of John the Baptist.

At the end of February, the group journeyed to the Jordan River. They worked for four weeks in Bethany and Jericho. The apostles concentrated on Jesus' request to minister to the sick and discovered that their message not only comforted sick people but also healed them. After visiting Lazarus in Bethany for several days, Jesus and the apostles traveled to celebrate the Passover in Jerusalem.

During these months, Jesus taught the apostles to recognize the differences between diseases of the body, diseases of the mind, and possessions by evil spirits. He knew the difference between spirit possessions and insanity, but it was not possible to make this matter fully understandable to the apostles. Jesus promised them that once he had ascended to the Father, evil spirits would never again be able to molest humans.

Jesus never tired of teaching the apostles; when he failed to reach them with one illustration, he would try again with a different way. Repeatedly he warned the apostles against formulating creeds and traditions as a means of guiding or controlling believers. Jesus tried to convince his disciples that they should live in such a way that people would become conscious of the kingdom by seeing it operating in their lives.

Jesus tried to explain to the apostles that his mission was not just to set an example for people on our planet, but to demonstrate a standard of life for all people on all worlds in the universe. He taught the attainment of salvation by faith alone. Jesus offered spiritual joy and divine communion in this world, and eternal life of spiritual progress in the next. He taught, "God is your Father, and religion—my gospel—is nothing more nor less than the believing recognition of the truth that you are his son." Jesus didn't ask his followers to think alike; he came to proclaim spiritual liberty and to empower individuals to live with originality and freedom before God. He did not desire that social harmony be purchased by sacrificing spiritual originality.

142—The Passover at Jerusalem

During the month of April, 27 AD, Jesus and the apostles taught daily in the temple in Jerusalem. They worked personally with people who later carried the gospel to other areas of the Roman empire and the East.

A Jewish trader, Jacob, asked Jesus to explain the difference between the angry God described by Moses and the loving God of Jesus. Jesus said, "When your children are very young and immature, and when you must chastise them, they may reflect that their father is angry and filled with resentful wrath. Their immaturity cannot penetrate beyond the punishment to discern the father's farseeing and corrective affection. But when these same children become grown-up men and women, would it not be folly for them to cling to these earlier and misconceived notions regarding their father? . . . And should not mankind, as the centuries pass, come the better to understand the true nature and loving character of the Father in heaven?"

Jesus was invited to visit the home of a wealthy Greek Jew named Flavius. Flavius had collected many works of art and was nervous about inviting the Master because he feared Jesus would take offense at them. Instead, Jesus showed great interest in the art. Sensing Flavius's discomfort, Jesus said, "Why should you expect to be rebuked? Moses' children have misunderstood him, and now do they make false gods of even his prohibitions of images and the likeness of things in heaven and on earth... I declare that in the coming kingdom they shall no longer teach, 'Do not worship this and do not worship that'; no longer shall they concern themselves with commands to refrain from this and take care not to do that; but rather shall all be concerned with one supreme duty. And this duty of man is expressed in two great privileges: sincere worship of the Infinite Creator, the Paradise Father, and loving service bestowed on one's fellow men. If you love your neighbor as you love yourself, you really know that you are a son of God."

A man from Damascus asked how he could know for certain that Jesus was sent by God; Jesus said that his message and his disciples should be judged by their fruits. Nicodemus, a member of the Sanhedrin, requested a private conference with the Master, during which Jesus said that children of God are born again, "born of the spirit." Nicodemus asked, "How can a man be born again when he is old?" Jesus spoke of entering the spiritual kingdom, saying, "That which is born of the flesh is flesh, and that which is born of the spirit is spirit."

Jesus taught the apostles that the concept of "kingdom" was not the best way to illustrate a person's relationship with God. He employed such words because the Jewish people were expecting a new kingdom to appear. Jesus told them that the people of other ages would better understand the gospel presented in terms expressive of a true family, founded on:

1. The fact of existence

2. Security and pleasure

3. Education and training

4. Discipline and restraint

5. Companionship and loyalty

6. Love and mercy

7. Provision for the future

By the end of April the opposition to Jesus in Jerusalem was so strong that he decided to go south to work in Bethlehem and Hebron. No public preaching was done. During part of this time, Jesus visited with Abner in the Nazarite colony. By the first week of June, the mood in Jerusalem had quieted down enough that the apostles returned. Jesus and the apostles lived in tents in the garden of Gethsemane for the entire month of June, never preaching publicly. They spent their weekends with Lazarus in Bethany.

The Jerusalem Jewish leaders saw that Jesus did no public preaching and decided to leave him alone. At the end of June, Simon, an influential member of the Sanhedrin, espoused Jesus' teachings publicly. A new agitation against the Master sprang up. Jesus and the apostles left Jerusalem for Samaria.

143—Going through Samaria

Jesus and his apostles spent the month of July near Bethel, Arimathea, and Thamna. During the first half of August, they preached in the Greek cities of Archelais and Phasaelis. Here they had their first experience with a group that was almost exclusively Roman, Greek, and Syrian, and the apostles met with new objections to the Master's teachings. These gentiles told the apostles that Jesus' words were fit only for weaklings and slaves.

Jesus said, "Do you, my chosen apostles, resemble weaklings? Did John look like a weakling? Do you observe that I am enslaved by fear? The Paradise ascent is the supreme adventure of all time, the rugged achievement of eternity. The service of the kingdom on earth will call for all the courageous manhood that you and your coworkers can muster. You are the first volunteers of a long line of sincere believers in the gospel of this kingdom who will astonish all mankind by their heroic devotion to these teachings."

It was mid-August when the apostles set out for the city of Sychar in Samaria. It was a test of loyalty for the apostles to visit Samaria, as there had been bad blood between Jews and Samaritans for more than six hundred years. During this trip the apostles learned to overcome much of their prejudice against Samaritans.

At Jacob's well near Sychar, Jesus encountered a woman named Nalda. During this conversation Jesus told Nalda, "You have received that living water, and a new joy will spring up within your soul, and you shall become a daughter of the Most High." That evening Nalda brought a crowd from Sychar to hear Jesus speak about self-mastery as the measure of spiritual development.

The apostles never ceased to be shocked by Jesus' willingness to talk with women. It was difficult for Jesus to convince them that even so-called immoral women have souls and can become daughters of God.

Jesus and the apostles camped in the heart of Samaria until the end of August.

144—At Gilboa and the Decapolis

Jesus and the apostles spent September and October in seclusion on the slopes of Mount Gilboa. John the Baptist was still imprisoned, and Herod was suspicious of the relationship between John and Jesus. Jesus spent this time working quietly, rehearsing the apostles, allowing opposition to die down, and awaiting the fate of John.

The theme of discussions in September centered around prayer and worship. The apostles knew that Jesus did not approve of formal prayers or public prayer, yet believers frequently asked to be taught how to pray. Jesus shared the prayer he had taught his siblings in Nazareth:

> Our Father who is in heaven,
>   Hallowed be your name.
> Your kingdom come; your will be done
>   On earth as it is in heaven.
> Give us this day our bread for tomorrow;
>   Refresh our souls with the water of life.
> And forgive us every one our debts
>   As we also have forgiven our debtors.
> Save us in temptation, deliver us from evil,
>   And increasingly make us perfect like yourself.

Jesus taught that prayer should be personal, spontaneous, and persistent— "the breath of the soul." The apostles learned to pray in solitude. Prayer is a technique of detachment from the daily routine of life and often leads to worship. Effective prayer should be unselfish, believing, sincere, intelligent, and trustful. The earnest repetition of any petition sincerely uttered in faith, no matter how ill-advised, never fails to expand the soul's capacity for spiritual receptivity.

Around the first of October, Philip met some of John's apostles at the village market. The two groups arranged a three-week meeting at the Gilboa camp. During the first week, Jesus stayed and listened to the deliberations of the twenty-four men but refrained from advising them about the issues they grappled with.

During this conference, the twenty-four believers reached several agreements together. They decided to teach believers the new prayer that Jesus had suggested. They agreed that as long as John lived, joint meetings would be held every three months, and that only the apostles of John would baptize believers. If and when John died, the apostles of John would follow Jesus, and both groups would then use baptism as a symbol of the divine Spirit.

The apostles left the Gilboa camp early in November, working quietly in the Greek cities of Scythopolis, Gerasa, Abila, and Gadara. John the Baptist was executed in January. When messengers brought news to Jesus about the death of John, he called the twenty-four together and said, "The hour has come to proclaim the kingdom openly and with power. Tomorrow we go into Galilee."

145—Four Eventful Days at Capernaum

Jesus and the apostles returned to the Zebedee's home in Capernaum in preparation for their first public tour in Galilee. At the synagogue that week, Jesus preached about religion as a personal experience. He said that the approach to God should be attempted as a child of God, rather than as a child of Israel. The people of Capernaum were astonished at how Jesus taught as one with authority rather than as a scribe.

At the end of this particular sermon, a man suffered an epileptic attack. Jesus took the man's hand just as he began to recover. The inaccurate report spread that Jesus had cast a demon out of the man, healing him. That same afternoon, Jesus visited Peter's mother-in-law, who was sick with a fever and chills. It happened that her fever broke just at the time when Jesus was with her. The apostles saw this coincidence as another miracle, and spread the news to the people of the city.

By the time Jesus sat down to dinner, all of Capernaum was stirring. Scores of afflicted people made their way to the Zebedee home in Bethsaida. Peter's wife heard voices in the front yard, and saw the large company assembling. A voice from the crowd called, "Master, speak the word, restore our health, heal our diseases, and save our souls." Peter asked Jesus to heed their cry, and Jesus replied that if it were the will of his Father in heaven, he would desire to see the afflicted made whole. In that instant, all six hundred and eighty-three people were healed.

Of all who witnessed this healing, Jesus was the most surprised. The apostles were overjoyed; to them this was possibly the greatest day in their time spent with the Master. Jesus was disturbed by what had happened and refused to be congratulated. The majority of those who were healed that evening were not permanently uplifted spiritually by this display of mercy. Miracles were not part of Jesus' plan. They were incidental occurrences that happened because a divine being with almost unlimited creative powers lived in the flesh.

Jesus was so distressed that he couldn't sleep. He didn't wish to avoid physical healing altogether, but he knew that teaching and religious training were more important. The Master rose early the next morning and went into the hills to pray for wisdom and judgment.

Peter, James, and John went searching for Jesus. When they found him, they asked him to tell them why he was troubled. The Master spent more than four hours explaining the reasons why the kingdom of God could not be based on wonder-working and physical healing, but the apostles could not understand him.

Meanwhile, crowds of afflicted people and curiosity-seekers had gathered at the Zebedee home, clamoring to see Jesus. Andrew went in search of Jesus to ask him to work with the new crowd, but Jesus refused to return to the house. The crowd was dismissed and the apostles prepared for travel.

The apostles were saddened to leave the interested multitudes in Capernaum. Peter believed that one thousand believers were ready to be baptized, but Thomas said, "The Master has spoken. No matter if we cannot fully comprehend the mysteries of the kingdom of heaven, of one thing we are certain: We follow a teacher who seeks no glory for himself."

146—FIRST PREACHING TOUR OF GALILEE

The first public preaching tour in Galilee lasted for almost two months. One of the remarkable events of this tour took place at Jotapata, where Jesus spoke to the apostles about prayer and worship. He taught that:

Prayer doesn't change God's attitude toward man, but changes man's attitude toward God.

Praying for people cannot replace ministering to their needs.

Prayers of thanksgiving are appropriate for groups, but personal prayers should be made privately.

Believers should pray for the extension of the kingdom and the spiritual progress of others, but should avoid materialistic prayers.

Prayer helps increase the capacity for the presence of divine spirit.

One day in the city of Iron, a man approached Jesus and asked to be healed of his leprosy. Since lepers were forbidden to engage in public worship, this man believed he could not be close to God unless he was cured. Jesus cured him. He asked that the man tell no one, but the man immediately spread the word of his cure. Such a crowd of sick people gathered that Jesus was forced to leave the city.

In Cana a man named Titus came to Jesus and asked him to cure his son. Jesus said, "The power of God is in your midst, but except you see signs and behold wonders, you refuse to believe." But Titus pleaded until Jesus assured him that his son would live. The man returned home to find his son recovering. Titus and his family believed incorrectly that they had witnessed one of the Master's miracles.

Jesus left Cana to travel to Nain. On the way he met a funeral procession bearing the son of a widow. Jesus examined the boy and said, "Your son is not dead; he sleeps." When the boy sat up and began to talk, the villagers thought another miracle had taken place. No matter how Jesus tried to explain to them that the boy had never been dead, they would not listen. Word traveled through Galilee and Judea that Jesus had raised this boy from the dead.

147—THE INTERLUDE VISIT TO JERUSALEM

Jesus and the apostles traveled to Jerusalem to celebrate the Passover in April, 28 AD. They set up camp in Gethsemane and moved between there and Bethany to avoid crowds of followers. The apostles were somewhat restless.

John brought Jesus to a nearby hot spring reputed to cure the sick of everything that ailed them. John hoped that Jesus, seeing the sick people there, would feel compassion for them, work a miracle, and win Jerusalem to the gospel. Again, Jesus attempted to explain to John that wonders and miracles were no substitute for teaching the gospel.

That same evening, Nathaniel asked Jesus to teach them how the golden rule could be applied universally. Nathaniel used the example of a lustful man, asking "How can we teach that this evil-intending man should do to others as he would they should do to him?" The apostles disappointed Jesus because they failed to interpret his teachings from the spiritual perspective. He described the levels of application of the golden rule, from the lowest level of the flesh, through the levels of feelings, mind, brotherly love, and morality. Spiritually interpreted, the golden rule means that we should treat others as we believe God would treat them.

A wealthy Pharisee, Simon, invited Jesus to his home for a meal. The Pharisee custom was to leave the doors open when they entertained so beggars could come in for food. During this dinner, a new convert to the kingdom, a former brothel owner, came in and stood behind Jesus as he ate. She had brought a flask of lotion with which to anoint his feet, and as she did so, she began to kiss his feet and weep with gratitude. Simon thought to himself that if Jesus were really a prophet, he would know what a sinner this woman was.

Jesus knew what Simon was thinking and said, "A certain wealthy moneylender had two debtors. The one owed him five hundred denarii and the other fifty. Now, when neither of them had wherewith to pay, he forgave them both. Which of them do you think, Simon, would love him most?" In the ensuing discourse, Jesus described how those who have the most sins forgiven may be led to love God most deeply. God is available to everyone who sincerely seeks Him, even the most humble sinner.

Jewish leaders in Jerusalem wanted to be rid of Jesus. They tried to get Herod to arrest him, but Herod refused. The priests then sent six spies to follow Jesus so they could gather evidence of blasphemy, a crime that could be tried by the Sanhedrin themselves.

The spies soon witnessed an infraction against Jewish law. Some of the apostles had plucked ripe grain from the roadside and eaten it. The spies told Jesus that harvesting grain was the same as working on the

Sabbath. Jesus pointed out that the Sabbath was made for man, not man for the Sabbath. "If you are here present with us to watch my words, then will I openly proclaim that the Son of Man is lord even of the Sabbath." The spies were confounded.

Jesus and the apostles traveled to Bethsaida by boat, trying to escape the crowd that followed them. By the next day, the spies had caught up with them. One evening in Bethsaida, one of the spies asked Jesus why he did not insist his disciples fast and pray as the Pharisees and John the Baptist taught. Jesus replied that praying is natural for the children of God but fasting is not. "My disciples show wisdom in that they do not bring too much of the old order over into the new teaching of the gospel of the kingdom of heaven... the sons of God shall experience freedom from fear, and joy in the divine spirit." Jesus taught that it was faith that makes man secure with God, not afflictions of the body or fasting. It is right that old truth should be kept and new falsehood rejected, but one must also have the courage to accept new truth.

148—TRAINING EVANGELISTS AT BETHSAIDA

Between May and October, 28 AD, Jesus and the apostles ran a camp for prospective evangelists in Bethsaida. David Zebedee was camp supervisor and Peter was in charge of the school. The apostles taught groups of trainees in the morning, and the trainees and apostles together taught visitors in the afternoons. Several thousand people attended this camp during the five months it existed.

While in Bethsaida, Jesus spent much of his time in the hills "about his Father's business." The apostles taught their own personal interpretations of the Master's truth, which Jesus harmonized during his weekly instructions.

One evening Jesus defined evil, sin, and iniquity. Evil is unintentional transgression of divine law and a measure of human imperfection. Sin is the deliberate transgression of the Father's will—a measure of unwillingness to be led. Iniquity is persistent transgression of divine law.

Nathaniel asked why God permits afflictions. Jesus explained that God does not send afflictions to men, but that our world has been upset by sins of those disloyal to God. He said people bring a lot of unnecessary pain to themselves by refusing to heed the divine will. Humans suffer from the accidents of time and from immaturity. God never sends afflictions as arbitrary punishment for wrongdoing, neither does material wealth indicate God's favor.

One day while Jesus was speaking in the synagogue, the leader of the Pharisee spies convinced a man with a deformed hand to ask Jesus whether it was lawful for him to heal on the Sabbath. Jesus asked whether this man would rescue a sheep that fell into a pit on the Sabbath. The man said yes. The audience agreed. Jesus then looked at the audience and said, "I know wherefore you have sent this man into my presence. You would find cause for offense in me if you could tempt me to show mercy on the Sabbath day." "How much more valuable is a man than a sheep! I proclaim that it is lawful to do good to men on the Sabbath day." The man was healed.

The angry spies hurried to Tiberias to report this to Herod, but Herod was not interested. This protest against meaningless Sabbath restrictions was the first miracle Jesus worked as a direct response to his enemies.

Meanwhile in Jerusalem, an influential member of the Sanhedrin was publicly baptized in a fountain by Abner. The donation this convert made to the apostolic funds helped launch nearly one hundred newly trained evangelists from the camp. This conversion caused some consternation in Jerusalem among Jesus' enemies. Messengers set out to bring the six spies home.

During the final days of the camp, a paralyzed man sought healing while the Master was teaching in the Zebedee home. The house was so crowded that the man's friends could not get him into the room. They climbed a ladder onto the roof, lifted the man up with them, removed some roof tiles, and lowered the man into the room directly in front of the Master. The paralytic asked for healing, saying, "I am not like those who received healing and immediately forgot your teaching. I would be made whole that I might serve in the kingdom of heaven." Jesus, seeing the man's faith, replied, "Son, fear not; your sins are forgiven. Your faith has saved you."

The Pharisees thought this was blasphemy, and began to murmur among themselves. Jesus said, "But that you who witness all this may finally know that the Son of Man has authority and power on earth to forgive sins, I will say to this afflicted man, Arise, take up your bed, and go to your own house." The man stood up and walked out of the room, much to the astonishment of everyone present.

At about this time the messengers of the Sanhedrin arrived to instruct the spies to return to Jerusalem. The leader and two others returned, but three of the spies had come to believe in Jesus and were baptized into the kingdom.

149—The Second Preaching Tour

The second public teaching tour of Galilee began early in October, 28 AD. Each apostle traveled with about a dozen of the newly trained evangelists. James, John, and Jesus traveled together, observing the work of the new people. It was during this time that David Zebedee started the messenger service that would faithfully serve Jesus and his disciples as long as Jesus lived.

Jesus' fame as a healer spread throughout Syria and Palestine. An unexplained healing phenomenon continued throughout the rest of Jesus' life. Scores of people were spontaneously healed even though Jesus did not deliberately intend to heal them. Three factors influenced these cases: strong, living faith in a person who sought healing for spiritual benefits; the great compassion of Jesus, who possessed nearly unlimited healing powers; and that Jesus was the personified expression of God's will on this planet.

During this tour, Jesus taught that anger is a failure of the spiritual nature to control the intellectual and physical nature. He discussed the desirability of a well-balanced character. On the subject of happiness, Jesus said that some people are naturally more happy than others, but much depends on our willingness to be led by the Spirit. He advised his followers not to look for false peace and fleeting joy, but for faith and the assurance of divine sonship that brings supreme joy of the spirit.

One evening, Philip asked Jesus to explain why the scriptures commanded men to fear the Lord, while Jesus taught that men should love God fearlessly. Jesus answered, "I have come into the world to put love in the place of fear, joy in the place of sorrow, confidence in the place of dread, loving service and appreciative worship in the place of slavish bondage and meaningless ceremonies. But it is still true of those who sit in darkness that 'the fear of the Lord is the beginning of wisdom.' But when the light has more fully come, the sons of God are led to praise the Infinite for what he is rather than to fear him for what he does."

The second preaching tour ended on December 30. The evangelists discussed their experiences with each other in Bethsaida before taking a two-week break.

150—THE THIRD PREACHING TOUR

During the third preaching tour, the evangelists traveled together in small groups, covering central and southern Galilee.

Jesus chose ten women as teachers for this tour: Susanna, the daughter of the Nazareth chazan; Joanna, the wife of Herod's steward; Elizabeth of Tiberias and Sepphoris; Martha, the sister of Andrew and Peter; Rachel, Jude's sister-in-law; Nasanta, the daughter of Elman; Milcha, the cousin of Thomas; Ruth, the daughter of Matthew Levi; Celta, the daughter of a Roman centurion; and Agaman, a widow from Damascus. Later Rebecca, daughter of Joseph of Arimathea, and Mary Magdalene joined the women. The women's corps elected Suzanna as their chief and Joanna as treasurer.

The formation of this group was a shock to the twelve apostles. They had heard Jesus say that all people are equal as sons and daughters of God, yet they were stunned when he formally commissioned women as religious teachers. The enemies of Jesus held this against him, but women everywhere approved of this acknowledgment of a woman's place in religious work.

At Magdala the women demonstrated the wisdom of their group's existence when they freely entered the "evil resorts" to preach to the prostitutes there. It was during one of these visits that Martha and Rachel converted Mary Magdalene, who later became the most effective preacher in the women's corps.

Jesus and the apostles traveled to Nazareth. Nazareth had changed since Jesus' boyhood days and many of Jesus' childhood friends were dead or gone. Nazarenes had become increasingly influenced by the low moral standards of nearby Sepphoris, and some resented that Jesus had not done any miracles for them.

On the Sabbath, Jesus spoke in the synagogue on the subject of "Sons and Daughters of God." Many of the people were pleased with his gracious talk, but his disciples were aware of a group of belligerent thugs that Jesus' enemies had hired to cause trouble. Simon Zelotes became angry and the mob became aroused. They grabbed Jesus and took him to the edge of a hill, intending to push him over. At the edge of the cliff, Jesus suddenly turned on his attackers, quietly folded his arms, and walked unmolested through the mob. Jesus escaped harm, but the episode had a sobering effect on his followers. The apostles began to understand what Jesus meant when he told them that peace would not always attend their preaching.

151—Tarrying and Teaching by the Seaside

Jesus and his preachers gathered by the sea at Bethsaida, quietly ministering while they waited to travel into Jerusalem for the Passover. It was about this time that Jesus began to employ parables. Jesus used parables so those people who wanted the truth could learn, while his enemies would hear without understanding. Parables appeal simultaneously to different levels of intellect and spirit—they stimulate the imagination, provoke critical thinking, and promote sympathy without arousing antagonism. Parables use material reality to introduce spiritual lessons.

One of Jesus' first parables was:

"A sower went forth to sow, and it came to pass as he sowed that some seed fell by the wayside to be trodden underfoot and devoured by the birds of heaven. Other seed fell upon the rocky places where there was little earth, and immediately it sprang up because there was no depth to the soil, but as soon as the sun shone, it withered because it had no root whereby to secure moisture. Other seed fell among the thorns, and as the thorns grew up, it was choked so that it yielded no grain. Still other seed fell upon good ground and, growing, yielded, some thirtyfold, some sixtyfold, and some a hundredfold."

The apostles tried to unravel the meaning of Jesus' parable. Peter came to the conclusion that the parable was an allegory and tried to figure out the meaning of each part. Nathaniel also tried to assign a meaning to each detail but came to a different interpretation. Thomas, remembering that Jesus had warned them not to invent spiritual applications for every detail, interpreted the parable of the sower to mean that no matter how faithfully one teaches the gospel, degrees of success will vary due to conditions that cannot be controlled.

Jesus commended Thomas. He reiterated the danger of trying to make allegories out of parables. Jesus told them that it might be profitable to thus speculate in private, but not to offer such lessons in public work. Jesus also advised his men to adjust their presentations of truth to the hearts and minds of each audience.

The next day Jesus taught many other parables, relating the kingdom to a grain of mustard seed, leaven, a treasure hidden in a field, a merchant seeking pearls, and a sweep net.

The crowds increased as the week passed. Jesus became weary and decided to travel across the sea to rest for a few days in Kheresa. When the group reached the outskirts of Kheresa, a lunatic named Amos rushed up to them, saying, "I am possessed of many devils, and I beseech you not to torment me." Jesus took Amos by the hand and told him that he was not possessed, and commanded him to come out of his spell. Amos was so swayed by Jesus' words that he was immediately restored to his right mind. A crowd from the village had gathered, as well as some pig herders.

The herders hurried to the village to tell people that Jesus had cured Amos. Just then, dogs charged an untended herd of swine, driving them over a cliff into the sea. This occurrence prompted the legend that Jesus cured Amos by casting his devils into the swine. The whole village believed this, and Amos' belief in this erroneous tale had much to do with the permanency of his cure.

The next day the swine herders asked the apostles to leave, fearing they would lose too many pigs if Jesus stayed. Jesus left Kheresa without the much-needed rest he had sought.

152—EVENTS LEADING UP TO THE CAPERNAUM CRISIS

Jesus' reputation as a healer was growing. The apostles and the common people seemed unable to discern the difference between true miracles and coincidence. Jesus' attempts to explain his apparent miracles as natural phenomenon had little effect, partly because people enjoyed the idea of miracles so much.

The story of Amos' cure reached Capernaum even before Jesus returned from Kheresa. A great crowd was waiting for him when his boat landed. Jairus, a leader from the Capernaum synagogue, asked Jesus to come to his house because his daughter was close to death. As Jesus walked to Jairus's house, he felt a "living energy" drawn from him. A sick woman in the crowd had touched his hem and was healed of her ailment. Jesus stopped to assure her that it was her faith, and not the touch of his hem, that had cured her. This miracle was genuine although unintended.

When the group arrived at Jairus's house, they were informed that the child was already dead, but Jesus saw that she was only sleeping. He asked her to arise, which she did. Jesus tried to explain to the family and the apostles that she had only been in a coma, but they all believed he had raised her from the dead. Nothing Jesus said could convince them otherwise.

Jesus continued to teach in Capernaum. Soon, he was so tired that he instructed his disciples to go home for a week, but half of his followers refused to leave. The crowds continued to grow. Jesus and the apostles tried to leave unnoticed. They went to Magadan Park on the opposite shore of the lake, hoping for a few days rest. Over five thousand people followed them. A rumor was spreading that Jesus had chosen this secluded spot as the place in which he wanted to be crowned king. The crowds refused to leave even after their food supplies were depleted.

Jesus decided to feed the people and asked Philip what food they had to share. Philip brought him five loaves of bread and two dried fish. Jesus took the loaves, gave thanks, broke the bread, and passed it to his apostles who distributed it to the multitudes. He did the same with the fish. The crowd ate until they were full, and when they were done, the apostles gathered up the leftovers—twelve baskets full. This was the first and only nature miracle that Jesus ever performed with conscious preplanning. It was a genuine supernatural ministration.

The crowds finished eating and began to shout, "Make him king!" But Jesus said, "You would make me king, not because your souls have been lighted with a great truth, but because your stomachs have been filled with bread. How many times have I told you that my kingdom is not of this world? Go hence to your own homes. If you must have a king, let the Father of lights be enthroned in the heart of each of you as the spirit Ruler of all things."

The people were stunned; the apostles were speechless. Of the five thousand who were fed, only five hundred continued to follow the Master. Jesus asked Andrew to take the apostles to Bethsaida to pray while he went into the hills to be alone.

When Jesus later rejoined the apostles at Zebedee's home, he tried to explain once and for all why the kingdom could not be inaugurated with miracle-working.

"And now do you all see that the working of miracles and the performance of material wonders will not win souls for the spiritual kingdom? We fed the multitude, but it did not lead them to hunger for the bread of life neither to thirst for the waters of spiritual righteousness. When their hunger was satisfied, they sought not entrance into the kingdom of heaven but rather sought to proclaim the Son of Man king after the manner of the kings of this world, only that they might continue to eat bread without having to toil therefor. And all this, in which many of you did more or less participate, does nothing to reveal the heavenly Father or to advance his kingdom on earth. Have we not sufficient enemies among the religious leaders of the land without doing that which is likely to estrange also the civil rulers? I pray that the Father will anoint your eyes that you may see and open your ears that you may hear, to the end that you may have full faith in the gospel which I have taught you."

In April, 29 AD, Jesus and the apostles traveled once again to Jerusalem for the Passover. They traveled quietly, dividing into pairs to stay in various homes. During this trip, the apostles learned how bitter the talk against their Master was beginning to turn.

153—THE CRISIS AT CAPERNAUM

Returning from Jerusalem to Bethsaida, Jesus seemed preoccupied. The apostles were downhearted. Andrew went to the Capernaum synagogue to secure permission for Jesus to speak on the following Sabbath day.

More that fifty Pharisees and Sadducees from Jerusalem gathered on the Sabbath in the synagogue along with leaders from neighboring synagogues. Jesus, knowing that Jewish leaders intended to initiate open opposition to the gospel, took the offensive. Jesus understood that half-hearted followers were going to reject him and that his disciples would get the training they needed to fully assert their growing faith in the gospel.

Jesus began his sermon by reading sections of Deuteronomy and Jeremiah about people who didn't listen to the word of God. He asked the congregation what signs they needed as evidence of his mission. He berated those who had pursued him looking for miracles and would have crowned him king as reward for bread for which they had not labored. Jesus told them they needed to look for spiritual food that nourishes eternal life. "He who comes to me shall not hunger, while he who believes me shall never thirst. Will you now take the bread of the spirit as you then so willingly ate the bread of this world?"

When asked why he and the apostles did not wash their hands properly before they ate, Jesus said, "It is not that which enters into the mouth that spiritually defiles the man, but rather that which proceeds out of the mouth and from the heart... Do you not know it is from the heart that there come forth evil thoughts, wicked projects of murder, theft, and adulteries, together with jealousy, pride, anger, revenge, railings and false witness? And it is just such things that defile men, and not that they eat bread with ceremonially unclean hands."

One of his enemies brought a young man who was possessed and asked if Jesus could cure him. Jesus banished the evil spirit. Immediately the lad behaved normally, and the people marveled. The Pharisee charged that Jesus' power to cure the lad was from Satan. Jesus replied, "How can Satan cast out Satan?" He warned them against ascribing works of God to the devil, declaring that those who knowingly blasphemed against God would not be forgiven.

This meeting lasted for more than three hours. When Jesus finished, his somewhat frightened apostles led him home to Bethsaida. They were amazed at Jesus' sudden use of such militant tactics. Jesus secluded himself while the apostles ate supper.

A little after midnight Jesus gathered the disciples and tried to comfort them, saying, "I realize that this sifting of the kingdom distresses you, but it is unavoidable. Why is it that you are filled with fear and consternation when you see the kingdom being divested of these lukewarm multitudes and these halfhearted disciples? My beloved, you must remember that it is the spirit that quickens; the flesh and all that pertains thereto is of little profit. The words which I have spoken to you are spirit and life."

Jesus fully understood how men prepare themselves for courageous performance during a crisis by the slow process of reiterated choosing between the recurring situations of good and evil. He knew that when his followers met the final test, they would make their decisions in accordance with habitual mental and spiritual attitudes. Jesus subjected his chosen messengers to repeated rehearsals in disappointment, and provided them with frequent opportunities for choosing between the right and wrong ways of meeting spiritual trials.

154—LAST DAYS AT CAPERNAUM

Jewish leaders pressured Herod to arrest Jesus, but Herod sent them away. The Sanhedrin ordered all the synagogues in Palestine closed to Jesus and his followers. Five members of the Sanhedrin resigned in protest. Although this unprecedented mandate over the independent congregations was unusual, all but one synagogue complied.

In May the Jewish leaders tried again to have Herod arrest Jesus. Herod refused, but decreed that the Sanhedrin could seize Jesus on religious charges and take him to Jerusalem for trial. Meanwhile, Jesus and his disciples rested; no public teaching took place during this time.

Citizens of Capernaum gathered to discuss their opinions of Jesus. A few believed that Jesus was the Messiah. Others thought he was a harmless religious fanatic, a dangerous agitator, in league with the devil, or crazy. This was the lowest point of Jesus' popularity. When news of Herod's decree reached Capernaum, Jesus prepared to flee. He called an early morning meeting to give instructions to the disciples.

Jesus' family learned of his pending arrest and decided to try to meet with Jesus to talk some sense into him. Ruth was the only person in Jesus' earth family who still believed in her brother's mission. The Pharisees had been trying to convince Mary that Jesus was mad, and she wavered between love and fear. Jesus' brothers felt disgraced and embarrassed by him. The family decided that while Joseph kept Ruth quiet, Mary, James and Jude would try to dissuade Jesus from his plans.

When the family reached the Zebedee's house, it was so crowded that they could not enter. Not realizing that Jesus' enemies were so nearby at the time, they waited on the back porch and sent word to Jesus that they needed to see him.

When Jesus heard they were waiting, he said, "Say to my mother and my brothers that they should have no fear for me. The Father who sent me into the world will not forsake me; neither shall any harm come upon my family. Bid them be of good courage and put their trust in the Father of the kingdom. But, after all, who is my mother and who are my brothers? I have no mother; I have no brothers. Behold my mother and behold my brethren! For whosoever does the will of my Father who is in heaven, the same is my mother, my brother, and my sister."

Jesus finished his message to the disciples, intending to go out to the garden to meet his family privately. But just then a messenger arrived warning of the imminent arrival of the authorities sent from Tiberias to arrest Jesus. Jesus and the apostles hurried through the front door onto boats and escaped by rowing across the Sea of Galilee to Kheresa. The Jewish authorities arrived soon thereafter and wasted a week looking for Jesus near Capernaum.

155—Fleeing through Northern Galilee

Once safely across the Sea of Galilee, Jesus sent twelve evangelists with Peter to Chorazin while he and the other apostles went to Caesarea-Philippi. Peter's group taught about the spiritual aspects of the gospel, but won few new converts.

The apostles held many private meetings with local believers. Although a little depressed about the quiet phase of preaching they had entered, the apostles learned much from their daily conferences with Jesus. Jesus told them that people can best be taught to love God by first being taught to love other people. Jesus saw true religion as loyalty to one's highest convictions. Religion lessens the strain of existence and gives one courage for dealing with daily life.

After two weeks the groups reunited and traveled to the Phoenician coast to avoid their enemies. Over lunch, Jesus discoursed on religion. He spoke so well that by mid-afternoon the apostles asked him to stop walking and tell them more.

Jesus discussed three kinds of religious devotion: primitive religion—the religion of fear; religion of civilization—established religious authority; and true religion—the religion of the spirit in human experience. He stated that until the world was more fully civilized, superstitious ceremonies would persist; many people would continue to prefer religions of authority to the faith adventure of a spiritual quest. Religions of authority provide a haven for those who are fearful and uncertain, but they do not provide for the thrill of truth, intellectual discovery, and personal religious experience. The religion of the spirit means effort, struggle, conflict, faith, determination, love, loyalty, and progress.

Jesus asked, "Are you fearful, soft, and ease-seeking? Are you afraid to trust your future in the hands of the God of truth, whose sons you are? Are you distrustful of the Father, whose children you are? Will you go back to the easy path of the certainty and intellectual settledness of the religion of traditional authority, or will you gird yourselves to go forward with me into that uncertain and troublous future of proclaiming the new truths of the religion of the spirit, the kingdom of heaven in the hearts of men?"

He said, "I have called upon you to be born again, to be born of the spirit. I have called you out of the darkness of authority and the lethargy of tradition into the transcendent light of the realization of the possibility of making for yourselves the greatest discovery possible for yourself, in yourself, and of yourself, and of doing all this as a fact in your own personal experience."

Jesus explained that God does not reveal himself to one generation and then withhold himself from the next. All things are sacred in the lives of those who are spirit led, and those who are born of the spirit can hear God's word no matter where it appears. Jesus taught the apostles that there are two demonstrations that reveal a person is God-knowing; first, the fruits of the spirit evident in the believer's daily life, and second, the believer's willingness to risk everything in the pursuit of God and eternal life.

156—SOJOURN AT TYRE AND SIDON

Jesus and the apostles spent two and a half weeks in Sidon. A woman, Norana, hearing that Jesus was near, brought her daughter to be healed. The apostles explained that the Master was resting and could not be disturbed, but Norana refused to leave.

Finally Simon Zelotes chastised her, saying, "Woman, you are a Greek-speaking gentile. It is not right that you should expect the Master to take the bread intended for the children of the favored household and cast it to the dogs." Norana replied, "I am only a dog in the eyes of the Jews, but as concerns your Master, I am a believing dog." As they exchanged words, Norana's daughter went into convulsions.

Norana pleaded with Simon, saying, "If our need does not impress you, it would appeal to your Master, who I have been told loves all men and dares even to heal the gentiles when they believe. You are not worthy to be his disciples. I will not go until my child has been cured."

Jesus, hearing this conversation, went outside and said, "O woman, great is your faith, so great that I cannot withhold that which you desire; go your way in peace. Your daughter already has been made whole."

Jesus used this woman's faith to demonstrate to the apostles that even gentiles could acquire faith. His lesson was driven home during the next few weeks by the great success the preachers had in winning converts among the gentile population. Many non-Jews grasped the fact that not only was Jesus like God, but that God was like Jesus.

In Sidon, Jesus' instructions centered on spiritual progression. He declared that we must either go forward in righteousness or retrogress into sin; that we must not only cease to do evil but must actively learn to do right.

In Tyre, Jesus used a parable about a foolish carpenter to admonish men not to waste time measuring and smoothing rotten wood that later will be rejected as unfit for use. He warned against supplanting one desire for another by sheer will power; saying that we should develop a love for higher conduct so as to be delivered from temptation through spiritual transformation rather than through suppression of mortal desires.

Jesus asked his followers to love people who were not easy to love because those are the people who have the greatest need for love. He also advised them to step aside from the rush of life to refresh and renew their spirits in worship.

While Jesus was away from Galilee, opposition to his teachings subsided. The mandate to shun him from the synagogues backfired; local resentment began to build against the Pharisees and Sanhedrin. Even Herod Antipas had a change of heart. He sent word that although he had signed a warrant for the arrest of Jesus in Galilee, no such order was in effect in Perea. The Master, free to travel outside of Galilee, made plans to sojourn near Caesarea-Philippi.

157—At Caesarea-Philippi

Before setting out for Caesarea-Phillipi, Jesus and the apostles camped again at Magadan Park. Believers, evangelists, and the women's corps came in from Capernaum for a conference during which it was decided that a united preaching effort would be made throughout the Decapolis after Jesus returned from Caesarea-Philippi.

The next day as Jesus and the apostles stopped for lunch, Jesus asked, "Who do men say that I am?" The apostles answered him, saying that people thought he was a prophet, an extraordinary man, a person feared by his enemies, a man in league with the devil, or maybe even John the Baptist risen from the dead.

Then Jesus asked, "But who say you that I am?" Simon Peter leapt to his feet and said, "You are the Deliverer, the Son of the living God." When the rest indicated that they agreed, Jesus replied, "This has been revealed to you by my Father. The hour has come when you should know the truth about me." The apostles sensed that a great event had taken place.

The next day, Jesus asked them again if they believed that he was the Son of God, and again they asserted their belief in him. Jesus began to have confidence in the faith of his apostles. He said, "This is a revelation of the spirit of my Father to your inmost souls. I am led to declare that upon this foundation will I build the brotherhood of the kingdom of heaven. Upon this rock of spiritual reality will I build the living temple of spiritual fellowship in the eternal realities of my Father's kingdom. All the forces of evil and hosts of sin shall not prevail against this human fraternity of the divine spirit." Jesus told the apostles that he was vesting them with authority over the social and economic features of the kingdom, "the keys" of the outward kingdom.

The important new concept of the apostles grasped during this episode was that Jesus was truly divine. For years Jesus had announced himself as the Son of Man, and now he could disclose that he was also the Son of God, two natures combined in one person. With this announcement, Jesus entered the final stage of his earthly career. Throughout the rest of his human life, he lived openly as the personification of God on earth.

The apostles were stunned by many new teachings from Jesus that day. In the evening, Andrew spoke individually with each of the other apostles. His discussion with Judas troubled him so much that he sought advice from Jesus. Jesus told Andrew that there was nothing more they could do for Judas, and that he should say nothing to the others about it.

Judas had been shocked by John the Baptist's death, hurt by Jesus' rebukes, disappointed when Jesus refused to become king, and dejected over the depletion of their treasury when public opinion turned against them. But his biggest error was that during the times that Jesus sent the apostles out to pray for guidance in solitude, Judas indulged in fear, doubt, and thoughts of revenge instead of praying.

158—The Mount of Transfiguration

Jesus traveled to Mount Hermon to meet with Gabriel and Father Melchizedek. While nine apostles rested at the foot of the mountain, Peter, James, and John accompanied Jesus up the mountainside. Jesus then took leave of his three men, asking that they wait for him while he met with his Father's messengers.

Jesus' first conference with the universe personalities lasted for three hours. Gabriel brought assurance of the fulfillment of Jesus' bestowal on behalf of the Eternal Mother-Son. Father Melchizedek confirmed the satisfaction of the Infinite Spirit. Jesus was pleased at these testimonies, but he also noted that God the Father did not indicate that his work was finished. When he rejoined the apostles, Jesus told them that he had chosen to complete his full mortal life.

After supper, Peter, James, and John fell asleep by the fire. They awoke to a crackling sound and were amazed to see Jesus with two beings. Jesus, Gabriel, and Father Melchizedek were glowing with a heavenly light and conversing in another language. The three apostles were frightened by what they saw, but as the vision faded, they became so excited from the experience that they wanted to stay and live on the mountain. As they presented this idea to Jesus, a cloud appeared above them and they heard a voice saying, "This is my beloved Son; give heed to him." Jesus asked them not to tell anyone what they had seen until after he had risen from the dead. His men were shocked by his words.

Meanwhile down at the base camp, the nine apostles fell into their persistent habit of talking about who would be most esteemed in the coming kingdom. As they argued amongst themselves, a man, James of Safed, brought his son to be healed by Jesus.

Simon and Judas told James that he did not need to wait for Jesus; that since they now held the keys to the kingdom, they would heal the boy themselves. Simon laid his hands on the boy and tried to heal him, but failed. Onlookers mocked him. Then Andrew tried and failed. Andrew asked James to stay until Jesus returned.

Shortly before breakfast the next morning, Jesus, Peter, James, and John reached the camp of the apostles. The anxious father knelt at Jesus' feet, relating the boy's symptoms and the apostles' failure. James begged that his son be healed. Jesus told him not to question God's love, but to have sincere faith that all things were possible to one who believes. James replied, "Lord, I believe. I pray you help my unbelief." Jesus healed the boy.

That evening, the apostles asked Jesus to tell them why they had failed to heal James's son. Jesus told them that instead of praying for deeper understanding of the Father's will, they had fallen into the contemplation of their places of honor in the material kingdom. They continued to cling to the concept of a kingdom that did not exist, and refused to accept that the kingdom of heaven was not of this world. Jesus said, "Spiritual greatness consists in an understanding love that is Godlike and not in an enjoyment of the exercise of material power for the exaltation of self. In what you attempted, in which you so completely failed, your purpose was not pure. Your motive was not divine. Your ideal was not spiritual. Your procedure was not based on love, and your goal of attainment was not the will of the Father in heaven."

Jesus said that he was entering the last phase of his work on earth. The apostles were dismayed as he discussed his own death and resurrection. Jesus told them plainly that he would suffer many things at the hands of the priests of Jerusalem, and that he would be killed and then rise from the dead.

Peter jumped up and declared that these things would never happen. Jesus rebuked him, saying, "When you talk in this manner, you are not on my side but rather on the side of our enemy. In this way do you make your love for me a stumbling block to my doing the Father's will."

The Master continued, "If any man would come after me, let him disregard himself, take up his responsibilities daily, and follow me. For whosoever would save his life selfishly, shall lose it, but whosoever loses his life for my sake and the gospel's, shall save it. What does it profit a man to gain the whole world and lose his own soul? What would a man give in exchange for eternal life?"

The apostles reeled from the rebuke. They were horrified by the idea that Jesus would suffer and die even as their hearts were stirred by the Master's appeal. Jesus and the twelve started walking toward Capernaum to their camp at Magadan Park.

159—THE DECAPOLIS TOUR

When Jesus and the apostles reached Magadan Park, they were greeted by a group of one hundred evangelists who were ready to start a four-week tour of the Decapolis. Each apostle worked with a small group of evangelists in the towns and villages, while Jesus and the women's corps rotated between the various groups. Hundreds of believers were won for the kingdom during this tour, and the apostles gained valuable experience working without daily contact with Jesus.

On this tour Jesus declared that there is more joy in heaven over one sinner who repents than over ninety-nine righteous persons who need no repentance. He instructed his disciples to forgive their brethren not just seven times, as was taught in the scriptures, but seventy times seven. The Master advised his followers that all who believe the gospel would not be subject to their direction, saying, "Rejoice that already our teaching has begun to manifest itself beyond the bounds of our personal influence." He also clearly stated that the Father does not limit the revelation of truth to any one generation or to any one people.

Jesus took the best of the known scriptures and wove them into the teachings of his new gospel. His religion put the spirit of positive action into play. Jesus taught that one should not just believe what the gospel says, but should also actively do those things that the gospel requires.

The Master's teaching about turning the other cheek was not that people should passively submit to indignities but that they should actively be alert for opportunities to overcome evil with good. He emphasized that goodness is always more powerful than evil. Jesus described three possible ways of dealing with evil:

1. To return evil for evil: the unrighteously positive method

2. To suffer evil without complaint: the negative method

3. To return good for evil: the righteously positive method

Jesus said, "Believing the gospel will not prevent getting into trouble, but it will insure that you shall be unafraid when trouble does overtake you. If you dare to believe in me and wholeheartedly proceed to follow after me, you shall most certainly by so doing enter upon the sure pathway to trouble. I do not promise to deliver you from the waters of adversity, but I do promise to go with you through all of them."

160—Rodan of Alexandria and
161—Further Discussions with Rodan

While the rest of the apostles took a week's rest with family and friends, Nathaniel and Thomas remained in Magadan to engage in discussion with a Greek philosopher, Rodan. Rodan gave a series of ten talks to Nathaniel, Thomas, and a group of two dozen believers. Rodan had embraced the gospel and was synthesizing his own philosophy with the teachings of Jesus. He believed that the religion of Jesus transcended all former concepts because it declared that the divine source of values, the eternal center of the universe, is personally attainable by every mortal who chooses to seek God.

Rodan asked, "But are we willing to pay the price of this entrance into the kingdom of heaven? Are we willing to be born again? To be remade? Are we willing to be subject to this terrible and testing process of self-destruction and soul reconstruction?" Rodan was mindful that the Master had declared that whomever would save his life must lose it.

One thing that Rodan and Jesus' apostles disagreed about was the personality of God. Rodan believed that the heavenly Father could not be a person as man conceives of personality. This disagreement bothered Thomas and Nathaniel so much that they asked Jesus to intervene, but the Master refused.

Rodan believed that personality could only exist in the context of full and mutual communication between beings of equality. He maintained that since God is the Creator of all other beings, there are none equal to him in the universe, and no one for him to communicate with as an equal. Thomas tried to convince Rodan that God was a personality, but after two days, the most Rodan would concede was that Thomas had proven the reality of God, not his personality.

After Thomas gave up, Nathaniel succeeded. Nathaniel reasoned that since the Eternal Son and the Infinite Spirit are equal to God, that meant that even by Rodan's definition there was a possibility that God had personality. Rodan accepted this possibility. Then Nathaniel reasoned that since Jesus was equal to God, and Jesus was able to communicate with humans, this proved that God and humans can intercommunicate. Also, since Jesus and the Father were one, the personality of Jesus demonstrated the personality of God. Finally, God must be a personality, since he is the Creator of all personality as well as the destiny of all personality.

Rodan accepted that God was a person. The three men spent two more days discussing the divine nature of Jesus. The apostles told Rodan their reasons for accepting the Master's divinity:

Jesus said he was divine.

He never made mistakes; he was consistently sinless.

He healed diseases and professed to forgive sin.

He seemed to know people's thoughts.

He seemed to have foreknowledge of things, even his own death.

He knew what was happening away from his immediate presence.

He spoke with the authority of a divine teacher.

John the Baptist had declared Jesus to be the Son of God.

Jesus talked about God as an ever-present associate.

He appeared to communicate directly with God.

162—At the Feast of the Tabernacles

In October, 29 AD, Jesus and the apostles stayed in or near Jerusalem. Jesus spent most of his time during October between the apostles in Bethany and Abner's group in Bethlehem. Abner was the leader of the former followers of John the Baptist.

Jesus' apostles many times had asked the Master to preach the gospel in Jerusalem, to which he had always replied that his hour had not yet come. Now that Jesus was being pursued by the Sanhedrin, the apostles pleaded with him not to go into Jerusalem. Jesus responded, "But the hour has come."

People from as far away as Spain and India were gathered in Jerusalem for the feast of the tabernacles. Jesus boldly entered the city on several occasions to teach publicly in the temple.

Jesus' appearance at this feast confused both his followers and his enemies. Abner and his associates had done much to create favorable opinion for Jesus' gospel, so his enemies were afraid to be too outspoken against him. Some members of the Sanhedrin believed in Jesus, and others were adverse to arresting him while so many people were in town. The Sanhedrin also conjectured that Jesus appeared so openly in their midst due to some promise of protection by the Romans. So the Master taught unmolested.

The crowds who listened to Jesus had various opinions: he was the Messiah, a good man, a prophet, a meddler, a madman. Even his enemies marveled at his teachings. One man asked Jesus how he could teach so fluently when he had not been taught by the rabbis. Jesus said that his teaching was not his own, but God's.

One of the men in the crowd asked Jesus why the rulers sought to kill him. He replied, "The rulers seek to kill me because they resent my teaching about the good news of the kingdom, a gospel that sets men free from the burdensome traditions of a formal religion of ceremonies which these teachers are determined to uphold at any cost... they well know that, if you honestly believe and dare to accept my teaching, their system of traditional religion will be overthrown, forever destroyed."

Eber, an officer of the Sanhedrin, was sent to arrest Jesus. As Eber approached, Jesus said, "I know you have been sent to apprehend me, but you should understand that nothing will befall the Son of Man until his hour comes." Jesus continued to speak about the love of the Father. He proclaimed that he had come that all might have eternal life. When Jesus finished, Eber refused to arrest him; he returned to the Sanhedrin and told his superiors that Jesus was speaking words of mercy and hope, cheering and comforting the downhearted. He questioned what was wrong in such teachings, even if Jesus was not the Messiah. The Sanhedrin disbanded in confusion.

A man who had known Jesus in childhood conspired with agents of the Sanhedrin to trap Jesus. The man had married a woman, Hildana, and set her up as a prostitute. The husband betrayed his wife to the Sanhedrin's men so they could use her to set a trap for Jesus.

The Sanhedrin agents brought Hildana to Jesus saying, "Master, this woman was taken in adultery—in the very act. Now, the law of Moses commands that we should stone such a woman. What do you say should be done with her?" If Jesus upheld the law of Moses, he would be speaking against the Roman authorities. If he forbade the stoning, the Sanhedrin could accuse him of setting himself above Jewish law. If he said nothing, they would accuse him of cowardice.

Jesus looked over the crowd, saw the husband, and walked over to where he stood. Jesus wrote a few words in the sand. When the man read them, he quickly left the scene. The Master then stood before the agents of the Sanhedrin and wrote on the sand again. One by one, these men also went away. Finally, Jesus wrote words in front of the man taken with Hildana, who also took his leave. Jesus said, "Woman, where are your accusers? Did no man remain to stone you?" Hildana replied, "No man, Lord." Jesus replied, "I know about you; neither do I condemn you. Go your way in peace." Hildana later became a disciple of the kingdom.

The former apostles of John the Baptist were influenced by the courage Jesus displayed in his public preaching during the feast of the tabernacles, and also by the sympathetic understanding of his private work with them in Bethlehem. During this time, Abner and Jesus consolidated their two groups. Early in November, Abner and his group joined Jesus in his work. They labored with the apostles until the crucifixion.

163—ORDINATION OF THE SEVENTY AT MAGADAN

Jesus returned to Magadan, where he met with Abner and his disciples, the women's corps, the evangelistic corps, and about one hundred and fifty other disciples from various parts of Palestine. The entire group began a course of intensive training. Jesus talked to the believers each morning. Peter taught methods of public preaching, Nathaniel taught about the art of teaching, and Thomas explained how to answer questions.

The selection of the seventy was decided by a committee of Andrew, Abner, and the acting head of the evangelistic corps. When these three judges were not unanimous in their opinion, they brought the candidate to Jesus.

One disciple brought before Jesus asked that he be allowed first to return home to await the imminent death and burial of his father. Jesus said the man could remain a faithful disciple while ministering to loved ones, but if he wanted to be ordained, he must let others bury the dead. Another wanted to go home to comfort his family. He was told that he must choose one or the other.

A rich man, Matadormus, a former member of the Sanhedrin, pleaded with Jesus to allow him to become one of the newly ordained messengers. Jesus said he would accept Matadormus if he was willing to pay the price. Matadormus replied. "Master, I will do anything if I may be allowed to follow you." Jesus told him to go and sell all that he owned, and bestow the proceeds to the poor.

Matadormus had been raised to believe that wealth was a sign of the favor of God. Jesus knew that he couldn't be an ordained teacher until he was free of his love of wealth. Jesus also saw that Matadormus could have become the leader of the group, but unless Matadormus gave up his wealth he would not be accepted by others who had truly given up everything.

Matadormus couldn't do it. Jesus was sad that Matadormus did not choose ordination, for he greatly loved him. Sometime later, Matadormus did obey Jesus' request and became treasurer of the church in Jerusalem. But his delay deprived him of the chance for personal association with the Master during his last few months on earth.

Later Peter asked, "Shall we require those who follow you to give up all their worldly goods?" Jesus replied that this was necessary only for those who would become apostles. "Whatever thing or person comes between you and the love of the truths of the kingdom, must be surrendered. If one's wealth does not invade the precincts of the soul, it is of no consequence in the spiritual life of those who would enter the kingdom."

At the end of this two-week training period Jesus ordained seventy new teachers of the gospel. During the ordination ceremony, Jesus instructed them to:

Give the gospel to gentile and Jew alike.

Refrain from the expectation of miracles.

Proclaim a spiritual brotherhood rather than a worldly kingdom.

Stay in the first worthy house offered in each city.

Tell believers that the time for an open break with the Jerusalem Jewish leaders had come.

Reveal that man's only duties are to love God completely and to love his neighbor as himself.

Peter also spoke to the new teachers, asking them to:

Pray for more laborers for the kingdom.

Expect hostility and persecution.

Trust the Father to provide food and shelter.

Attend to their business with enthusiasm and without distraction.

Show kindness and courtesy toward all.

Minister to those sick in mind and body.

When the ordination sermon was over, Abner assigned them to preach for six weeks in Galilee, Samaria, and Judea. The seventy set out in pairs on their mission. Jesus and the apostles broke camp early in December and set off to establish headquarters in Perea.

After they left, David Zebedee curtailed his messenger service. He organized a camp near the vacated Magadan site for housing pilgrims who arrived daily from throughout the Roman empire. Within a week, David's camp was prepared to accommodate fifteen hundred visitors.

On December 30, the seventy messengers assembled at the Perea headquarters to exchange their stories of the completed six-week tour. Jesus rejoiced to see men continue the proclamation of the gospel without his immediate presence. The Master addressed them, saying,

"To you and to all who shall follow in your steps down through the ages, let me say: I always stand near, and my invitation-call is, and ever shall be, Come to me all you who labor and are heavy laden, and I will give you rest. Take my yoke upon you and learn of me, for I am true and loyal, and you shall find spiritual rest for your souls."

Preparation for the three-month Perean mission, the Master's last mission, began. Jesus no longer needed to travel to teach people; increasingly, people came to him. He and the apostles spent much of the time during the Perean tour in camp teaching the multitudes, while the seventy and the women's corps went out two by two into the cities.

164—At the Feast of Dedication

In December, 29 AD, to give the Jerusalem leaders one more opportunity to embrace the gospel, Jesus took Nathaniel and Thomas to Jerusalem to attend the feast of the dedication.

On the way, they stopped for the night in Jericho. During a discussion with the local people, a lawyer began asking questions, hoping to entrap or embarrass Jesus. "Teacher, I should like you to tell me just who is my neighbor?" Jews generally looked upon all non-Jews as less than human, and Jewish law defined neighbors as "the children of one's people."

Jesus, knowing the lawyer's motive, responded by telling a story. A traveler was robbed, beaten, and left half dead on the roadside. Soon, a priest passed by. When he saw the unfortunate traveler he crossed to the other side of the road and continued his journey. Likewise, a Levite passed by without stopping. Later, a Samaritan came upon the wounded man. Moved with compassion, he bound the man's wounds, brought him to an inn, and cared for him. Jesus then asked the lawyer, "Which of these three turned out to be the neighbor of him who fell among the robbers?" And the lawyer replied, "He who showed mercy on him." Jesus answered, "Go and do likewise." By turning the lawyer's question back to him, Jesus simultaneously taught a lesson to his followers, renounced the Jewish attitude toward Samaritans, and avoided the lawyer's trap.

In Jerusalem, the Master met with a group of educated men in the home of Nicodemus, many of whom were or had been members of the Sanhedrin. They listened to his teachings intently and offered to help him in winning over the others. Jesus declined, saying that he would wait for his Father's guidance.

The next morning, on the Sabbath, Jesus and the two apostles encountered a well-known blind beggar named Josiah near the temple. As an open challenge to the Sanhedrin, Jesus decided to restore Josiah's sight. He spat on the ground and mixed some clay, which he placed over Josiah's eyes. Jesus told Josiah that his eyes would be restored when he washed the clay away in the pool of Siloam. Josiah obeyed him, and when his sight was restored, he returned to his usual place and began telling people what happened.

An intense public discussion arose. The Sanhedrin convened in direct violation of the rule that forbade meeting on the Sabbath, and summoned Josiah for questioning. After hearing the story, the leaders fell to arguing whether this act was one of God or of the devil. A serious division arose among them.

The Sanhedrin sent for Josiah's parents and questioned them, and then resumed Josiah's interrogation. Josiah became impatient with his questioners, asking them, "I have told you how it all happened, and if you did not believe my testimony, why would you hear it again? Would you by any chance also become his disciples?" As the Sanhedrin broke up in confusion, Josiah said, "Look then, all of you, upon me and realize what has been done this day in Jerusalem! I tell you, if this man were not from God, he could not do this."

During the time the session was in progress, Jesus was teaching close by, but the Sanhedrin were afraid to send for him. The opportunity they had so diligently sought was given them voluntarily by the Master, but they feared even calling him as a witness. Later, as Jesus continued to teach, some of the Jewish leaders baited him. One man asked, "If you are the Messiah, why do you not plainly tell us?"

Jesus said, "I have told you about myself and my Father many times, but you will not believe. The teacher of truth attracts only those who hunger for the truth and who thirst for righteousness. My sheep hear my voice and I know them and they follow me. And to all who follow my teaching I give eternal life; they shall never perish, and no one shall snatch them out of my hand. The Father and I are one." Many who heard would have liked to stone him, but Jesus left the temple unharmed.

When Jesus heard later that Josiah had been cast out of the synagogue, he invited him to come with them to the camp in Pella. Josiah proved to be a worthy recipient of the Master's miracle by becoming a lifelong preacher of the gospel.

165—THE PEREAN MISSION BEGINS

In January, 30 AD, Abner dispersed the entire group of evangelists into the cities and villages of Perea. This region, evenly divided between gentile and Jew, turned out to be the most fruitful in acceptance of the Master's teachings. The Perean mission lasted for three months. Jesus divided his time between teaching the multitudes at Pella and assisting the traveling preachers.

Over three hundred Pharisees and others from Jerusalem had followed Jesus to Pella after the feast of the dedication. Soon after they arrived Jesus addressed the crowd, saying that he knew there were some among them who would die for him and others who wanted to kill him.

Jesus told a parable in which he described himself as a true shepherd, one who gathers his flock in times of danger and who would lay down his life for his fold. He openly declared that no other person could take away his life: "I have the right and the power to lay down my life, and I have the same power and right to take it up again. You cannot understand this, but I received such authority from my Father even before this world was." His words prompted astonished discussion among his friends as well as his enemies. The next day, half of the Jerusalem Pharisees cast their lot with Jesus.

Toward the end of January, Jesus spoke on trust and spiritual preparedness. He advised his followers not to fear their religious enemies who have no power other than to kill the body. The apostles were instructed not to be concerned for their sustenance: "Which of you by anxiety can add a handbreadth to your stature or a day to your life? Since such matters are not in your hands, why do you give anxious thought to any of these problems? Seek the greater thing, and the lesser will be found therein; ask for the heavenly, and the earthly shall be included. The shadow is certain to follow the substance." Jesus also asked his followers not to be anxious about how to answer the questions of their enemies, saying, "...for the spirit that dwells within you shall certainly teach you in that very hour what you should say in honor of the gospel of the kingdom."

One young man went privately to Jesus and asked him to help him regain his inheritance which was being withheld by his brother. Jesus replied that his covetousness in the matter of his material inheritance was causing him to miss an opportunity to learn about his heavenly inheritance. After advising him to take his complaint to the proper authorities, Jesus sent the man away, saying, "My son, what shall it profit you if you gain the whole world and lose your own soul?"

166—LAST VISIT TO NORTHERN PEREA

A wealthy Pharisee named Nathaniel invited Jesus to breakfast with a group of Pharisees as the guest of honor. Many of the guests knew of Jesus' teachings, and were not surprised when he came to the table without washing his hands, but Nathaniel and an unfriendly Pharisee started whispering about it. Jesus rebuked them, saying, "How carefully you cleanse the outside of the cups and the platters while the spiritual-food vessels are filthy and polluted! You make sure to present a pious and holy appearance to the people, but your inner souls are filled with self-righteousness, covetousness, extortion, and all manner of spiritual wickedness."

After a lengthy dissertation, Jesus left. Some of the Pharisees who heard him that day became believers, but most continued to oppose him.

The next day, Jesus explained to the apostles that gentiles and less orthodox Jews were more accepting of the gospel than orthodox Jews. He pointed out how their message had been readily received by the Galileans and Samaritans. Just then, the apostles encountered a group of lepers—nine Jews and one Samaritan. When the lepers saw Jesus coming near they called him to have mercy and heal them.

Simon Zelotes wanted Jesus to pass the lepers by without stopping, but the Master seized the opportunity to reinforce his lesson. Jesus told the lepers that they would be made whole if they went and presented themselves to the priests. They set out to do as Jesus asked, and as they left they were made whole.

When the Samaritan saw that he was healed, he returned to Jesus, fell on his knees, and gave thanks, while the others continued on their way. Jesus remarked, "You see how it is that the children of the house, even when they are insubordinate to their Father's will, take their blessings for granted...but the strangers, when they receive gifts from the head of the house, are filled with wonder and are constrained to give thanks in recognition of the good things bestowed upon them."

One day, a believing Pharisee asked, "Lord, will there be few or many really saved?" The Jewish people had been taught that only Jews would be allowed into the kingdom of heaven, and that the way to eternal life was straight and narrow. Jesus said, "I declare that salvation is first a matter of your personal choosing. Even if the door to the way of life is narrow, it is wide enough to admit all who sincerely seek to enter, for I am that door. And the Son will never refuse entrance to any child of the universe who, by faith, seeks to find the Father through the Son." Jesus declared that whether few or many are to be saved altogether depends on whether few or many heed his invitation: "I am the door, I am the new and living way, and whosoever wills may enter to embark upon the endless truth-search for eternal life."

Thomas asked whether spiritual beings are concerned with events in the material world, and whether angels could prevent accidents. Jesus replied that believing prosperity was a sign of divine approval or that adversity was a sign of God's displeasure was superstitious. "The Father causes his rain to fall on the just and the unjust; the sun likewise shines on the righteous and the unrighteous." Jesus continued to teach them, saying that matters of sickness and health are the result of material causes rather than divine favor or disfavor, but he found it difficult to dissuade the apostles from their long-held beliefs.

Jesus and the apostles traveled to Philadelphia, where Abner was teaching three times daily in the synagogue.

167—THE VISIT TO PHILADELPHIA

Over six hundred people accompanied Jesus on his visit to Philadelphia in February. No miracles happened during the preaching tour through the Decapolis and, except for the cleansing of the lepers, there had been none so far in Perea. During this tour the gospel was being taught without miracles and for the most part without the presence of Jesus or the apostles.

One day a wealthy Pharisee in Philadelphia invited Jesus to breakfast. A large number of visitors, including many Pharisees, also attended. Near the end of the meal a diseased man came in from the street. One Pharisee voiced his objection that the sick man was allowed to enter the room, but Jesus smiled so warmly at the man that he drew closer and sat down on the floor.

Jesus asked the men gathered, "Is it lawful to heal the sick and afflicted on the Sabbath day, or not?" No one replied. Jesus took the sick man's hand and said, "Arise and go your way. You have not asked to be healed, but I know the desire of your heart and the faith of your soul." Addressing the guests Jesus continued, "Such works my Father does, not to tempt you into the kingdom, but to reveal himself to those who are already in the kingdom."

Jesus told a parable: A ruler invited guests to a wedding supper. When the time for the feast arrived his friends did not attend, and the ruler sent his servants out into the street to fill the house with the poor, the lame, the blind, and the outcasts. One of the Pharisees listening understood Jesus' meaning and was baptized into the kingdom that same day.

On the Sabbath, Abner arranged for Jesus to teach in the synagogue. After the service the Master spoke to a woman bowed down by depression and fear. Believing in him, she straightened up for the first time in years and began to glorify God.

The chief ruler of this synagogue was an unfriendly Pharisee who objected to this healing because he believed that healing was work and should not be performed on the Sabbath. Jesus responded, asking, "Does not everyone of you, on the Sabbath, loose his ox from the stall and lead him forth for watering? If such a service is permissable on the Sabbath day, should not this woman, a daughter of Abraham who has been bound down by evil these eighteen years, be loosed from this bondage and led forth to partake of the waters of liberty and life, even on this Sabbath day?" As a result of this public criticism, the ruler of the synagogue was deposed and was replaced by one of Jesus' followers.

A messenger from Bethany brought news that Lazarus was very sick. Jesus told his apostles to prepare to travel to Judea. The apostles thought it was too dangerous for Jesus to travel to Bethany and they pleaded with him not to go.

Jesus told the apostles that Lazarus was dead. The Master wanted to give the Jews one more chance to believe in his Father's message. He told his men that even if no more Jews were brought into the kingdom, the trip to Bethany would give the apostles a new belief in the gospel that would strengthen them when after he was gone.

The apostles saw that Jesus would not be dissuaded. Some were reluctant to accompany him, but Thomas rallied them, saying, "We have told the Master our fears, but he is determined to go to Bethany. I am satisfied it means the end; they will surely kill him, but if that is the Master's choice, then let us acquit ourselves like men of courage; let us go also that we may die with him."

On the way to Judea, Jesus told the parable of the Pharisee and the publican. A Pharisee stood in the temple and prayed, giving thanks that he was not like other men, and listing all the good deeds he had done. The publican stood with his eyes turned down, asking for God's mercy on his sins. Jesus said, "I tell you that the publican went home with God's approval rather than the Pharisee, for every one who exalts himself shall be humbled, but he who humbles himself shall be exalted."

In Jericho, Jesus was asked to discuss marriage. While he was reluctant to make pronouncements about marriage and divorce, Jesus taught that marriage was honorable and was to be desired by all men. He denounced the lax divorce laws used by the Pharisees on the grounds that they were unjust to women and children.

Jesus' message about marriage and children spread all over Jericho. The next morning, scores of mothers came to where Jesus lodged to have the Master bless their children. The apostles tried to send the women away, but Jesus reproved them, saying, "Suffer little children to come to me; forbid them not, for of such is the kingdom of heaven." He laid his hands on the children, and spoke words of courage and hope to the mothers. Women's status was much improved by Jesus' teaching, and so it would have been throughout the world if his followers had not departed from his teachings.

168—THE RESURRECTION OF LAZARUS

When Jesus arrived in Bethany on March 2, 30 AD, Lazarus had been dead for four days. Many people were comforting Mary and Martha, including some who were enemies of Jesus. Martha said to Jesus, "Master, if you had been here, my brother would not have died!" Jesus replied, "Only have faith, Martha, and your brother shall rise again."

As the grieving sisters led him to the tomb, Jesus wept. He felt deep affection and sympathy for Martha and Mary. He resented the outward show of mourning by some of the insincere in the crowd, and hesitated to bring Lazarus back to the certain bitter persecution that he would endure.

A group of forty-five people gathered before the tomb, along with a vast assembly of celestial beings who awaited the command of their beloved Sovereign. When Jesus asked that the stone be taken away from the front of the tomb, Martha and Mary were filled with conflicted emotions. Martha said, "Must we roll away the stone? My brother has now been dead four days, so that by this time decay of the body has begun."

Jesus asked, "Did I not tell you at the first that this sickness was not to the death?" His apostles and some of the neighbors rolled the stone away. They could see the form of Lazarus, wrapped in linen, lying in the cave.

Jesus began to pray aloud, and then he cried out, "Lazarus, come forth!" Lazarus, still wrapped in the grave cloths, sat upright. Everyone except his sisters and the apostles fled.

Lazarus asked why he was in the garden wrapped in linens. He had no memory of his death. After Martha explained what had happened, Lazarus went to the Master, knelt at his feet and offered praise to God. Jesus lifted his friend and said, "My son, what has happened to you will also be experienced by all who believe this gospel except that they shall be resurrected in a more glorious form. You shall be a living witness of the truth which I spoke—I am the resurrection and the life."

By noon the next day the story of Lazarus had spread throughout Jerusalem. People flocked to Bethany to see him. The alarmed Pharisees called a meeting; the miracle had strengthened the faith of believers but only made the Sanhedrin more determined to destroy Jesus.

One of the Pharisees made a proposal advocating Jesus' immediate death without trial. The resolution did not come to a vote that day because fourteen members of the Sanhedrin resigned in protest. Two weeks later, five other members were expelled on the suspicion that they believed Jesus' gospel.

Although the Sanhedrin admitted that Lazarus had been resurrected from the dead, they attributed this and all of Jesus' miracles to the work of the devil. No matter the source of his power, the Jewish leaders believed that if he were not stopped all the common people would soon believe in him.

On the following Sunday morning, Jesus and the apostles traveled back to Pella. On the journey, the apostles asked Jesus questions concerning the answers to prayer. Jesus taught them that prayer is an effort of the finite mind to approach the Infinite. He assured the apostles that all spirit-born prayers are certain of an answer, even when they appear to go unanswered. Some prayers can only be answered in eternity or when a person advances to higher spiritual levels. Sometimes people don't recognize the answers to their prayers.

Lazarus remained at his home in Bethany until the week Jesus was killed. When Lazarus was warned that the Sanhedrin were planning to kill him as well, he fled to Perea. Mary and Martha later joined their brother in Philadelphia where he served as treasurer of the church under Abner.

169—Last Teaching at Pella

Jesus and the apostles returned to the camp at Pella, where the assembled crowds had already learned of the resurrection of Lazarus. Jesus preached in Pella, telling the stories of the lost sheep, the lost coin, and the prodigal son. He grouped these three stories together to demonstrate that God knows when we are lost, is diligent in his search for those who are lost, and that when a lost soul returns to God, he is accepted with joy.

Jesus taught that when people seek God, God is likewise seeking them. He said that there is more joy in heaven over one sinner who repents that in ninety-nine who need no repentance. Jesus emphasized that he and God actively search for lost souls and use every resource possible to find those in need of salvation.

One evening Jesus told the parable of the shrewd steward to illustrate to his followers that they should arrange their lives to provide for present joy as well as future enjoyment of the treasures in heaven. He said, "He who is faithful in little will also be faithful in much, while he who is unrighteous in little will also be unrighteous in much. If you have not shown foresight and integrity in the affairs of this world, how can you hope to be faithful and prudent when you are trusted with the stewardship of the true riches of the heavenly kingdom?"

Jesus always had trouble explaining to the apostles that the Father in heaven was not a king. People of Jesus' time were accustomed to kings and emperors, and Jewish lore had long told of the coming of the kingdom of God. For this reason, Jesus referred to the spiritual brotherhood as the kingdom of God, but he never referred to his Father as a king.

Meanwhile in Jerusalem, the priests created these accusations against Jesus:

He is a friend of sinners; he even eats with them.

He blasphemes by saying that God is his father.

He heals disease on the Sabbath and flouts the sacred law of Israel.

He does miracles by the power of devils.

170—THE KINGDOM OF HEAVEN

The term, "kingdom of heaven" was one that had many meanings in Jesus' era. Jewish people thought the kingdom would mark the coming of the Messiah who was to establish Jewish power on earth. Persians believed that a divine kingdom would be established miraculously at the end of the world.

Jesus taught that the kingdom of heaven centered in the Fatherhood of God and the brotherhood of man. He taught the apostles to pray, "Your kingdom come, your will be done." He earnestly sought, without success, to have them exchange the phrase "the kingdom of God" for "the will of God." The apostles' distorted ideas were compounded after his death by their belief that Jesus would return within their lifetimes to establish the new kingdom in power and glory.

The kingdom of God in this world is the supreme desire to do the will of God and an unselfish love of others. Humans enter the kingdom by faith, sincerity, trust in the Father, open-mindedness, truth-hunger, and the desire to find God and be like Him. Acceptance of God's forgiveness creates a path that ensures the continuing progress of children of God toward righteousness.

True righteousness is the natural result of unselfish love for others. Although righteousness is more than merely doing good works, the true religion of the kingdom unfailingly manifests itself in social service. Jesus did not concern himself with morals and ethics as such, rather, he was concerned with an inward spiritual fellowship with God that out-wardly manifests as loving service. Religion is personal, but the results of religion are familial and social.

Jesus observed five phases of the kingdom of God: personal experi-ence of spiritual relationship with God, enhanced social ethics resulting from the influence of God's spirit in the heart, supermortal brotherhood of spiritual beings in heaven and on earth, hope of a more perfect fulfill-ment of God's will in the next age of humanity, and the spiritual age of light and life on earth.

Features of the kingdom of heaven are: pre-eminence of the individ-ual; will as determining factor in man's experience; spiritual fellowship with God the Father; supreme satisfaction of loving service; and the transcendence of the spiritual over the material in human personality.

The world has yet to seriously implement Jesus' ideals of the king-dom of heaven. Jesus' teachings nearly failed because of his followers' distortion of his concepts. Jewish believers persisted in regarding him as the Messiah who would return to establish a kingdom on earth. Gentile Christians accepted the doctrines of Paul, who described Jesus as the re-deemer of the church.

The church as a social outgrowth of the kingdom is desirable, but not if it becomes an institutional substitute for the kingdom of heaven. Jews thought of the kingdom as the Jewish community; gentiles thought of it as the church. Jesus taught that it was all people who confess their faith in the Fatherhood of God, and declare their wholehearted dedication to doing his will. The Christian church is the cocoon in which Jesus' con-cept of the kingdom now slumbers. Someday, a new John the Baptist will revive the actual teachings of the Master, and the religion of Jesus will replace the religion about Jesus.

171—On the Way to Jerusalem

On March 12, 30 AD, Jesus announced that he and the apostles would travel to Jerusalem for the Passover. His followers, in spite of all that Jesus taught about his kingdom not being of this world, assumed that he was going there to establish the temporal kingdom of Jewish supremacy.

Salome, mother of the Zebedee brothers, came to Jesus with James and John. She asked him to promise that her sons would sit beside him in the kingdom, one on his right side and the other on his left. Jesus grieved that his beloved apostles still did not understand the nature of his kingdom. He assured them that they would indeed drink of his cup of bitterness and share in his humiliation, but it was not his place to give what Salome asked. Later, when Salome witnessed the Master crucified between two criminals, she remembered her ill-conceived request.

The other apostles were upset to learn that James and John had gone secretly to Jesus seeking preference. They began again to argue among themselves. Jesus spoke to them, saying, "Whosoever would be great among you, let him first become your servant. I declare to you that the Son of Man came not to be ministered to but to minister; and I now go up to Jerusalem to lay down my life in the doing of the Father's will and in the service of my brethren."

One thousand people traveled with Jesus as he made his final journey to Jerusalem. At a ford in the Jordan river, the Master discoursed on the cost of being his disciple. Jesus warned his followers that they would face bitter persecutions and crushing disappointment; they must be willing to renounce all that they were and to dedicate all that they had. He frequently repeated that his kingdom was not of this world. His apostles considered what Jesus said but clung to the belief that after a period of adversity, the kingdom would be established just as they desired.

As the group traveled the number of followers shrunk to less than two hundred. On March 29, they camped at Livias. Here Simon Zelotes and Simon Peter obtained over one hundred swords that they distributed and wore concealed beneath their cloaks.

Jesus warned his men not to put their trust in the uncertainties of the flesh. He told them plainly that he would be delivered to the priests and put to death in Jerusalem. The Master asked them not to be dismayed and to remember that he would rise again on the third day. The stunned apostles would not accept what he was telling them. They were so attached to their old beliefs that they could not believe that Jesus really meant he would be killed by his enemies in Jerusalem.

In Jericho, a tax collector named Zaccheus wanted to see Jesus so much that he had climbed a sycamore tree to get a good view. As Jesus passed by, he looked up at Zaccheus and said, "Make haste, Zaccheus, and come down, for tonight I must abide at your house." The people who witnessed this were surprised that Jesus wished to stay with this publican, and one of the Pharisees commented on Jesus' willingness to lodge with a sinner who robbed his own people.

When Zaccheus heard this, he responded, "Men of Jericho, hear me! I may be a publican and a sinner, but the great Teacher has come to abide in my house; and before he goes in, I tell you that I am going to bestow one half of all my goods upon the poor... I am going to seek salvation with all my heart and learn to do righteousness in the sight of God." And when Zaccheus finished, Jesus said, "Today has salvation come to this home, and you have become indeed a son of Abraham. And marvel not at what I say nor take offense at what we do, for I have all along declared that the Son of Man has come to seek and to save that which is lost."

The next day, when the apostles stopped for lunch, Jesus told a parable. A nobleman entrusted each of his stewards with one pound to invest during the nobleman's absence. When an accounting was later required, the first steward had increased his pound tenfold. He was given authority over ten cities. The second servant had earned five pounds, and was made ruler of five cities. The last steward had wrapped his pound in a napkin to keep it safe. His master took it from him and gave it to the servant who had ten cities, saying, "To every one who has shall be given more, but from him who has not, even that which he has shall be taken from him."

172—GOING INTO JERUSALEM

Jesus and the apostles arrived in Bethany on the afternoon of March 31st. Six days before the Passover, the people of two towns, Bethany and Bethphage, honored Jesus and Lazarus by attending a banquet at the home of Simon. Since all Jews were under order to deliver

Jesus to the Sanhedrin on sight, this feast was held in defiance of the priests.

Near the end of the banquet, Mary, sister of Lazarus, went to Jesus and opened a large container of expensive ointment. She anointed Jesus' head and feet with it, and then wiped his feet with her hair. The crowd murmured. Judas thought that the Master should rebuke this wastefulness. He whispered that the oil should have been sold and the proceeds given to the poor.

Jesus said, "Let her alone . . . you have the poor always with you so that you may minister to them at any time it seems good to you; but I shall not always be with you; I go soon to my Father. This woman has long saved this ointment for my body at its burial, and now that it has seemed good to her to make this anointing in anticipation of my death, she shall not be denied such satisfaction. In the doing of this, Mary has reproved all of you in that by this act she evinces faith in what I have said about my death and ascension to my Father in heaven."

Judas felt humiliated. It was at this moment that Judas made his first conscious decision to seek revenge against Jesus.

Jesus, having decided to make a public entrance into the city, recalled a scripture that had sometimes been associated with the anticipated Messiah: "Rejoice greatly, O daughter of Zion; shout, O daughter of Jerusalem. Behold, your king comes to you. He is just and he brings salvation. He comes as the lowly one, riding upon an ass, upon a colt, the foal of an ass." Warrior kings entered cities riding horseback, but a king on a peaceful mission always entered riding an ass. Jesus used this symbol in an attempt to reinforce the idea that his kingdom was not an earthly one.

Several hundred people gathered to escort Jesus into Jerusalem. As they moved toward Jerusalem, the procession became increasingly festive. The crowd began to shout the psalm, "Hosanna to the son of David; blessed is he who comes in the name of the Lord." Jesus was lighthearted until he reached the brow of Olivet, where he stopped. Silence came over the crowd as they beheld him weeping at the thought of the fate of Jerusalem.

David Zebedee and his men had been spreading the word that Jesus was about to make his entry into the city, and several thousand pilgrims poured out of the city to greet him. The Pharisees were unhappy about this unanticipated acclaim; it prevented them from arresting the Master immediately. There was no deep significance in this outburst of public enthusiasm. The people who cheered Jesus so joyously as he entered the city quickly rejected him when they realized later that he would not inaugurate an earthly kingdom.

Jesus and the apostles strolled about the Jerusalem temple but did no preaching that day. When they returned to Bethany that evening the apostles were full of mixed emotions. Andrew had been worried that the other apostles, especially those with swords, would be swept away by the emotion of the day. Simon Peter was disappointed that Jesus had wasted an opportunity to preach in the temple. James Zebedee could not understand why Jesus would accept the crowd's acclaim, then refuse to speak once they had safely entered the temple.

John Zebedee suspected that Jesus had been emulating the Scripture that described the Messiah riding into Jerusalem on an ass. Nathaniel, besides being aware of the symbolism of Scripture, also reasoned that without the demonstration Jesus would not have reached the temple without being arrested; he was not surprised that once inside the city the Master had no further use for the cheering crowds. Matthew also recalled the Scripture. He was elated at the thought that something spectacular was about to happen, and when nothing occurred, he became depressed.

Philip's enjoyment in watching Jesus being honored was offset by his worry that he, Philip, would be required to feed the multitude. Thomas, at first bewildered by the Master's motives, soon realized that the crowd was keeping the Sanhedrin at bay. By the end of the day, Thomas was cheered by Jesus' cleverness at outwitting the priests. Simon Zelotes had visions as they entered the city of the nationalists taking action, of himself in command of the kingdom's military forces, and of all the Sanhedrin dead. By the anticlimactic evening, Simon was crushed emotionally; it was not until long after the resurrection that he recovered from his depression and disappointment. The Alpheus twins had a perfect day; they enjoyed every moment.

Judas Iscariot was still stewing over the Master's rebuke of him the previous day. The idea of coming into Jerusalem this way seemed ridiculous to him. He considered leaving but decided not to because he still had possession of the apostolic funds. Judas was especially humiliated by the ridicule of some of his Saducean friends, who laughed as they teased Judas about his Master riding into town on an ass.

173—MONDAY IN JERUSALEM

Priests in Jerusalem profited enormously from businesses in the temple courtyards. Many worshipers bought overpriced sacrificial animals guaranteed to pass the required pre-sacrifice inspection. Extensive amounts of foreign currencies were converted because shekels were required for the temple head tax; moneychangers charged thirteen cents for each ten-cent coin.

On Monday morning Jesus and the apostles arrived at the temple to preach. As Jesus began, a hundred steer bellowed as they were led through the courtyard and a violent argument arose at the table of one of the money lenders.

To the amazement of the apostles, Jesus stepped down from the teaching platform, took a whip from the boy who was driving the steer, and drove the cattle from the temple. He then opened all of the pens and released the other animals while the assembled crowds began to overturn the lenders' tables. In less than five minutes, all commercial activity in the temple ceased.

This cleansing of the temple discloses the Master's attitude toward the commercialization of religion, as well as his disdain for all forms of unfairness at the expense of the poor and the unlearned. This episode also demonstrates that Jesus did not disapprove of the employment of force against the unfair practices of unjust minorities who entrench themselves behind political, financial, or ecclesiastical power. Shrewd, wicked, and designing men are not to be permitted to organize themselves for the exploitation and oppression of others.

By the time Roman guards arrived, the temple was calm. Jesus was preaching, "You have this day witnessed that which is written in the Scriptures: 'My house shall be called a house of prayer for all nations, but you have made it a den of robbers.'" The apostles were so stunned by their Master's actions that they could only watch in amazement.

When the priests heard the news, they were dumbfounded; they were more determined than ever to destroy Jesus. The priests agreed that Jesus must be destroyed but were unwilling to arrest him publicly. They decided to attempt to discredit him in front of his audience.

A group of priests asked Jesus who had given him authority to do the things he did. Jesus answered with a question, asking them whether

John the Baptist got his authority from heaven or from men. The elders found themselves confused. If they answered "from heaven", Jesus would be able to logically ask why they did not believe in him. If they answered "from men", they were afraid that the crowd would turn on them, because people generally believed that John was a prophet. So they were compelled to express no opinion, and answered that they didn't know. And Jesus said, "Neither will I tell you by what authority I do these things." The Sadducees and the Pharisees asked no more questions that day.

While the priests lingered, Jesus told a parable about a landowner with two sons. The landowner asked one son to work in the vineyard. At first the son refused, but after his father left, this son repented and went to work. The landowner also asked the second son to work, and he agreed, but when his father left, he didn't work. Jesus asked, "Which of these sons really did his father's will? …now do I declare that the publicans and harlots, even though they appear to refuse the call to repentance, shall see the error of their way and go on into the kingdom of God before you, who make great pretensions of serving the Father in heaven while you refuse to do the works of the Father."

The Master told another story about a man who rented his vineyard out to tenants. When he sent servants to collect the rent payment, the tenants beat the servants and sent them away empty-handed. Repeated attempts by the lord's servants to collect the rent failed. His favorite steward and his son were sent, and the tenants killed them both. Jesus asked the people to imagine what the lord would do to these wicked tenants. Some of them understood that this parable referred to the Jewish nation's rejection of Jesus and the prophets.

Jesus then told the parable of the wedding feast. A king sent messengers to invite guests to a feast celebrating his son's wedding, but the guests didn't come. Some guests openly rebelled against the king, killing his messengers. The king ordered his armies to destroy the rebels. He then sent his servants out to gather people, good and bad, rich and poor, to fill the wedding hall. When the king entered the hall he saw a man without a wedding garment. This surprised the king, who had provided the wedding garments for free. The unprepared man was cast out and the king said, "I will have none here except those who delight to accept my invitation, and who do me the honor to wear those guest garments so freely provided for all."

A man asked Jesus what sign the Master would give to prove that he was truly the Son of God. Jesus said, pointing at his own body, "Destroy this temple, and in three days I will raise it up." But they did not understand him. Even the apostles did not understand until after his resurrection.

As they made their way out of the city that afternoon, the apostles sensed that something of tragic import was about to happen.

174—TUESDAY MORNING IN THE TEMPLE

On Tuesday morning, Jesus went to Jerusalem with four of the apostles while the rest set up camp at Gethsemane. On the road to Jerusalem, James and Peter asked Jesus to help them understand divine forgiveness. Jesus explained that mature relationships prevent any estrangement that would require either a child's repentance or a parent's forgiveness. A good parent sees the immaturity of his child in light of his own understanding, and the divine parent possesses infinite sympathy and understanding. Jesus said that when we love others, we have already forgiven them. This quality of forgiveness is Godlike. An immature child may feel a sense of separation due to guilt over wrongdoing, but the true parent is not conscious of separation. Sin is an experience of creature consciousness: it is not a part of God's consciousness. Inability to forgive others is a measure of immaturity.

Soon Jesus and the four apostles arrived at the temple. No sooner had Jesus begun to teach than a group of students who had been coached by the Pharisees asked, "Is it lawful for us to give tribute to Caesar?" The priests reasoned that this question, if answered affirmatively, would alienate the multitude, who resented Roman rule. If Jesus answered negatively, it would give them cause to go to the Roman authorities and have him charged with inciting rebellion.

Jesus told them to show him a coin. As he looked at it he asked them whose image was on the coin. The students answered, "Caesar's." And Jesus said, "Render to Caesar the things that are Caesar's and render to God the things that are God's." The students marveled at the wisdom of his answer.

A lawyer representing a group of Pharisees asked Jesus to name the greatest commandment. Jesus answered: "There is but one commandment, and that one is the greatest of all, and that commandment is: 'Hear

O Israel, the Lord our God, the Lord is one; and you shall love the Lord your God with all your heart and with all your soul, with all your mind and with all your strength.' This is the first and great commandment. And the second commandment is like this first; indeed, it springs directly therefrom, and it is: 'You shall love your neighbor as yourself.' There is no commandment greater than these; on these two commandments hang all the law and the prophets." The lawyer who asked the question perceived that the Master had answered wisely. That evening this same man was baptized near Gethsemane.

Other groups had been instructed to ask Jesus questions, but when they saw what was happening, they decided to keep quiet. When Jesus saw that no more questions were forthcoming, he asked the audience a question, "What do you think of the Deliver? That is, whose son is he?" One of the scribes replied, "The Messiah is the son of David." Jesus then referenced a Psalm attributed to David, "The Lord said to my lord, sit on my right hand until I make your enemies the footstool of your feet." Jesus asked, "If David calls him Lord, how then can he be his son?" The priests saw the dilemma and would not answer. No more questions were asked in the temple that morning.

At lunch time, a group of Greek gentile believers were invited by Andrew and Philip to meet with Jesus. As he spoke during the meal, Jesus remarked that this would be the first and last time that he would instruct a group that was composed equally of Jews and gentiles. He looked at the Greeks and said:

"He who believes this gospel, believes not merely in me but in Him who sent me. When you look upon me, you see not only the Son of Man but also Him who sent me. I am the light of the world, and whosoever will believe my teaching shall no longer abide in darkness. If you gentiles will hear me, you shall receive the words of life and shall enter forthwith into the joyous liberty of the truth of sonship with God."

"But to both Jew and gentile I declare the hour has about come when the Son of Man will be glorified. You well know that, except a grain of wheat falls into the earth and dies, it abides alone; but if it dies in good soil, it springs up again to life and bears much fruit. He who selfishly loves his life stands in danger of losing it; but he who is willing to lay down his life for my sake and the gospel's shall enjoy a more abundant existence on earth and in heaven, life eternal." Having thus spoken, Jesus led the way back to the temple.

175—THE LAST TEMPLE DISCOURSE

Jesus returned to the temple accompanied by Joseph of Arimathea, thirty Greeks, several disciples, and eleven of the apostles—all but Judas. He delivered his final discourse in the temple. Jesus explained once again that his proclamation of the truth of sonship with God was open to all. He said that he had persistently sought peace but that the rulers of Israel would not have it. "There cannot be peace between light and darkness, between life and death, between truth and error." He offered mercy once more to the leaders who were about to reject him.

Jesus spoke about the long history of mercy that his Father had bestowed on the Jewish people, and about the prophets that had been sent generation after generation. He warned them that they were in danger of losing their status as the custodians of divine law. Jesus offered them one more chance to repent, to seek God and the kingdom of heaven.

Jesus faulted the scribes and Pharisees for being hypocrites, for refusing to enter the kingdom, for preventing others from entering the kingdom, for refusing to show mercy to the poor, for being false teachers, for dishonesty, for being strict about tithes while disregarding laws on faith, mercy, and judgment, for rejecting truth and spurning mercy, and for making an outward show of religion while their souls were steeped in iniquity. He warned them that if they persisted in their evil ways an accounting would be required. Jesus finished his speech and left the temple with his followers.

The apostles were confused. The crowds who heard Jesus were stunned. That evening all of Jerusalem discussed the question of Jesus' fate. More than thirty prominent Jews met that night and agreed that if Jesus was arrested, they would make an open acknowledgment of their allegiance to him.

Judas returned to the temple in time to hear the last half of Jesus' discourse. Although he clung more firmly than ever to his plan to forsake the gospel, Judas left the temple with the other apostles and remained with them that night at Mount Olivet.

The Sanhedrin's answer to the Master's offer of mercy was their unanimous vote to sentence him to death, a sentence declared even before Jesus was arrested. The Sanhedrin gave orders that Jesus was to be apprehended in secret and brought to court Thursday at midnight. The angels and celestial beings attending the Master were eager to assist him but were powerless to act against his wishes.

176—Tuesday Evening on Mount Olivet

On Tuesday evening as the Master and his men left Jerusalem for the Gethsemane camp, Jesus declared to his apostles that the temple in Jerusalem would be destroyed. He admonished them not to be overly concerned about being delivered to the authorities, thrown out of the synagogue, put in prison, or even put to death for the gospel's sake. He advised the apostles to remain in the city until Roman troops invaded Jerusalem, at which time they should flee into the mountains.

The apostles were bewildered by the Master's predictions. In spite of his attempts to dissuade them, many apostles assumed that the destruction of Jerusalem would coincide with Jesus' promised return.

"Have I not all this time taught you that your connection with the kingdom is spiritual and individual, wholly a matter of personal experience in the spirit by the faith-realization that you are a son of God? What more shall I say? The downfall of nations, the crash of empires, the destruction of the unbelieving Jews, the end of an age, even the end of the world, what have these things to do with one who believes this gospel, and who has hid his life in the surety of the eternal kingdom? What does it matter to you who believe this gospel of the kingdom if nations overturn, the age ends, or all things visible crash, since you know that your life is the gift of the Son, and that it is eternally secure in the Father?"

"Every generation of believers should carry on their work, in view of the possible return of the Son of Man, exactly as each individual believer carries forward his lifework in view of inevitable and ever-impending natural death."

Jesus told a story about a man who, before embarking on a journey, divided his treasures among his servants to be cared for while he was gone. Most of the servants invested their talents to increase their master's wealth, but one servant buried the talent entrusted to him in the ground. When the master returned, he commended those servants who had invested their talents wisely, and he increased their responsibilities. But the servant who buried his talent in the ground was chastised, and his talent was taken from him. "To every one who has, more shall be given, and he shall have abundance; but from him who has not, even that which he has shall be taken away. You cannot stand still in the affairs of the kingdom."

"Truth is living; the Spirit of Truth is ever leading the children of light into new realms of spiritual reality and divine service. You are not given truth to crystallize into settled, safe, and honored forms. Your revelation of truth must be so enhanced by passing through your personal experience that new beauty and actual spiritual gains will be disclosed to all who behold your spiritual fruits and in consequence thereof are led to glorify the Father who is in heaven."

177—Wednesday, the Rest Day

On Wednesday Jesus suggested that the apostles take some free time, asking only that they not go into Jerusalem. Jesus prepared to go into the hills alone to commune with his Father. David Zebedee proposed to send three men along for protection but Jesus declined the company.

Just before Jesus set out, John Mark brought him a basket of food and water. As Jesus reached for the basket the boy begged to come along. Holding fast to the lunch, John Mark promised that he would not disturb the Master and that he could watch the basket while Jesus prayed. Jesus relented, "Since with all your heart you crave to go with me, it shall not be denied you. We will go by ourselves and have a good visit."

The apostles spent most of the day visiting with disciples. As the day passed, they grew increasingly anxious about Jesus' safety. They were lonely for him. Nathaniel voiced the opinion "…that what is wrong with most of us is that we are only half-hearted. We fail to love the Master as he loves us. If we had all wanted to go with him as much as John Mark did, he would surely have taken us all."

That afternoon, David Zebedee received word that his mother was on her way to Jerusalem accompanied by Jesus' mother and family. David kept the news of their pending arrival to himself.

Soon after Jesus left camp, Judas slipped away to meet with Jesus' enemies at the home of the high priest Caiaphas. His Sadducean friends told Judas that his reversal of opinion on Jesus would be hailed as a great event and that he would receive high honors from the Sanhedrin.

Judas was convinced that Jesus was going to allow himself to be defeated by the Jewish rulers, and Judas could not endure that humiliation.

He entertained the idea that Jesus was probably not sound of mind. Judas resented Jesus for not assigning him greater honor, and was indignant to think that James, Peter, and John had been closer to the Master. This meeting with the Sanhedrin gave Judas an opportunity to secure glory for himself while taking revenge on those whom he now so bitterly resented.

Judas presented his case to Caiaphas and the other Jewish leaders, offering to help them arrest Jesus in a private place. An agreement was made that Judas would deliver Jesus to the temple guards late Thursday evening. Judas was pleased that he had found a way to salvage the lost glory he had dreamed of in the new kingdom for immediate honor in the old. The other apostles also craved honor, but their love for Jesus was a more powerful influence on them than their desire for personal glory.

Evening came. Jesus returned to camp and tried to cheer his followers, but they were so downhearted by their sense of impending disaster that it was nearly an impossible task. The apostles had begun to realize the terrible isolation that was about to visit them, and none of them felt prepared.

During his evening talk Jesus warned his disciples to beware the support of the multitudes who believe the truth superficially but do not allow it to grow roots in their hearts. "Those who know the gospel only in the mind, and who have not experienced it in the heart, cannot be depended upon for support when real trouble comes." Knowing that this was their last evening together Jesus sent them to sleep, saying, "Go to your sleep, my brethren, and peace be upon you till we rise on the morrow, one more day to do the Father's will and experience the joy of knowing that we are his sons."

178—Last Day at the Camp

After breakfast Thursday Jesus led fifty disciples to a secluded place above the camp to deliver his farewell discourse. He spoke for nearly two hours on the subject of the relationship between earthly kingdoms and the kingdom of heaven. Jesus taught that while earthly governments may use physical force to maintain law and order, in the kingdom of heaven believers will not, although social groups of believers are right to maintain order and discipline among their membership.

Awareness of spiritual sonship should help mortals become ideal earthly citizens. There is no conflict between cosmic and earthly citizenship unless human rulers usurp the spiritual honor and worship that belongs to God. Material-minded people will only know of spiritual light when those who possess it draw near them in unselfish social service.

Jesus taught, "As faith-enlightened and spirit-liberated sons of the kingdom of heaven, you face a double responsibility of duty to man and duty to God while you voluntarily assume a third and sacred obligation: service to the brotherhood of God-knowing believers."

Jesus admonished his followers not to worship earthly rulers and not to use temporal power to further the spiritual kingdom. He asked them to offer loving service to believers and unbelievers alike; sincere and loving service is a mighty social lever. Jesus advised them to become experts at adjusting misunderstandings and disagreements, and to seek to live peacefully with all people.

Jesus warned his followers that in the near future they should expect trouble, persecution, and death. He told them that the manner in which they suffered for the gospel would enlighten their backward brethren. He asked that they remain faithful to the kingdom even in times of peace, always laboring to persuade people but never trying to compel them.

He gave them much instruction in dealing with other people in the work of spreading the gospel. "The revelation I have made to you is a living revelation, and I desire that it shall bear appropriate fruits in each individual and in each generation in accordance with the laws of spiritual growth, increase, and adaptive development. You are not to attack the old ways; you are skillfully to put the leaven of new truth in the midst of the old beliefs. Let the Spirit of Truth do his own work." Few who heard Jesus speak that morning comprehended anything he said, but the Greeks understood him best. The apostles were bewildered by his references to generations of believers.

David Zebedee learned of the plan to arrest Jesus—including Judas' part in the plot—but when he tried to speak to Jesus, Jesus asked him to remain silent. Philip asked Jesus what plan should be made for the Passover meal. Judas tried to eavesdrop on this conversation, but David quickly drew Judas aside to discuss the status of the apostolic funds. During this conversation, Judas turned over the money in his possession to David.

Meanwhile, Philip, Peter, and John learned that Jesus had made plans to have supper that evening at John Mark's parents house in Jerusalem.

They went into the city to make the arrangements, then returned to the camp to lead the rest of the group back into Jerusalem.

To avoid the crowds, the group traveled by way of the western brow of Mount Olivet. As they paused to look down on the city, Jesus told his men that he would soon leave them to return to the work the Father had given him. He warned them not to needlessly expose themselves to danger when he was taken, saying that if the Father wished his departure, nothing the apostles could do would change things. The Master asked them not to be misled into any foolish plan to defend him. He spoke to them of cities whose builder is God and worlds whose habit of life is righteousness and joy in the truth. He told them that they would one day sit with him on high when their work on earth was finished. The apostles then stood up and made their way into the city, where John Mark welcomed them into his parent's home.

179—The Last Supper

The apostles arrived at John Mark's house, wondering why Jesus had decided to celebrate Passover one day early. They went immediately to the upper chamber while Jesus spoke with the family downstairs.

As the apostles entered the supper room, they noticed water pitchers, basins, and towels that were set aside for washing their feet. Noticing that no servant was present to perform this task, they began to wonder which of them would have to act the servant and wash the feet of the others. Looking at the table that was prepared for them, they also wondered whether they should seat themselves, or wait for Jesus.

Judas went to the seat of honor at the left of the host's seat, and sat down. The others fell into dispute. John Zebedee immediately sat in the next highest seat, at the right of the host. Peter became angry that these two would presume to seat themselves nearest the Master, and so he marched around the table to sit at the lowest seat, hoping that Jesus would call him to displace one of those in the most honored seats. The rest of the apostles chose places around the table, continuing their arguments until Jesus appeared and took his seat.

James Alpheus brought Jesus the first cup of water and wine, and Jesus held the cup saying, "Take this cup and divide it among yourselves and when you partake of it, realize that I shall not again drink with you the fruit of the vine since this is our last supper. When we sit down again in this manner, it will be in the kingdom to come."

After drinking the first cup, Jewish custom dictated that the host should wash his hands. Knowing that Jesus never observed this rite, the apostles were curious when they saw him rise from the table and move toward the water pitchers. They were shocked when the Master poured water into one of the foot basins and prepared to wash the feet of Simon Peter. As Jesus knelt before Peter, all twelve men rose to their feet in amazement.

Embarrassed, Peter asked Jesus if he really intended to wash his feet. Jesus replied, "You may not fully understand what I am about to do, but hereafter you will know the meaning of these things." Peter exclaimed, "Master, you shall never wash my feet!" And each of the apostles nodded their agreement.

Jesus said, "Peter, I declare that if I do not wash your feet, you will have no part with me in that which I am about to perform." Peter thought for a moment and said, "Then, Master, wash not my feet only but also my hands and my head." Jesus set about to wash each of the apostles' feet in turn.

When Jesus finished, he asked his followers what lesson they thought they should learn from the fact that their Master had so willingly done a service that they refused to do for each other. He spoke of how his life had been one of service to them, and told them that they were slow to realize that greatness in the spiritual kingdom is not obtained the same way as power in the material world. He chastised them for arguing among themselves about the seating arrangements and compared their behavior to that of the Pharisees. He told them that he loved each of them just as he did the others and that there was no place of preferment at his table.

During the second course, the Master told them again that he would not be with them the next evening. "Now has my hour come, but it was not required that one of you should betray me into the hands of my enemies." When the twelve heard this remark, they began to look at each other and inquire, "Is it I?" When Judas asked, Jesus replied, "You have said." The others didn't hear the words Jesus spoke to Judas. They continued to murmur among themselves until Jesus said, "I sorrow that this evil should have come to pass and hoped even up to this hour that the power of truth might triumph over the deceptions of evil, but such victories are not won without the faith of the sincere love of truth."

Jesus then leaned over to Judas and told him to go quickly. Judas rose from the table and left the room. The other men, seeing him leave, assumed that Jesus had sent Judas out on some errand and still did not guess that he was the traitor.

Over the third cup of wine, Jesus said, "Take this cup, all of you, and drink of it. This shall be the cup of my remembrance. This is the cup of the blessing of a new dispensation of grace and truth. This shall be to you the emblem of the bestowal and ministry of the divine Spirit of Truth. And I will not again drink this cup with you until I drink in new form with you in the Father's eternal kingdom."

And when they finished, Jesus broke the bread, saying, "Take this bread of remembrance and eat it. I have told you that I am the bread of life. And this bread of life is the united life of the Father and the Son in one gift. The word of the Father, as revealed in the Son, is indeed the bread of life." They meditated for a few moments, and Jesus said, "When you do these things, recall the life I have lived on earth among you and rejoice that I am to continue to live on earth with you and to serve through you." They ended the Passover meal by singing the 118th Psalm.

180—The Farewell Discourse

When the Psalm ended, Jesus told the apostles, "When I enacted for you a parable indicating how you should be willing to serve one another, I said that I desired to give you a new commandment; and I would do this now as I am about to leave you. You well know the commandment which directs that you love one another; that you love your neighbor even as yourself. But I am not wholly satisfied with even that sincere devotion on the part of my children. I would have you perform still greater acts of love in the kingdom of the believing brotherhood. And so I give you this new commandment: That you love one another even as I have loved you. And by this will all men know that you are my disciples if you thus love one another."

"I am the true vine, and my Father is the husbandman. I am the vine, and you are the branches… Herein is the Father glorified: that the vine has many living branches, and that every branch bears much fruit." Jesus told his men that if they would live within him, his spirit would so infuse them that they "may ask whatsoever my spirit wills and do all this with the assurance that the Father will grant us our petition."

This particular teaching has been much misinterpreted through the centuries. Some people believe mistakenly that invoking Jesus' name is a magic formula for getting what they want from God. Prayer is not a way to get God to bow to the will of mortals, but a way for humans to learn God's will. Once a person is truly aligned with Jesus they can be certain that all of their desires will be compatible with God's will.

The Master continued his advice, telling the apostles not to be discouraged when faint-hearted believers turned against them. He advised them to remember how he also suffered for the sake of the gospel. He promised that he would not leave them alone in the world, and that when he was gone his spirit would come to help them. Jesus said that he was going to the Father, and that they could not follow yet.

Thomas said, "Master, we do not know where you are going, so of course we do not know the way, But we will follow you this very night if you will show us the way." And Jesus answered, "Thomas, I am the way, the truth, and the life. No man goes to the Father except through me. If you know me, you know the way to the Father." Philip said, "Master, show us the Father, and everything you have said will be made plain." Jesus replied, "Philip, have I been so long with you and yet you do not even now know me? Again do I declare: He who has seen me has seen the Father."

Jesus spoke more about the Spirit of Truth. "I have loved the Father and have kept his word; you have loved me, and you will keep my word. As my Father as given me of his spirit, so will I give you of my spirit. And this Spirit of Truth which I will bestow upon you shall guide and comfort you and shall eventually lead you into all truth." Jesus told them that they would be indwelt by the Father and the Son, and that those gifts of heaven would work together to help them remember all that Jesus had taught.

"This new teacher is the Spirit of Truth who will live with each one of you, in your hearts, and so will all the children of light be made one and be drawn toward one another. And in this very manner will my Father and I be able to live in the souls of each one of you and also in the hearts of all other men who love us and make that love real in their experiences by loving one another, even as I am now loving you."

The Spirit of Truth leads the human mind to spiritual meanings. It is the spirit of living, growing, expanding, adaptive truth. Truth cannot be imprisoned in formulas or creeds, but it can be known and lived. Static truth is dead; living truth is dynamic. The Spirit of Truth helps humans interpret their experiences in a spiritual way.

The Spirit helps God-knowing people apply the golden rule in such a way that others receive the highest possible good from such contact. The golden rule cannot be properly understood as dogma, it can only be understood by living. No amount of piety can compensate for an absence of sincere and generous friendliness, any more than formal worship can atone for a lack of genuine compassion for others.

Jesus warned his apostles that the authorities might turn strongly against them. He reminded them again that his spirit would be with them throughout their sufferings, even though he would be leaving them. "And so are you about to sorrow over my departure, but I will soon see you again, and then will your sorrow be turned into rejoicing, and there shall come to you a new revelation of the salvation of God which no man can ever take away from you." Even after this frank discussion the apostles could not comprehend that Jesus was leaving.

181—Final Admonitions and Warnings

Before returning to camp, Jesus gave the apostles his last words of comfort and advice. He told them that when he was released from mortal form he could return as an indwelling spirit to guide each one of them. Jesus told them that everyone who received his spirit would be enlightened, cleansed, and comforted. He asked them not to feel troubled or fearful, because in him they would all triumph in faith.

The peace that Jesus gives to his followers is not that of a stoic prepared to endure the worst, nor that of an optimist who longs for future peace. Some stoicism and optimism are serviceable in life, but neither is the cause of that superb peace the Master brings. The peace of Jesus is based on human faith in God's overcare. It is the assurance of a child who knows that his universe career is safely in the keeping of a wise, loving, omnipotent Father.

As the apostles were still seated at the table in John Mark's home, Jesus moved around the table to speak to each of his men individually. Jesus asked John to continue to act in his stead in all matters pertaining to his earth family, and to dedicate his life to teaching others how to love as Jesus had loved. John wept as he asked Jesus how he could learn to love his brethren more. Jesus told him that he would love others more after he learned to love God more. Jesus told John to try to live peacefully with everyone, and not to strive with the people he was trying to win for the kingdom.

Jesus observed that Simon was still set on making a kingdom according to his own liking. He knew that none of his apostles were more sincere or honest than Simon, and that none would be more upset when Jesus was gone. The Master warned Simon about rendering unto Caesar what was Caesar's, and told him that throughout Simon's discouragement Jesus' spirit and the apostles themselves would be at hand. He warned him that people who fight with the sword perish with the sword. Jesus promised that Simon would see the kingdom that he longed for, but not in this lifetime.

The Master advised Matthew that the apostles would soon be scattered to the ends of the earth proclaiming the gospel. When Matthew asked how they would know where to go and who would send them, Jesus replied that the Spirit of Truth would lead them. He told Matthew to show the world what God could do for a tax-gatherer who dared to follow the Son of Man. He asked that Matthew serve by showing that God was no respecter of persons, that all believers are children of God.

Jesus asked James to allow the new teacher to give him compassion and tolerance. He warned James to remember that wisdom embraces discretion as well as courage, and that there would be times when it was better to placate the wrath of unbelievers so as to continue to live and preach another day. Jesus also told James that he and his brother would be separated, and that one would die long before the other.

When Andrew spoke with the Master, Jesus released Andrew from his duties as administrator and thanked him for his faithful service. He asked that Andrew hold the apostles together until the Spirit of Truth arrived to guide them individually. Andrew was instructed to do his best to promote harmony among the various groups of gospel believers.

Jesus counseled the Alpheus twins that when their time with him was finished they would return to their previous work, and that someday they would sit with him on high. He asked the twins to dedicate their lives to enhancing common toil. He said that to them all things had become sacred, and their labor had become a service to the Father.

The Master reminded Philip of the many foolish questions Philip had asked. Philip always wanted to be shown, and Jesus assured him that very soon he would see great things. Jesus predicted that since the world is filled with people who look at life the way Philip did, he would have great work to do. He told Philip that when his life was finished, he would come to Jesus in his kingdom, and that Jesus would then take great pleasure in showing him "that which eye has not seen, ear heard, nor the mortal mind conceived."

Nathaniel was warned that his frankness might interfere with getting along well with others. He was told that his lessons must be adapted to the intellectual status and spiritual development of the person he was addressing. "Sincerity is most serviceable in the work of the kingdom when it is wedded to discretion." Jesus cautioned Nathaniel that he was handicapped by a tendency to interpret the gospel according to Jewish teachings, and that what Nathaniel did not learn from Jesus, he would be taught by "that master of all teachers—actual experience."

Jesus advised Thomas that even though he had often lacked faith, he had never lacked courage. Jesus had confidence that false prophets would not deceive Thomas, and he asked Thomas to dedicate his life to showing how the human mind could triumph over the inertia of intellectual doubt.

To Peter, Jesus revealed his distress that years of such close association had not done more to help Peter think before he spoke. "What experience must you pass through before you will learn to set a guard upon your lips?" Jesus told Peter that he was destined to make much trouble for himself if he didn't overcome this fault.

Jesus then addressed all of the apostles, saying, "This night you will all be in great danger of stumbling over me."

Peter replied, "No matter if all my brethren should succumb to doubts because of you, I promise that I will not stumble over anything you may do."

Jesus then foretold that Peter would deny Jesus three or four times that very evening. "But remember my promise: When I am raised up, I will tarry with you for a season before I go to the Father. And even this night will I make supplication to the Father that he strengthen each of you for that which you must now so soon pass through. I love you all with the love wherewith the Father loves me, and therefore should you henceforth love one another, even as I have loved you."

182—IN GETHSEMANE

Late Thursday night Jesus led the eleven apostles back to camp where he asked them to kneel in a circle as he prayed. He asked God to help them and to keep them faithful until the Spirit of Truth arrived. "You gave me twelve men, and I have kept them all save one, the son of revenge, who would not have further fellowship with us. These men are weak and frail, but I know we can trust them; I have proved them; they love me, even as they reverence you." Jesus prayed for their strength and courage, and finished by saying, "This world knows very little of you, righteous Father, but I know you, and I have made you known to these believers, and they will make known your name to other generations. And now I promise them that you will be with them in the world even as you have been with me — even so."

Jesus revealed God's name to the world as never before. In revealing himself to Moses, all the Father could communicate was "I AM that I AM." Jesus' life enlarged the revelation of the name of God to all generations:

I am the bread of life.

I am the living water.

I am the light of the world.

I am the desire of all ages.

I am the open door to eternal salvation.

I am the reality of endless life.

I am the good shepherd.

I am the pathway of infinite perfection.

I am the resurrection and the life.

I am the secret of eternal survival.

I am the way, the truth, and the life.

I am the infinite Father of my finite children.

I am the true vine; you are the branches.

I am the hope of all who know the living truth.

I am the living bridge from one world to another.

I am the living link between time and eternity.

As the apostles made their way back to camp they had a discussion about Judas. John Mark and David Zebedee told Jesus privately that they knew Judas intended to betray him to his enemies. Jesus asked them not to be troubled by it.

Before they retired, Simon Zelotes offered the apostles weapons. Each man took a sword except for Nathaniel, who pleaded with the others to remember that Jesus didn't want them to use force to establish the kingdom of heaven. Nathaniel said he would pray but he would not arm himself. When Andrew heard Nathaniel's speech he turned his sword back in. Nine men remained armed.

After the men went to their tents, Jesus requested a messenger from David. Jesus sent the messenger to Philadelphia to warn Abner of what was to come and to promise that Abner would see Jesus again shortly. Jesus also asked the chief of the visiting Greeks not to be disturbed about what was to take place.

None of the apostles expected anything to happen that evening; only David and John Mark realized that their Master's enemies would come that very night. David bade farewell to Jesus, saying, "Master, I have had great joy in my service with you. My brothers are your apostles, but I have delighted to do the lesser things as they should be done, and I shall miss you with all my heart when you are gone." Jesus replied, "David, my son, others have done that which they were directed to do, but this service have you done of your own heart and I have not been unmindful of your devotion."

Jesus withdrew with Peter, James, and John to a nearby ravine. His heart was heavy with sorrow. The trial Jesus faced appeared more appalling to him as the evening wore on. He was weary, and anxious for the safety of the apostles. Parting with his men was a great strain. The divine Jesus knew that he had done his best, but the human Jesus wished he could have done more.

Jesus desired that the three apostles keep him company as he prayed, but they kept falling asleep. Three times Jesus went aside to pray for assurance from his Father, and three times he returned to find his friends sleeping. During his prayers an angel came to strengthen him. Jesus was convinced that his Father was going to let events take their natural course.

183—The Betrayal and Arrest of Jesus

The Master awakened Peter, James and John, and suggested that they return to their tents to rest. Back at the camp, the apostles slept but the Greeks were still awake. Jesus unsuccessfully tried to convince them all to return to their tents. Failing to disperse them, Jesus went to sit by an olive press near the entrance of Gethsemane, hoping to avoid a confrontation between his followers and those who were coming to arrest him.

Meanwhile, Judas went to the captain of the temple guards. A delay in Jerusalem caused the guards to miss finding Jesus in the Mark home. This upset Judas. He knew that only two apostles had been armed during supper, but sixty followers and many weapons were available in Gethsemane.

Judas and the guards returned to the temple. Judas told the Jewish rulers that they would have to look for Jesus in Gethsemane. He requested armed guards. Jewish authorities took this request to the Roman commander, who refused and sent them to his superior officer. They finally obtained permission for the armed guards from Pontius Pilate, who granted their petition, thinking that he could later undo any harm that might be committed that night.

About sixty people accompanied Judas to Gethsemane. Judas walked ahead of the group, hoping to make it look like he was not associated with the others. He pretended that he was coming to warn Jesus of the pending arrest with the thought that this might keep the other apostles from turning against him in anger.

When Peter, James, and John saw the armed band approaching, they rushed to the olive press along with thirty disciples. Jesus made one last effort to save Judas from betraying him. Before Judas could speak, Jesus approached a Roman guard, asked whom he was looking for, and identified himself as Jesus of Nazareth.

But Judas wanted to make a show of his part in the betrayal to ensure his claim on financial compensation. Judas stepped up to Jesus placing a kiss on his brow, saying, "Hail, Master and Teacher." Jesus replied,

"Friend, is it not enough to do this! Would you even betray the Son of Man with a kiss?"

The apostles were stunned. Jesus again asked the guards who they sought. Again the captain said, "Jesus of Nazareth." Jesus said, "I have told you that I am he. If, therefore, you seek me, let these others go their way. I am ready to go with you."

One of the guards began to tie Jesus' hands behind his back. This upset Peter and the others so much that they drew their swords and rushed forward, but Jesus forbade them. The captain feared that these followers would come later to rescue Jesus and ordered their arrest, but they fled. John Mark ran to David and informed him of what was happening. Together they woke the other apostles.

John Zebedee and Peter followed Jesus and the guards while the others met by the olive press to decide what should be done. Simon Zelotes made an impassioned case for trying to rescue Jesus. Nathaniel reminded them of the Master's teachings about non-resistance and his recent instruction that they should save their own lives so they could preach the gospel to the world. James Zebedee reminded them how Jesus had forbidden the use of force during the arrest. Thomas convinced them that they could do nothing to save Jesus, since Jesus himself had refused both human and divine intervention.

The men were persuaded to separate. David agreed to remain in camp to field messages. The apostles went into hiding in Bethany, Bethphage, and Jerusalem. Shortly after daylight, Jude arrived in camp and learned that his brother had been placed under arrest.

A dispute arose between the Jewish captain of the guards and the Roman captain of the soldiers about where Jesus was to be detained. The Jewish captain wanted Jesus taken to Caiaphas, the acting high priest, but the Roman guards were under orders to bring him before Annas, the former high priest. As they marched along discussing this issue, John Zebedee stepped up between the guards to be near his Master. The temple guards tried to arrest John, but the Romans stopped them. Since Roman law provided that any prisoner could have someone stand with him before his judges, the Roman captain ordered that John be allowed to accompany Jesus unmolested. Due to this intervention, John was able to be near Jesus throughout the trial and crucifixion, relaying information to David's messengers as events unfolded.

From the time of his arrest until his appearance before Annas, Jesus said nothing at all.

Great misunderstandings are associated with the events that ended the Master's life on earth. It was the will of the Father that Jesus should experience mortal life from birth to death, but God had nothing to do with the brutality and torture that were inflicted on Jesus. The inhuman and shocking final hours of Jesus' life were in no way the divine will of God; these cruelties were the work of evil men.

Just as ordinary people cannot expect to have their last hours on earth made easy by divine intervention, Jesus steadfastly refused to extricate himself from his situation by divine means.

184—Before the Sanhedrin Court

Jesus was brought before Annas at his palace on Mount Olivet. Annas knew that the Sanhedrin waited for Jesus at Caiaphas's palace but it was illegal to convene a court before three in the morning.

Annas was the most powerful person in Jewry during that era. Annas had taken a positive interest in Jesus when he was younger, but the recent assault on the money-changers in the temple had turned Annas against him. Annas charged Jesus with disturbing the peace and questioned him about the names of his disciples. Jesus did not reply.

Annas was disturbed by Jesus' silence. He reminded Jesus that he had some power over the pending trial. Jesus said, "Annas, you know that you could have no power over me unless it were permitted by my Father. Some would destroy the Son of Man because they are ignorant, they know no better, but you, friend, know what you are doing. How can you, therefore, reject the light of God?" Annas continued to question the Master, but his mind was already set that Jesus must be either banished or killed. As dawn approached he sent Jesus under guard to Caiaphas.

While Annas was questioning Jesus, Simon Peter waited shivering in the palace courtyard. John Zebedee knew Annas' doorkeeper and requested that Peter be allowed to enter. Peter was nervous about being inside the enemy's courtyard. He was unarmed and confused; he should have been with the other apostles in hiding.

The doorkeeper came up to Peter as he warmed himself by the fire and asked, "Are you not also one of this man's disciples?" Peter immediately replied, "I am not." Another servant said that he thought he had seen Peter in the garden with Jesus, but Peter denied that he knew the Master. The portress drew him aside privately and asked him once again why he denied being a disciple. Peter cursed her, insisting that he never even heard of Jesus before. Twice more he was asked, and twice more Peter denied Jesus.

As he uttered his final denial, Peter heard a cock crow. He was reminded of what Jesus had predicted earlier that night. Guilt washed over Peter as the palace doors opened and guards led Jesus out. Jesus saw the despair on Peter's face, and looked on him with such pity and love that Peter never forgot the look as long as he lived. Jesus and the guards left the palace, and Peter wept bitterly. He joined his brother Andrew in hiding.

Jesus' trial before the Sanhedrin began at half past three in the morning. Since the Sanhedrin had already agreed that Jesus was guilty, they were now concerned with developing charges that would justify a death penalty. More than twenty false witnesses were on hand. Their testimony was so trumped up that even the Sanhedrin were ashamed to listen.

After some time Caiaphas shouted to Jesus, "Do you not answer any of these charges?" Jesus stood in silence. Caiaphas, no longer able to watch Jesus standing there in quiet composure, shook his finger in the Master's face and said, "I adjure you, in the name of the living God, that you tell us whether you are the Deliver, the Son of God." Jesus answered, "I am."

Caiaphas angrily declared that they had witnessed blasphemy, and the court cried out for his death. Annas wanted the trial to continue until they showed charges that transgressed Roman law, but the rest of the Sanhedrin were eager to finish the trial. Jewish law forbade them to work past noon the day before Passover, and Pilate was only in Jerusalem for a short while. Caiaphas hit Jesus.

Annas was truly shocked when the other Sanhedrin left the room, spitting at Jesus and slapping him as they passed by. In this unprecedented confusion, the first session of the trial ended.

In order to pass a death sentence, two sessions of court were required, one day apart. The Sanhedrin waited one hour. Jesus spent the break in the audience chamber with guards and servants who mocked him, spit on him, and beat him. When the abuse began, Jesus made John leave the room.

Throughout his suffering, Jesus was silent. A shudder of indignation filled the universe as celestial observers witnessed the sight of their Sovereign submitting himself to ignorant, misguided people. These were the moments of the Master's greatest victories.

At half past five the court reassembled. Jesus was sent into the side room where John waited, while the Sanhedrin drew up a three-point indictment. This entire procedure was against Jewish law for many reasons: false witnesses, lack of witnesses for the defense, failure to wait one day between sessions, absence of witnesses to verify charges in the final indictment, and the fact that the prisoner was never told the charges against him. By six in the morning, the trial was over. Jesus was led away to appear before Pontius Pilate.

185—THE TRIAL BEFORE PILATE

Pontius Pilate had committed several errors early in his administration which incurred the displeasure of the emperor Tiberius. This situation gave the Judean Jewish leaders some leverage over Pilate. They had learned to use the threat of civil uprising to manipulate him.

The Sanhedrin brought Jesus before Pilate and asked permission to have him executed. Written charges were presented: perverting the nation and stirring people to rebellion, forbidding the people to pay tribute to Caesar, claiming to be king of the Jews and founding a new kingdom.

Jesus had not been legally convicted of any of these charges. Neither Jesus nor John responded to them when read aloud. Pilate was convinced that the proceeding was irregular and took Jesus and John into an inner chamber for a private examination.

After dismissing the first two charges, Pilate asked Jesus if he were king of the Jews and whether he was trying to found a new kingdom. Jesus replied, "Do you not perceive that my kingdom is not of this world?" Pilate asked, "Then you are a king after all?" Jesus answered, "Yes, I am such a king, and my kingdom is the family of the faith sons of my Father who is in heaven."

Pilate did not understand Jesus but he was convinced that he was nothing but a harmless visionary. He went back outside and told the priests that he had questioned Jesus and found no fault in him. The crowd became angry. One of the Sanhedrin declared that Pilate would long regret letting Jesus go.

Pilate, feeling pressured, announced that since Jesus was a Galilean he would send him to Herod, who had jurisdiction over Galilee. Jesus was brought before Herod but refused to answer Herod's questions. Herod sent him back to Pilate.

Pilate still wanted to set Jesus free. It had long been the custom to release a condemned man at Passover. It occurred to Pilate that he could release Jesus under this excuse. But the crowd called for the release of Barabbas, a man condemned for robbery and murder. Pilate was angry that the Jews requested mercy for a murderer instead of Jesus, but was afraid to defy the aroused Jews. "What shall I do with him who is called the king of the Jews?" And the crowd shouted, "Crucify him!" Pilate responded, "Why would you crucify this man? What evil has he done?" But they continued to cry out for his crucifixion.

Pilate decided to try one more tactic. He ordered the guards to scourge Jesus, hoping that this punishment would be enough to appease the crowds' anger. When the punishment ended, Pilate brought the prisoner before the crowd. The sight of the Master at this point was enough to send "a mighty shudder through the realms of a vast universe," but the crowd continued to shout for his death. Pilate knew Jesus was innocent, but he was unwilling to defy the Jewish leaders. Pilate released Barabbas.

Pontius Pilate's life ended in suicide. His wife Claudia became a believer in Jesus and contributed to the spread of the gospel.

186—Just Before the Crucifixion

The executive business of the universe nearly came to a complete halt as Gabriel and the celestial hosts observed what they termed "Pilate on trial before Jesus." When Jesus was arrested, he knew that his work in the flesh was finished. He understood the way he would die, and the details of his trial were of little concern to him. Jesus pitied Pilate and sincerely tried to enlighten him as the entire universe looked on.

Jesus was convinced that it was the will of God that the course of human events should unfold without celestial or divine interference. Jesus' love for mortals was evident in his patience in the face of the jeers and beatings of the soldiers and servants. Jesus' life was revelation of God to man, and in the final episodes of his earthly career, he made a new and touching revelation of man to God.

At about half past eight that Friday morning, Jesus was turned over to the soldiers who would crucify him.

Judas went to Caiaphas to claim his reward. Before he could enter the Sanhedrin's chamber, a servant took him aside and handed him thirty pieces of silver. Judas was stunned at this aloof treatment. He tried to go inside to speak to Caiaphas but he was refused admittance. Judas felt humiliated. Judas later saw Jesus' cross being lifted onto Golgotha from afar and was so overwhelmed that he ran back to Caiaphas's chamber. He stammered that he had sinned and had been insulted and he repented in what he had done. He threw the silver onto the floor and left. In his despair, Judas went outside the city gates and killed himself.

A detachment of temple guards went to Gethsemane to arrest the Master's followers, but they had scattered. Upon hearing that Gethsemane was empty, the Sanhedrin were satisfied that there was no further danger of an uprising. They adjourned their meeting to prepare for the Passover.

David Zebedee was the only disciple who took Jesus literally when he said he would rise again on the third day. He dismissed his messengers for the Passover, instructing them to report to him again first thing Sunday morning.

Humans, not God, planned the death of Jesus. The truth that men, by faith, can become spirit-conscious children of God does not depend on the death of Jesus. Mortals are the children of God, and the only thing required to actualize this truth is spirit-born faith. The love of God for his creatures is an inherent universe fact that is independent of the bestowal missions of the Creator Sons. The Father loved man just as much before Jesus lived on earth as he did afterward.

187—THE CRUCIFIXION

Jesus arrived at Golgotha in the company of two condemned robbers and a group of Roman soldiers. The soldiers removed Jesus' clothing and dressed him in a loincloth. They bound his arms to the crossbeam before nailing his hands to the wood. They hoisted the crossbeam onto the upright timber and nailed it into place. The soldiers bound Jesus' feet and nailed them to the cross, using one long nail to pierce both feet. It was half past nine in the morning.

The Creator Son's death on the cross took five and a half hours. He won two men for the kingdom during his crucifixion; the first, one of the two thieves hanging beside him, the other, the Roman centurion who was captain of the guard. Shortly before three in the afternoon, Jesus spoke his last words: "It is finished! Father, into your hands I commend my spirit."

John Zebedee, Jude, Ruth, Mary Magdalene, and Rebecca were with the Master when he died.

188—THE TIME IN THE TOMB

It was customary to throw the bodies of those who had been crucified into an open burial pit. To prevent this from happening to Jesus, Joseph of Arimathea and Nicodemus gained permission from Pilate to take the Master's body for proper burial.

Over the violent objections of the Sanhedrin, Joseph and Nicodemus took possession of Jesus' body on Golgotha. The body was carried to a tomb owned by Joseph, where it was wrapped in bandages saturated in myrrh and aloe, covered with a linen sheet, and placed on a shelf. The men who tended to this sad task were Joseph, Nicodemus, John Zebedee, and the Roman centurion. The centurion then signaled his men to roll the heavy stone into place to cover the entrance to the tomb.

Mary Magdalene, Mary the wife of Clopas, Martha the aunt of Jesus, and Rebecca of Sepphoris lingered near the tomb until after dark. They had followed the funeral procession at a distance because it was not permitted for women to associate with men at such a time. These four women saw that Jesus had been given a hasty burial; they agreed to return after the Sabbath to properly prepare his body.

Jesus' enemies remembered reports that Jesus would rise from the dead on the third day. The chief priests requested that a Roman guard be stationed in front of the tomb so that Jesus' followers couldn't steal his body and then pretend he had risen. Ten Roman soldiers joined ten Jewish guards to watch over the burial site. They placed a second stone in front of the first and attached Pilate's seal to it to make certain nothing would be disturbed. These men stayed on guard in front of the tomb continuously through the hour of the resurrection.

There are significant lessons attached to Jesus' death on the cross. Jesus lived and died for the whole universe. His life on earth shed light on the mortal pathway to salvation, and his death forever made evident the certainty of survival after death. Jesus' death portrays the full devotion that he had for even the lowest members of his creation.

The triumph of the death on the cross is summed up in the attitude of Jesus toward his assailants. The Master neither condemned nor condoned sin. Divine love doesn't merely forgive sins, it absorbs and destroys them. The cross became an eternal symbol of the victory of love over hate and truth over evil when Jesus prayed, "Father, forgive them, for they know not what they do." His devotion to mortals was contagious throughout the universe. On millions of worlds evolving creatures were inspired by the sight of Jesus laying down his life in unselfish devotion to human beings.

The cross is the abiding symbol of sacred service, representing the devotion of one's life to the welfare and salvation of others. When intelligent people look upon Jesus as he offers up his life, their own hardships and grievances hardly seem worth complaining about. The Master's death on the cross stimulates the universal realization of the Father's eternal love and the Son's unending mercy.

189—THE RESURRECTION

As Jesus' body lay in the tomb, the chief archangel stationed on Urantia called a meeting to consider techniques for restoring Jesus' life. The angels were advised by Gabriel that Michael already had whatever power he needed to take up his life again. Michael's personalized Adjuster also advised them, saying, "Those things which you ordinarily do for the creature, you may not do for the Creator." And so the council of celestials waited patiently for further events to unfold.

At two forty-five Sunday morning, a commission of seven Paradise personalities arrived on the scene. Vibrations began to emanate from the tomb, and at two minutes past three, Jesus came forth. The form in which the Master appeared during this final episode of earthly life was that of a resurrected morontia ascender. The mortal body still lay in the sepulchre undisturbed. The soldiers were still on guard, the seal of Pilate still unbroken.

Jesus' physical body could not be removed from the tomb the same way his morontia form was released. The chief archangel received permission from Gabriel to dissolve the mortal body of Jesus. He invoked the "process of accelerated time" in order that the hosts of heaven would be spared the sight of the slow decay of the human form of their Creator.

Secondary midwayers rolled away the huge stones from the tomb. The mortal remains of the Master then went through the usual disintegration process, but without the time factor. The physical dissolution of Jesus' body happened nearly instantaneously. When the guards at the grave saw the stones begin to move, they fled in fear back to the city.

That morning, ten of the apostles were staying at the Mark home. Thomas was in solitude at the home of Simon of Bethphage. The women were at the home of Joseph of Arimathea, and other disciples were gathered at the home of Nicodemus.

Five women started out before daybreak with bandages and embalming lotions, intending to anoint and rewrap the body of Jesus. It was half past three when these women arrived at the tomb. They were surprised to see the stone already rolled away from the entrance; they had wondered how they would get into the tomb. As the others stood by fearfully Mary Magdalene went inside the sepulchre.

Mary saw that Jesus' body was gone; only the grave cloths remained on the shelf. She cried out in alarm and the other women panicked. They fled all the way to the Damascus gate before they rallied and returned to the tomb. Mary showed her friends that the tomb was empty. They conjectured that the body had been moved to another place. As the women discussed what they should do they noticed a stranger standing nearby.

Mary Magdalene rushed over to him, asking, "Where have you taken the Master? Where have they laid him?" The stranger did not answer. Mary began to weep. Jesus then asked, "Whom do you seek?" And Mary told him that they were looking for Jesus, and asked again where he had been taken. Jesus asked, "Did not this Jesus tell you, even in Galilee, that he would die, but that he would rise again?" And then he spoke to Mary in a familiar voice, saying simply, "Mary." She recognized the voice of her Master and knelt at his feet. Mary tried to embrace Jesus' feet but he prevented her. He asked the women to go back into the city to tell the apostles that he had risen.

The women hurried to the Mark home and related what they had seen and heard. The apostles did not believe them. Peter and John ran out to look at the empty tomb for themselves. They could not understand what could have happened, thinking that perhaps the body had been stolen by the guards.

Mary returned to the tomb disheartened that the apostles did not believe her. After Peter and John left the Master appeared to her again, asking her to have courage. Jesus asked Mary to tell the apostles that he would soon appear before them. Mary returned to the city to speak once more with the apostles. They still did not believe, but when they heard Peter and John's reports they were filled with fear.

Mankind is slow to perceive that, in all that is personal, matter is the skeleton of morontia, and that both are the reflected shadow of enduring spirit reality. How long before you will regard time as the moving image of eternity and space as the fleeting shadow of Paradise?

190—MORONTIA APPEARANCES OF JESUS

Unsuccessful in their attempts to persuade the apostles that Jesus had risen, Mary Magdalene and the other women spread the news to the women gathered at Joseph's and to the men at Nicodemus's home.

David Zebedee and Joseph set out to inspect the tomb. They immediately went on to the Mark home and told the apostles that the tomb was empty. Only John Zebedee was faintly swayed. David declined to argue with the apostles. He took his leave of them saying, "You are the apostles, and you ought to understand these things. I heard the Master say that, after he should die, he would rise on the third day, and I believe him."

At half past nine that morning, a squadron of messengers assembled at the home of Nicodemus. David bid them to spread the message that Jesus had risen from the dead. Twenty-six runners set out to Bethany, Beersheba, Damascus, Sidon, Philadelphia, Alexandria, and other cities.

Jesus' family was staying in Bethany with Martha and Mary when David's messenger arrived with the news of the resurrection. As Jesus' brother James stood alone in front of Lazarus' empty tomb pondering what the messenger had told them, he became aware of a presence. He watched in amazement as a strange form appeared. Jesus said, "James, I come to call you to the service of the kingdom. Join earnest hands with your brethren and follow after me." The two brothers conversed for three minutes before Jesus said farewell. James rushed inside to tell the rest of his family what he had seen.

Two hours later Jesus appeared again at Lazarus's home, this time to almost twenty family members and believers.

The women assembled at Joseph's house were next to see Jesus. He greeted them: "Peace be upon you. In the fellowship of the kingdom there shall be neither Jew nor gentile, rich nor poor, free nor bond, man nor woman. You also are called to publish the good news of the liberty of mankind through the gospel of sonship with God in the kingdom of heaven. And I will be with you always even to the ends of the earth."

The Master next appeared to forty Greek believers who were staying at the home of Flavius.

Two brothers, Cleopas and Jacob, were walking outside of Jerusalem discussing the rumors of the resurrection when Jesus joined them on the road. He spoke to them at length. When they reached their home, the brothers invited Jesus inside. When they sat down to eat, they gave Jesus their bread to bless. He broke the bread and handed it to them. Suddenly Cleopas and Jacob realized who he was, and Jesus vanished. The brothers rushed to Jerusalem where they burst into the Mark home and excitedly told the apostles all that they had seen and heard.

Reports began to reach the Jewish rulers that Jesus had risen. The Sanhedrin called a meeting and decided that anyone who mentioned the resurrection would be banned from the synagogues. It was further suggested that the penalty should be death, but this didn't come to a vote because the meeting broke up in a panic. The Sanhedrin were about to discover that their problems with Jesus were only beginning.

191—APPEARANCES TO THE APOSTLES AND OTHER LEADERS

April 9th, resurrection Sunday, was a miserable day for the apostles. Thomas spent the day brooding alone in Bethphage. Peter vacillated between believing in the resurrection and doubting it. James wanted to go to the tomb to see for himself until Nathaniel reminded him that Jesus had warned against jeopardizing their own safety. Andrew was perplexed but was also grateful that he had been released from his leadership role.

Simon Zelotes spent most of the day lying on a couch, staring at the wall. Matthew was distracted by the fact that he had received the apostolic funds formerly carried by Judas, and he was worried about what to do with the money. Philip asked many questions. The Alpheus twins believed that Jesus was alive, because they had spoken with their mother who said she had talked to the resurrected Master.

Jesus delayed his first appearance to the apostles because he wanted them to think about what he had said about his death. The Master also wanted Peter to work through some of his problems, and Thomas to re-join his fellows.

Peter wondered if Jesus refrained from appearing to his men because of Peter's denials in Annas's courtyard. He went outside to the garden to think. As he contemplated events his faith increased. He spoke aloud, saying, "I believe he has risen from the dead; I will go and tell my breth-ren." At that very moment, Jesus appeared, saying, "Peter, the enemy desired to have you, but I would not give you up." Peter and Jesus spoke for almost five minutes before the Master vanished. Peter rushed into the upper chamber and told the apostles that he had seen the Master. The re-port had an influence on the apostles, but not enough to convince them of Jesus' resurrection.

Soon thereafter, Jesus appeared in their midst. "Peace be upon you. Why are you so frightened when I appear, as though you had seen a spirit? Did I not tell you about these things when I was present with you in the flesh?" Jesus told them that when they were all together again they would go into Galilee to enter into a new phase of service in the king-dom. The Master vanished.

On Monday, Jesus spent time visiting with morontia beings on Uran-tia. On Tuesday, he appeared to Abner, Lazarus, and over one hundred others at a meeting in Philadelphia which was called to discuss rumors of the resurrection. All day Wednesday Jesus visited morontia delegates from the mansion worlds of the local systems of Norlatiadek.

On Saturday, Peter and John went to Bethphage and brought Thomas to Jerusalem. Thomas continued to disbelieve the stories of the resurrec-tion. "I will not believe unless I see the Master with my own eyes and put my finger in the mark of the nails." At that moment, the morontia form of Jesus appeared. After speaking to the group, Jesus spoke to Thomas, saying, "I bid you be not faithless but believing—and I know you will believe, even with a whole heart."

Thomas fell onto his knees and exclaimed, "I believe! My Lord and Master!" And Jesus replied, "You have believed, Thomas, because you have really seen and heard me. Blessed are those in the ages to come who will believe even though they have not seen with the eye of flesh nor heard with the mortal ear." He instructed them to go to Galilee, and then disappeared. All eleven men were now fully convinced. They rose early the next day and started for Galilee.

It took nine days for the news of the crucifixion to reach Alexandria. On April 18th, Rodan gathered some eighty Greek and Jewish believers to hear the messenger's sad news. Just as his report ended the morontia form of Jesus appeared. Jesus' final words to this gathering were:

"As the Father sent me into this world, even so now send I you. You are all called to carry the good news to those who sit in darkness. This gospel of the kingdom belongs to all who believe it; it shall not be committed to the custody of mere priests. Soon will the Spirit of Truth come upon you, and he shall lead you into all truth. Go you, therefore, into all the world preaching this gospel, and lo, I am with you always, even to the end of the ages."

192—Appearances in Galilee

The apostles left for Galilee, followed by John Mark. Jewish leaders in Jerusalem, noting that the apostles were out of the public eye, decided that the Jesus movement had been squelched. The apostles arrived in Bethsaida late Wednesday. Simon Zelotes was so disheartened that he turned around and went home. Thursday night Peter suggested they go fishing. They fished all night without catching anything, and at dawn they decided to go ashore.

As they dropped anchor a man on the beach asked them whether they caught anything. When they told him they hadn't, he advised them to drop their net on the right side of the boat. The apostles did as they were told and their net was immediately filled. John Zebedee realized who the man on shore was and whispered to Peter, "It is the Master." Impetuously Peter jumped into the water and began to swim to shore, reaching Jesus just ahead of the others.

Jesus visited with John Mark and the apostles for more than an hour as they ate breakfast. After breakfast, he walked on the beach with them two by two, advising them, counseling them, and encouraging them to be strong during the trials ahead. Jesus left them with instructions that they were to find Simon Zelotes and return with him to a meeting the next day on the mount of the ordination near Capernaum.

At noon on Saturday Jesus appeared among his apostles at the site where they had first been ordained as ambassadors of the kingdom. The eleven men once again knelt in a circle around their Master as he reaffirmed their ordination. When the ceremony was complete, Jesus vanished.

Many believers arrived in Bethsaida to ask about the resurrection. Peter announced that a public meeting would be held the following Saturday afternoon. More than five hundred people gathered that day to hear Peter preach his first public sermon since the resurrection. Peter ended with these words: "We affirm that Jesus of Nazareth is not dead; we declare that he has risen from the tomb; we proclaim that we have seen him and talked with him." Just as Peter said this, Jesus appeared, saying only, "Peace be upon you, and my peace I leave with you."

The next day the apostles started back for Jerusalem where they headquartered in the home of John Mark. All except the Alpheus twins, Thomas, and Simon Zelotes, pledged themselves to preach the new gospel of the risen Lord. The subtle process of altering the religion of Jesus into a religion about Jesus had begun.

193—FINAL APPEARANCES AND ASCENSION

Jesus appeared in the courtyard of Nicodemus's home where the apostles, the women's corps, and about fifty other disciples were gathered. He commented on the diversity of believers this gathering represented and reminded them that the gospel was about the fatherhood of God and the brotherhood of men. Jesus warned them not to adjust their message because of the resurrection.

On May 13th Jesus appeared to Nalda and seventy-five Samaritans near Jacob's well at Sychar.

On May 16th Jesus appeared at Tyre in Phoenicia at the close of a meeting of believers; these believers carried the story to Sidon, Antioch, and Damascus.

On May 18th the Master made his final appearance on earth to the eleven apostles in the home of John Mark. Jesus led the apostles to the Mount of Olives where they looked out over Jerusalem. As the men knelt about Jesus in a circle he spoke his final instructions to them.

"I bade you tarry in Jerusalem until you were endowed with power from on high. I am now about to take leave of you; I am about to ascend to my Father, and soon, very soon, will we send into this world of my sojourn the Spirit of Truth; and when he has come, you shall begin the new proclamation of the gospel of the kingdom, first in Jerusalem and then to the uttermost parts of the world. Love men with the love wherewith I have loved you and serve your fellow mortals even as I have served you. By the spirit fruits of your lives impel souls to believe the truth that man is a son of God, and that all men are brethren. Remember all I have taught you and the life I have lived among you. My love overshadows you, my spirit will dwell with you, and my peace shall abide upon you. Farewell."

Jesus vanished from sight. He went to Edentia by way of Jerusem, where the Most Highs released him from morontia form and returned him to sovereignty on Salvington.

Peter called a meeting for disciples in Jerusalem that same morning. After Peter described their final meeting with the Master, the disciples began to pray in preparation for the reception of the promised Spirit of Truth.

194—BESTOWAL OF THE SPIRIT OF TRUTH

On Pentecost, one hundred and twenty believers gathered in prayer in Jerusalem after listening to Peter describe the farewell message of their Master. As they prayed, the became filled with a new consciousness of spiritual joy and power, followed by an urge to publicly proclaim the gospel. The Spirit of Truth, the promised new teacher, had arrived.

The apostles emerged from forty days in hiding and began to preach their new message in the temple. Peter delivered an appeal which won more than two thousand souls. The Jewish leaders were astounded at the boldness of the apostles.

Jesus' followers quickly discovered that the story of his resurrection held great allure. The gospel of the Fatherhood of God quickly changed into the gospel of the risen Lord Jesus Christ. The apostles proclaimed the facts of Jesus' life, death, and resurrection, and the fervent hope of his imminent return.

The Jesus brotherhood grew. Converts to the gospel prayed together, broke bread together, referred to each other as brothers and sisters. They ministered to the poor and shared their material possessions. The new fellowship spread rapidly for many years. Jewish leaders, seeing that they didn't pose any threat and that they continued to follow Jewish law, took little notice.

All went well in Jerusalem until pupils of Rodan began to make converts among the Hellenists. Greeks did not conform to Jewish practices and ceremonies and this eventually caused relations between the Jesus brotherhood and the Jewish leaders to deteriorate. One Greek convert, Stephen, was stoned to death as he preached, thus becoming the first martyr of the new religion.

Stephen's death brought about the formal organization of the early Christian church. Believers agreed to separate themselves from unbelievers. Within a month of Stephen's death, Peter and James were leading the new church in Jerusalem. Missionaries went forth throughout the Roman empire carrying the message of the new gospel, and relentless persecution by the Jews began.

Pentecost was a call to spiritual unity among believers. The Spirit of Truth descended in Jerusalem, Alexandria, Philadelphia, and all other places where true believers lived. The Spirit equipped teachers of the new faith with spiritual weapons: unfailing forgiveness, matchless good will, and boundless love. Among themselves, followers of Jesus were set free from discrimination based on sex, race, culture, and social status.

The life and death of Jesus eternally prove that goodness and faith will always be vindicated. Michael, as Jesus, revealed God to mankind as the Spirit of Truth reveals Michael to mankind. The mission of the Spirit is to foster and personalize truth and to destroy mortal feelings of orphanhood. The Spirit of Truth purifies the human heart and leads us to commit to the will of God and the welfare of humankind. The joy of this Spirit is a tonic for health, a stimulus for mind, and an unfailing energy for the soul. The Spirit of Truth brings a restatement of the message of Jesus to every new generation of believers, providing personal enlightenment and guidance for the spiritual difficulties of mortal life.

195—AFTER PENTECOST

The Roman Empire was receptive to the spread of Christianity. Conflicts between older religions and the budding new religion were solved through compromise. A revised version of Jesus' teachings blended with

Greek and Hebrew philosophy, Mithraism, and paganism to become Christianity.

Christianity started growing primarily in the lower classes. After the first century, the best members of the Greco-Roman culture were increasingly drawn in. Early leaders deliberately compromised the ideals of Jesus in the attempt to preserve his ideas. The eastern form of Christianity remained more true to the original teachings of Jesus, but was eventually lost in the rise of Islam. But someday the ideals of the Master will assert their power throughout the world.

The Roman empire was tolerant of strange peoples, languages, and religions; Christianity was opposed only when it seemed to be in competition with the state. The Romans were successful in governing the western world because of their honesty, devotion, and self-control, and these same qualities provided ideal soil for the spread of Christianity. Although the new religion came too late to save the Roman empire from its eventual moral decline, the empire did last long enough to insure the survival of Christianity.

Today Christianity faces a struggle more difficult than any it has known throughout history. The rise of science and materialism challenges religion. The higher a civilization evolves, the more necessary it becomes for people to seek spiritual reality to help stabilize society and solve material problems. Religion helps us develop faith, trust and assurance. Society without a morality based on spiritual reality cannot survive.

Science has destroyed childlike interpretations of life. True science has no conflict with true religion; but the change from an age of miracles to an age of machines has been upsetting to modern man. Religious leaders are mistaken when they try to lure people to spiritual practice with methods that were used in the middle ages. Religion must renew itself and find new ways to approach modern people.

Modern secularism sprang from two influences: atheistic science and the protest against the domination of western civilization by the medieval Christian church. For hundreds of years Western thinking has been progressively secularized; most professed Christians are actually secularists. Secularism is barren of spiritual values and satisfactions. It freed humankind from ecclesiastical slavery only to lead them into political and economic slavery. This philosophy leads to unrest, unhappiness, and disaster. The blessings of secularism—tolerance, social service, democracy, and civil liberty—can be had without sacrificing faith in God.

Christianity stands in need of the teachings of Jesus. "Urantia is now quivering on the very brink of one of its most amazing and enthralling epochs of social readjustment, moral quickening, and spiritual enlightenment." Religion needs leaders who will depend solely on Jesus and his teachings. The world must see Jesus living again in the experience of spirit-born mortals who reveal the Master to all people.

The true Church is invisible, spiritual, and characterized by unity rather than uniformity. If the Christian church would follow the Master, young people would not hesitate to enlist in his great spiritual adventure. It is not duty that will transform our world, but the "second mile" of freely-given service and devotion by followers of Jesus who truly live and love as he taught.

Christianity suffers a handicap because it is identified with western civilization—a society burdened with science without idealism, politics without principles, wealth without work, pleasure without restraint, knowledge without character, power without conscience, and industry without morality.

196—THE FAITH OF JESUS

Jesus magnificently demonstrated living faith in God. His faith was not merely intellectual; it was a profound conviction which securely held him in the living reality of God and destroyed every desire that conflicted with the will of the Father. Jesus was unquestioningly loyal to God's will.

Jesus trusted God as a child trusts his father. His complete dependence on God gave Jesus the assurance of absolute personal security. Jesus had confidence in the goodness of the universe. He wants his followers to believe in the reality of the Father's love so that they too can experience the confidence that comes from knowing they are children of God.

Jesus was the most truly religious person who ever lived on earth. If the religion of Jesus suddenly replaced the religion about Jesus, the social, economic, and moral transformations that would occur would be revolutionary.

Christianity is founded on the personal religious experience of Paul, but the gospel of the kingdom is founded on the personal religious experience of Jesus. We should not literally imitate Jesus' life; we need to trust God as Jesus trusts God and to believe in each other as he believes in us. The greatest of all human knowledge is knowing the religious life of Jesus and how he lived it.

Jesus' life reveals a pattern of religious growth that started with early primitive awe, moved through personal spiritual communion, and arrived at advanced consciousness of oneness with the Father. He grew from the humble mortal status that prompted his words, "Why do you call me good?" to the sublime consciousness of divinity which led him to say, "Which one of you convicts me of sin?"

Jesus did not believe, as Paul did, that the world was fundamentally evil. He viewed humans positively. Jesus saw men as sons of God and knew of the magnificent futures awaiting those who chose survival. Jesus was willing to devote himself to mortal service because of the high value that he placed on people. We are uplifted by his extraordinary faith in us.

There are three evidences that spirit indwells the human mind. The first is love—only a spirit-indwelt mind is capable of altruism. The second is wisdom—only a spirit-indwelt mind can discern that the universe is friendly. The third is worship—only a spirit-indwelt mind can realize the divine presence and seek experience with divinity.

The human mind does not create value. It can only discover, recognize, interpret, and choose values and meanings. Human survival is dependent on choosing those values selected by the indwelling Adjuster, the spirit-value sorter. Man's challenge on earth is to achieve better communication with this indwelling Monitor.

Be not discouraged; human evolution is still in progress, and the revelation of God in the world, in and through Jesus, shall not fail.

Printed in Great Britain
by Amazon

44587157R00169